"Matt's writings about Christianity is so spot on with the Spirit. This series keeps getting better. It's amazing how the Spirit of God leads us into the truth with Him in love." -*Amazon Customer*

"I would recommend this book to all Christians everywhere. Especially those who are weary and heavy laden." -*Amazon Customer*

"Absolutely wonderful book! I couldn't stop reading it!" -*Amazon Customer*

Matt McMillen is a bestselling Christian author and teacher of God's Word. His books and massive social media ministry has taught countless amounts of people their true identity in Christ. Matt's easy-to-understand biblical teachings have helped build confidence in his readers, break lifelong addictions, and find their true purpose for living: enjoying God's grace through Jesus Christ!

For more information on his ministry, visit:
www.mattmcmillenministries.com

THE
CHRISTIAN IDENTITY

VOLUME 2

Discovering What Jesus Has Truly Done to Us

MATT MCMILLEN

Citation: THE HOLY BIBLE, Copyright © 1973, 1978, 1984, 2011 by Biblica, Inc.®
Used with permission. All rights reserved worldwide.

Copyright © 2019 Matt McMillen
The Christian Identity, Volume 1
Discovering What Jesus Has Truly Done to Us

Published by: Matt McMillen Ministries
720 W. Karsch Blvd.
Farmington, MO 63640
matt@mattmcmillen.com

Printed in the United States of America

ISBN 978-0-9971533-5-4 (paperback)

For the grace teachers. Thank you for your bravery.
I look forward to meeting all of you in eternity.

Contents

"For you died, and your life is now hidden with Christ in God."

Colossians 3:3

Introduction

Who Are You, Christian?

"Grandma, why do you always say that?"

"Well, because I want it to get down into your soul."

As a young boy, and even into my teenage years, Grandma repeated a lot of the same things to me.

"Get down into my soul? Grandma, you're just being senile."

"Oh hush your mouth before I come smack it," she'd say with a grin and a wink.

So playful and funny, yet so wise. Like a warm blanket, the love she showed me as I grew up gives me comfort to this day. The things Grandma said and did, from my childhood, still stand out in my mind.

The older I became the more I understood what she was doing. Grandma was teaching me my identity. She wanted me to know who I am.

"Matthew, you're different. You're special, son."

She said this to all of us kids, not just me, as well as to everyone in the neighborhood. To those she counseled over the phone and at the table, the same words were given. We all felt as if we *were* different and we *were* special. We believed her.

The seeds she planted in our minds were seeds of identity. Grandma knew we'd need to stand on our identity as adults. She had lived enough life to know identity recenters us. She knew when we *don't* understand our identity, or when we forget, life can be extra hard. But when we understand who we are, no amount of difficulties can sway us from our righteous foundation.

Grandma also revealed no amount of success can teach us our identity nor can any number of failures. She made sure we *knew* only God can determine our identity.

As an unbeliever, God teaches a person their need for a Savior. As a believer, He's teaching us more and more about our heaven-ready status, our new birth. Confidence in being a member of His family, through faith in Christ, is God's desire. The enemy's desire is to make an unbeliever think they don't need Jesus, "You're completely self-sufficient."

For the believer, Satan's goal is to confuse us about who God has already made us to be. He wants you and I to commingle our *who* with our *do*. He wants us to think we *must* sustain our identity by whatever means necessary. But at the same time, he wants us to believe we can't *possibly* sustain our identity, by whatever means necessary.

One of his greatest deceptions, for Christians, is that we must change. The truth is we are no longer changing but growing. Why aren't we changing? Because our change, our new identity, only happens once. Christ only died once, and came back to life once. Our method of salvation accessed *His* death and life, once. He traded both off to us, once.

Once is an important word in regard to our identity. The author of Hebrews denotes "once for all" when explaining what Jesus has done to us, which is made us holy! (See Hebrews 10:10). This revelation in the mind of a Christian is paramount to enjoying Jesus within us. We've *been* changed. We are *new* creations. Now, we blossom.

Just as Grandma did for me with *her* words, the words in this book are meant to build up your confidence in who you currently *are*, Christian. I didn't write this book to change you. I wrote this book to help you understand you've been born again. Your birth into the family of God was a one-time event which happened the millisecond you accepted the truth: *Jesus forgave me. Thank you.*

We can't be unborn from our earthly parents. Just the same, we can't be unborn from our Heavenly Father. Birth is final. Birth creates *identity*.

Over the next month I hope to assist you in going deeper into the knowledge of God's grace. In the book of Acts, Paul called the gospel, the gospel *of* grace (see Acts 20:24). Grace is not a footnote to the gospel message but the tractor which tills the soil, the grain which is planted, the rain that falls, and the fertilizer which strengthens. Grace is everything. Grace is Jesus. Grace is completely unfair and that's how God likes it for His children.

Each devotional you're about to read can be found on my website for free. If you'd like to share them on social media, email them to loved ones, or print out to give away, simply go to www.mattmcmillen.com. As you read, if you have any questions, you can always email me at matt@mattmcmillen.com.

Please take your time with this book. Have an open mind and look to the Scripture I reference contextually. Try not to skip ahead and spend a full thirty days with me. A lot of the things you're about to read may not match up with the identity you've been taught to have. I'm still learning myself. That is, what Christ has truly done to me. We're all just scratching the surface of who God has changed us into being! Thankfully, we'll have an eternity to learn from Him!

Day 1

---∞∞∞---

Above All, Love Each Other Deeply

*"Above all, love each other deeply, because
love covers over a multitude of sins."*

1 Peter 4:8

In my mid-teenage years a friend of mine got ahold of a bottle of Jack Daniels. He downed the entire fifth–all of it. I had come home through the back door that evening and turned to my right, through a bedroom, because I heard his voice.

"Maaaaaaaaat. Matt. Matt… Matt… Matty Matt!"

Through this bedroom was a bathroom. In that bathroom was my friend in the bathtub, naked in the water.

"Oh gosh!" I exclaimed as I flinched and turned my head after seeing what I could never unsee.

"What are you *doing*?!" I barked, confused.

"Oh, I'm drunk as crap. HA! I just smashed a whole bottle of Jack… huh…"

I winced and looked back at him, covering up his lower half from my view with my left hand. He was obliterated and could hardly keep his eyes open.

"Geez. Okay. You're gonna be in some pain tomorrow when that wears off," I said not fully knowing that I, myself, would begin to deal with alcoholism shortly after this, not getting sober until I was 32.

I turned and walked out, then into the kitchen. Grandma was sitting at the table by the window. The look she gave me was one of concern and sadness. Grandpa had struggled greatly with the same addiction, so this wasn't the first time she'd dealt with such a situation, by far.

"I couldn't send him home like that."

"Yeah, I know."

My friend's dad was not very kind to him. He was always respectful and friendly to me, but not to his own son. He knocked him around like a grown man in a bar fight. Now, just so you know, this friend was my *best* friend. He always stuck by my side. Even as the new kid in the neighborhood he showed me kindness and companionship when no one else would. He meant a lot to me and still does to this day.

His dad, however, was … what's the word I'm looking for? … Macho? He always wanted to come across as ultra-masculine, tough, and a "man's man." He took out his chauvinism quite often on my buddy, sometimes knocking him across the room or across the head when I spent the night–which was always awkward.

My friend lived on the other side of the alley so he was always at our house. Even when I wasn't there he'd come hang out with my brothers, sister, or even Grandma and Dad. He was basically family. We all knew how *his* dad was, including Grandma, so when he got super-drunk that day she took care of him and didn't send him home. He would've gotten punched around so she tried to sober him up by putting him in the tub.

But even if my friend's dad wasn't overbearing, Grandma would've still taken care of him just the same. The love of Jesus–which is protecting others and covering for their mistakes–would've *still* been expressed through her because she knew who she was.

The words *love one another* are mentioned in the same sentence in the New Testament approximately 20 times, depending on the translation. Loving one another is the foundational fabric of the one true God. In fact, for believers, loving others is a part of who we are in our supernatural genetic makeup. We cannot get away from loving others, it's impossible. Even when people infuriate or annoy us, such attempts to shield them off by non-loving actions and attitudes could be compared to corking Old Faithful at Yellowstone.

We *are* loving, by nature. Old Faithful *does* explode, by nature. You can't stop either so don't even attempt to.

Try denying our loving nature as we might–because we're hurt or mad– we never feel more like ourselves than when we express love. Paul calls this built-in love *incorruptible* (see Ephesians 6:24). Incorruptible means *unable to die or decay, everlasting.*

This love which has been poured into the heart of every single Christian, evenly, is the love of God Almighty. Truthfully, it *is* God Almighty, Himself. Paul informs the Romans:

> *"And hope does not put us to shame, because <u>God's love has been poured out into our hearts through the Holy Spirit</u>, who <u>has been</u> given to us."*
> *(Romans 5:5)*

Do you see that, friend? You, dear believer, have God's Spirit in you, in full, right now, this moment. You lack nothing because you have Him. You *house* His incorruptible love.

Let me back up just in case you feel left out. If you've *not* yet believed Jesus, believe. Today is your day of salvation. Believe Jesus has forgiven you this moment and be saved for eternity. When you do this you'll receive the same Spirit of incorruptible love into *your* spirit. This is not a feeling but a fact of faith. The Bible never says to "feel" anything–although, sure, you could. God is not against feelings. But salvation isn't based on feelings. It's based on believing and knowing that Jesus has forgiven you.

Feelings come and go based on what's happening around us and in our mind at any given moment. Jesus *never* comes and goes. He stays.

When you believe this, at that exact millisecond your old spirit dies, you get a new spirit, and the Holy Spirit of Jesus infuses Himself with you permanently (see Galatians 2:20, Romans 6:6-10, 8:9, Colossians 3:3, 2 Corinthians 5:17, 1 Corinthians 6:17). No special event needs to happen–but again, if a special event *did* happen that's okay too. Just know that event didn't save you. Jesus did.

So if you've not yet believed, believe right now. Repent of unbelief, once, and you'll become a child of God forever (see John 1:12, 3:16-18, Acts 3:19, Hebrews 10:10,14).

As for the situation with my friend and Grandma, that moment in the late 1990's will forever be seared into my subconscious. I got to see parts of my friend I wish I never did, literally, but I also got to see my grandma loving him as Christ loves us all. No shame, no condemnation, just covering a multitude of mistakes in order to protect him from being harmed even worse. That's mercy. That's grace. That's love.

So today, my friends, know this: You have this same incorruptible love in you if you've ever trusted in Jesus. In your core, you want exactly what He wants. You can't deny this love because love *is* your nature. Just try withholding it and you'll see such never fits. Jesus wants you to love others and *you* want you to love others. The pain certain people have caused you might muffle this truth–and God shows you grace, especially during those frustrating times–but *you* love like a fish swims, Christian. Your mind will catch up to this truth over the course of your short life on this planet, even if you live an entire century. The older I get the more I realize Grandma *knew* this truth about *who* she was. She did what she did for so many people during her 89 years because she understood it was a natural thing to love others, deeply.

A prayer for you: *Heavenly Father, today I want to express my appreciation to you. I want to thank you for giving me yourself, and your love. This union we have is indescribable. On the days I start to lose patience with myself, you remind me how to love myself, because you are in me. This organic love cannot be explained in human languages, but you know, and I know. Thank you for this love. Thank you. Right now, I lift up all who are reading this, directly to you. For the Christians, what they've just read makes perfect sense. It clicked, and now they feel relief. Many of them were taught they have to prove their love to you and others, but Jesus did that for us and we are thankful. Now that same love is in us permanently. Keep taking them deeper into the knowledge of who you've remade them to be as your loving children. For the unbeliever, in regard to this love, maybe they're intrigued but can't wrap their minds around it. Let them know that's exactly where they need to be. Like a child, they simply need to trust you and believe in your Son. Thank you so much for Him, for your love, and for giving us all the opportunity to be one with you forever. Amen.*

Day 2

What If You've Already Been Changed?

*"Therefore, if anyone is in Christ, the new creation
has come: The old has gone, the new is here!"*

2 Corinthians 5:17

How would you live if you knew you didn't have to change?

Five years ago that question would have baffled me. After all, I could never reach the dangling carrot of "changing myself for the better."

Truth be told, for a time, I said the heck with it and *stopped* trying to change myself into being a better person. Licentiousness and debauchery was the result. But even then, God was renewing my mind to who I already was, I just didn't get it.

Then I fell off the cliff into the opposite direction. Legalism, pastoral approval, great-comissionism and self-righteousness ruled and ruined my days. I became uber-competitive in ministry and wanted to iron out everyone's incorrect theology. What madness. What *unrest*.

"I gotta change all these sinners and false teachers! I gotta change myself! The work is never done!"

In the midst of this confusion God's Holy Spirit would speak to *my* spirit, "Matthew, it's not your job to change anyone and *you* don't need to change either. You need to learn who I've already changed you into, and live."

This made no sense to me so I ignored it.

"That's too easy, and nobody teaches that in church."

Then it happened. I can remember the moment it hit me and where I was when I finally realized the second half of the gospel, "I'VE *BEEN* CHANGED!"

I was laying in bed, reading, before I went to sleep. "There's no more changing to be had! I am complete! My identity is final!"

This brought another question to mind, "When exactly did this happen?"

The answer was: *from the moment of my salvation.* From the millisecond I believed Jesus forgave me in the mid-1980's! My mind immediately backtracked! This twist ending caused me to see my entire life differently! I had a brand new perspective about my past!

"I WAS CHANGED THIS WHOLE TIME?! WOW!"

It's like when you first see the ending of the movie, *The Sixth Sense.* Your brain instantly tries to replay the film from the beginning to the end, now that you know Bruce Willis was dead the entire time!

"So *that's* why nobody ever talked to him or looked at him but only the boy! The boy was counseling another dead person, but the dead person thought he was counseling the boy! Crazy!"

In regard to my newly-discovered, heaven-ready identity, the same thing happened.

"I've been a new creation since I was eating pudding cups and playing with ninja turtle figurines! That's why sinning never felt right permanently!

That's why trying to earn God's approval never made any sense! That's why getting drunk all the time never fulfilled me! That's why legalism never set right in my soul! That's why going to a building to feel better, calling down God's Spirit, praising a pastor, or reading a book to become a better person was weird!"

I had been a child of God the whole time! I didn't *need* to change! I HAD ALREADY BEEN CHANGED! Instead, I needed to know *more about* my righteousness! I needed to be educated on what the Cross had not just done *for* me but *to* me! I had *been* reborn! I didn't need to keep *getting* reborn! I NEEDED TO LEARN AND GROW–I NEEDED TO MATURE–NOT BE BORN AGAIN AND AGAIN AND AGAIN BY WHAT I DO OR DON'T DO!

"Aaaaaaaaaahhhhhh!" I wanted to shout about this freedom from the rooftops!

…My spiritual rebirth was final, a long time ago. I wish I believed this truth sooner. Just like we can't be reborn physically once it's happened, we can't be reborn spiritually once it's happened. Birth is unchangeable, unsustainable, and unimprovable. This is why Jesus told Nicodemus–a devout, religious man–"You must be born again" (see John 3:1-8).

A long time ago, this happened to me. As I sat on that cold, hard pew, my spirit had been killed, buried, and reborn. I was resurrected, forever connected to God's Spirit through Jesus Christ (see John 1:12, Galatians 2:20, Romans 6:6-10, Colossians 3:3, 1 Corinthians 6:17).

My *gosh* how *awesome* is this? I didn't have to change–me, as in, my identity. Sure, my actions and attitudes would always be a work in progress, but not *me*. WHO I AM. No more changing was to be had from the time I knew Jesus saved me. The reality is, no Christian needs to change. We need to be ourselves and renew our thinking to who we are (see Romans 12:2, Philippians 1:6, 4:8, Colossians 1:22, 1 John 4:17,18).

What does this look like practically? Friend, think about it. If you *knew* Jesus took all your punishment, for every mistake–past, present, and future–you'd stop being afraid of God and you'd let Him love you. If you *knew* you were one of God's own kids, and you *knew* God is a good Father–not an abusive legalist–you'd stop hiding from Him and enjoy Him. You'd stop flinching. You'd let Him hug you more often, especially when you're hard on yourself. You'd stop with all the false humility each time He, or someone else, gives you an amazing compliment. You'd say, "Thank you," instead. You'd forgive those who hurt you a lot quicker because you'd know that *you*, yourself, are completely forgiven forever.

You'd let Him push up and out your stinking thinking, like splinters, rather than think He's changing you all the time. You'd listen more often when He corrects you because you'd know He only wants the best for you. But even when you don't, you'd still know He makes your crooked paths straight because He uses grace on you like He uses rain on flowers.

You'd look at all Scripture differently–with confidence–from Genesis to Revelation. You'd sin a lot less because you'd know that when you sin it's not natural, because you're a saint. You'd know you're a holy person by new birth–and nothing more.

You'd also know that no amount of unnatural choices–sinning–could cause the Father and Son to break their promise to each other. When you are faithless they remain faithful *for* you. You'd feel secure no matter what season of life you're going through, which would inspire you to live authentically, gracefully. Even in the pain.

If you knew you didn't have to change, you'd take the pressure off others because you'd know behavior does not define them either. You'd love them better, because you'd love yourself better, because you'd know God loves you, better.

You'd be comfortable in your own skin. You'd understand your righteousness. You'd understand your glory. Not a separate or conditional righteousness and glory, but *yours* (see 2 Corinthians 5:21, John 17:22).

You'd remove your masks. Those feeble coverings of posturing and addictions to achieve satisfaction and validation would fall away left and right. You'd know God is *always* well-pleased with who you are. You're His baby, no matter your age.

Mistakes would never define you, nor would achievements, nor would people. Only God.

If you knew you didn't have to change and that you've *been* changed, you'd enjoy the abundant life Christ has already given you, which is Himself.

So today, my friends, know this: Don't change, Christian, be yourself. You *can't* change anyway. God has already changed you into a whole new creation, a creation with whom He's immeasurably infatuated.

A prayer for you: *Dad, when I think about how far you've brought me in my thinking, I get choked up. I could write about this subject for days. When I think back on all those years you were renewing my mind to the truth of what you did to me when I first believed... I don't know what to say. Just, thank you. Right now, I lift up all who are reading this, directly to you. I understand, for many, what they've just read might have their heads spinning–I get it. I've been there and we both know it. You were with me as I sat through countless church services and in front of guest speakers where the emphasis was on getting ME to change. Do this, do that, start this, stop that, go there, be more, do more–on and on, but the focus was never on the Cross alone. Thank you for teaching me that the same Cross which*

crucified Jesus crucified me too. The same tomb in which He was buried, I was buried, and on that same Sunday He arose, I arose. I was made new, just like Him, in my spirit. No more changing was necessary but only the renewing of my mind into who you caused me to become. Please expose these truths in even greater ways to these wonderful people. In Jesus' name I pray, amen.

Day 3

Jesus Has Retroactive Blood

*"… the Lamb who was slain from
the creation of the world."*

See Revelation 13:8

Jesus' blood is timeless. From the moment it was shed it had the ability to
forgive present, future, and even *past* sins—the sins of those who believed
God *before* Jesus was born. But before I dive deeper into this opening statement, I want you, dear reader, to think of one word: *blood*.

I had a nice medium rare steak the other night. It was a little more rare
than medium, yet still delicious. Grace thought it was gross that blood was on
my plate after I cut into it, Jennifer quickly assured her, "That's not blood, it's
just juice coming from the steak."

But it was blood, a *tiny* bit anyway. Blood on my dinner plate was improper
to my daughter. Most people have this reaction to blood, we don't like to see
this red fluid. When we prick our finger and blood comes out, without hesita-
tion a majority of us will put our finger in our mouth. Gross. But why is it gross?

Because of blood. Blood is not supposed to come out of our body, it's supposed to stay in there so our knee-jerk reaction is normally off-putting when we see it.

Blood provides oxygen for our cells. Blood keeps us alive and moving. It gives us energy. It provides life. But also, blood *forgives* us. If there's anything you remember from this devotional, remember that blood forgives, and nothing else. God has a blood-based forgiveness economy. This is why Jesus had to die by bloodshed.

Christ symbolically explains this to the disciples at the Last Supper while holding up His wine:

> "This is *my blood* of the covenant, which is *poured out* for many *for the forgiveness of sins*." *(Matthew 26:28)*

Paul tells the Ephesians too:

> "*In him* we have redemption *through his blood, the forgiveness of sins*, in accordance with the riches of God's grace." *(Ephesians 1:7)*

There are many more biblical passages about how Jesus' blood forgives, but sadly, many of us have taken our focus off this truth and put it on ourselves. Ourselves didn't save us, ourselves can't keep us saved, and ourselves can't make us "more" holy. The reality is, our spirits are complete in Christ! This holy wholeness came by way of faith in what *He* did at the Cross. What did He do? Poured out His blood (see Colossians 2:9,10, Hebrews 10:10, John 19:30). Friend, whether we realize it or not, even *when* we believe, we are believing in the ability of Jesus' bloodshed to forgive us.

Typically, death is the result of major bloodshed, and *death* is the punishment required for every single sin, according to our Creator (see Romans 6:23). So, only blood can provide forgiveness. This is why Jesus had to die. He is our Judge, but also our Savior at the exact same time. Because of being born into sin, our punishment was spiritual death. Perfect blood was the requirement for restitution. Jesus paid off our fines in full (see all of Romans 5).

I don't want to be misunderstood. I'm not talking about Universalism. Not everyone is saved. We must believe in His blood's capability *to* forgive us—and that we need this forgiveness. *Then* it forgives, immediately, once. Why once? Because Jesus would have to be repeatedly crucified if this were not the truth (see 1 Peter 3:18, Hebrews 4:14-16, all of chapters 9 and 10).

The author of Hebrews explains this ad nauseam throughout their epistle. Painstakingly, he or she is making the case for Christ being *who* the Jewish people were waiting on for permanent forgiveness. Their religious customs handed down by Moses were but shadows—Christ was the One *making* that shadow. Many refused to look to the real thing lest they were cut off from God because of their obsession with Law (see Romans 11:23, Hebrews 6:4-8, 10:26-29).

The Jews were Hebrew people. Therefore the epistle of *Hebrews* is written to them. Yes, Jews *and* Gentiles would eventually read it, but this was not originally *for* the Gentiles because Gentiles were never given the subject matter in the letter: *the Old Covenant*. Consequently, the audience knew full well that God only forgives by way of b-l-o-o-d…blooooooooooood:

> *"According to the Law, in fact, nearly everything must be purified*
> *with blood, and <u>without the shedding of blood there is no forgiveness</u>."*
> *(Hebrews 9:22)*

Words did not forgive. Repentance of actions and attitudes did not forgive (the Jews were the best-behaved people on earth). Repeated confession did not forgive. Only blood had the ability to atone for or "cover up" their sins. This forgiveness event happened annually at the temple during the Day of Atonement with sacrificial animal blood. This is why Jesus is called *the Lamb,* a proper noun, by John the Baptist (see John 1:29). As a Jewish man, John knew lamb blood paid off his sins with God each year. The Holy Spirit revealed to him that Jesus was the final sacrifice for sin. This is also why he said, "He must increase, and I must decrease" (see John 3:30).

John wasn't talking about himself as a person, as so many use this verse out of context for. He was talking about his ministry of Mosaic Law. John was running around telling people, "Stop sinning or else!" (See Matthew 3:1,2). Jesus was running around telling people, "Believe I can forgive you, and I will" (see Mark 2:10, John 3:16-18).

The Law of Moses–613 commandments which included *the* Ten Commandments–which John preached, required animal blood to forgive every single transgression. The New Covenant–believe in Jesus and love as He loves us–which Jesus preached, required His *own* blood to forgive. The Law of Moses' bloody Day of Atonement happened once a year. Jesus' bloody day happened once for all time. These two Covenants were never allowed to conjoin. The Hebrew people had to pick one or the other (see Mark 2:22, John 13:34, 1 John 3:23, 5:3, Galatians 2:19, Romans 6:14, 10:4, Hebrews 8:13, 10:10).

Even more, the Jews felt relief for their commandment-breaking for the previous *year* as they walked away from the temple after handing off their livestock to be killed by a Levitical priest. Once they sinned again–by breaking one or more of Moses' commandments–they didn't neurotically start asking God for forgiveness or "change their ways" to *achieve* forgiveness. Instead, they worried nothing about their sins being forgiven until the following Day of Atonement. They knew without the shedding of blood there is no forgiveness, so they *waited* while feeling the burden of their mistakes.

We, as the modern church, have twisted *how* we are forgiven. Why? I believe mostly due to tradition. We've been taught wrong through poor interpretation of Scripture by our now-dead relatives. We think because it's old it's correct, just like the Jews did with Moses' teaching, and just like so many

Muslims do too–or any other old religion for that matter. From the foundation of the planet–not from the foundation of the Bible–if the Holy Spirit is not guiding us, we are wrong. We will even misinterpret God's perfect words *in* the Bible, apart from His Spirit. Satan loves this.

It also preaches well to tell people to beg God for forgiveness, *and* it conveniently extorts money from parishioners when "holy hierarchies" broker God's blessings. *Ahem* But I'll stay on course here about Jesus' blood.

Blood mattered. Not words. Not begging. Not even lifestyle change (that sentence will upset many legalistic demons who pester people, don't fall for it). Friend, blood *still* matters today, only there's no more animal sacrifices left to be made, and Jesus isn't going to die again *either*. He was the final sacrifice for sin and He did one better than just atone for sins–HE REMOVED THEM PERMANENTLY (see 1 John 3:5). The world's sin issue with God is over. Now, everyone has the opportunity to be reconciled with Him through faith in Jesus (see 2 Corinthians 5:17-21).

The main difference in the blood of animals and the blood of Jesus is that animal blood only forgave *past* sins–whatever a Jewish man or woman had accumulated a year at a time. Jesus' blood not only forgave past sins but also present sins and *future* sins. But what about the people who lived before the Cross? How did they receive forgiveness by way of Jesus' blood?

Because His blood is *retroactive* as well.

Through the bloodshed of Messiah at Calvary, He dealt with sin *once* and for all time. That is, the entire timeline of human history. The opening of Hebrews unrolls the truth; the truth that Jesus is a non-time-Creature:

> *"The Son is the radiance of God's glory and the exact representation of his being, <u>sustaining all things</u> by his powerful word. After he <u>had provided purification for sins,</u> he sat down at the right hand of the Majesty in heaven." (Hebrews 1:3)*

Sustaining all things? You cannot be bound by time if you're doing such. *Had* provided purification? That's past tense. Purification of what? Planet earth's sin-filled spirits–*our* spirits–*we* needed to be purified. Jesus provided a way for this purification with His own perfect blood. Now, to tap *into* this spiritual purification–which is supernatural perfection–we must simply believe He can and will forgive us. This one-time decision of faith in His blood causes us to be forgiven once and for all time:

"By this will we have been sanctified through the offering of the body of Jesus Christ once for all." (Hebrews 10:10)

Again, to God, every sin requires death. Jesus died. Because of His death we believe and receive *His* supernatural life into our own. Our spirits immediately die by faith. Once dead–not our physical body but our spirit–we are given new spirits while still *in* these fleshy-shells. Then, at the same time, His Spirit joins our spirit and lives through us as we allow Him to (see John 3:16, 14:19, 15:5, 19:30, Colossians 3:3,4, Galatians 2:20, 5:22,23, Romans 6:6-11,23, 1 Corinthians 6:17).

All of this happens because of His blood. We are made brand new in spirit (see 2 Corinthians 5:17-21, 1 John 1:8-10). Keep in mind, His blood was shed once, it won't be shed again and again in heaven for each future sin we commit, like the animal bloodshed each year (see Hebrews 10:4).

So when you sin, turn from it, repent, confess to a trusted friend–but never to *be* forgiven. You are 100% forgiven by God *already*. Turn from sin because sin never pays off and you weren't made to sin. But don't turn from sin to achieve more forgiveness. Jesus would have to die for more forgiveness, not *you* starting or stopping something.

For the person who believes God, Jesus' blood forgives past, present, and I repeat, even future sins. Remember, all of our sins were in the future when

Christ died. He's not bound by the notion of time in which He created. This is why in Revelation, John writes:

"… the Lamb who was slain from the creation of the world."
(See Revelation 13:8)

How was Jesus slain from the beginning of this physical universe? After all, the moment in *time* of His death had not yet come to pass. This is impossible to fathom as time creatures, which we are. You and I, we understand time based on the revolutions of the planets–*when* we eat, sleep, work, and play. We experience 24 hour days, weeks, months, the seasons, and years. God isn't confound to this. He is Spirit. He always has been and always will be (2 Peter 3:8, Exodus 3:14, Revelation 22:13).

So if I pull myself "up and out of time" as *I* know it, I can *kind* of get a sense of this, although ant-like in my perception of what God truly sees. God is *not* confined by what He's created. Think of Bill Gates. He created Windows. Microsoft Windows is being used everywhere by lots of people at this very moment. Is what he's created stopping Bill Gates from being who he is? No. Windows carries on, and Bill Gates does too. So, *time* is not stopping God *either*. He invented time and isn't bound by its "programming."

Because of this epiphany, we come to realize God can see the future. Is He controlling the future by controlling us? No. But He can still see down the timeline of His Creation just the same as we can see what's been recorded on our DVR. When we pick up the remote and play a show or watch a ballgame, we aren't controlling the actors or players–but, we control the remote. We are not bound by the time of the very people we're watching. Same with God and us. He isn't controlled by the time of this universe. He's holding the remote.

Therefore, the Lamb, who is Christ, *was* slain at the creation of the world because time does not shackle Him. Jesus' blood is not only proactive–forgiving the future sins of all humans who would ever believe in Him–but it's also retroactive. It forgives those who were born *before* His human life and human death. This is how Noah, Abraham, Issac, Jacob, and every person who *believed* God were righteous *before* the blood of Jesus was shed: *Messianic retroactive holy hemoglobin.*

Think about it. Jesus died a long time ago, so if *we* can receive forgiveness 2,000 years *later*, why can't *they* receive forgiveness thousands of years *before*? I mean, *both* of us are believing God. The answer is they can! Look!

"Abram believed the LORD, and he credited it to him as righteousness."
(Genesis 15:6)

Why was it credited? Why was his righteousness put on the books? Because Jesus *physically* had not came and went, and *He* is the only way to God. This passage is from Genesis! The very first book of the Bible! Thousands of years before the crucifixion!

But what I find even more amazing is that pre-Cross *Gentiles* had the option of receiving the righteousness of Jesus Christ too–not just the Jews. Rahab, a Gentile prostitute, she received righteousness by faith *before* Jesus was born, let alone sacrificed:

"Rahab the prostitute is another example. She was shown to be right with God by her actions when she hid those messengers and sent them safely away by a different road." (James 2:25)

She *believed* God. That belief caused her to act. Had she not believed Him *first* she wouldn't have helped the spies. Friend, God has always been interested in one main thing: "Do you believe me?"

Belief put Jesus' blood money into the accounts of the patriarchs–which included Gentiles! Who's to say there's not even *more* Gentiles, all throughout the world, who became righteous by faith who are *not* mentioned in the canon of the Bible? That's definitely something to think about!

Faith in God retro-acted the power of the Cross *into* the lives of people on planet earth *before* the Cross happened. Is this not cool or what?!

So the next time someone asks you, "If Jesus' blood forgives us, what about the people who lived before He died?"

Just reply with, "His blood goes backwards, too," and then smile. The Cross is timeless. Before the foundation of time, space, or matter, the power of the Lamb was in full effect.

So today, my friends, know this: The blood of Jesus Christ is not restrained by our idea of time. His blood has no beginning or end. All of the famous Old Testament believers who were mentioned in Hebrews 11? Those who were looking forward to the promise of Messiah? They *too* enjoyed His finished work by faith, just like you and I enjoy it today. Once we eject from this body, we'll all fully understand what Jesus Christ has done for us. So for now, let's let Him live *through* us.

A prayer for you: *Father, thank you for opening up my mind to understand that you are not defined by time. This has changed so much for me. Please continue to take me deeper into this truth, as well as your grace, and use me for your purposes. This is so much fun! Right now, I lift up all who are reading this, directly to you. For those who are obsessed with keeping track of their sins so they can confess them or turn from them–to*

try and try to please you by doing so—ease their minds. Let them know that Jesus has dealt with all of their sins at the Cross. Remind them that confession and repentance is normal and healthy for us saints, but neither can cause us to be more forgiven than we already are right now. The blood of Jesus was suffice! Thank you so much! Amen!

Day 4

What's the Real Greatest Commandment?

"A new command I give you: Love one another. As
I have loved you, so you must love one another."

John 13:34

"Matt, what's the *real* greatest commandment?"
Before I came to understand the New Covenant, if I was asked this question, my answer would've been wrong. I'd reply, "Love God with all my heart, soul, and mind–and the second greatest commandment is to love my neighbor as myself."

A majority of the Christian population would say, "What's wrong with that answer? It's biblical." And yes, it *is* biblical, but just because something is biblical doesn't mean it's written to Christians. This passage is from Matthew 22:36-39, and we Christians should know it, but if we aren't separating the Old and New Covenants as we read this section of Scripture confusion will happen.

Love God with everything I am? Love my neighbor as myself? This is *not* how God expects Christians to live. Why not?

1. Because Jesus is being literal. He wasn't saying, "Give it your best shot."
2. Because it is impossible to do this perfectly, which is required, in context.
3. Because this was spoken to legalists, not Christians.

Other than Christ, nobody has ever expressed such a love in the history of humanity and that's exactly why Jesus said it. This isn't the *true* greatest commandment–for Christians–but instead for Israelites according to the Old Covenant, the Law. We have something much better because of Jesus; something much easier, much lighter. I'll get to that shortly, and don't worry, God has rigged it to where Christians have a love for Him and others which will never go away. We've been reborn with an incorruptible love in our genetic spiritual makeup. Like a fish in water swims, we love as we live (see Ephesians 6:24, 1 John 3:9, 4:20, Galatians 5:22,23).

What blew my mind was when I finally understood the context of Matthew 22:36-39:

This is the two greatest commandments *in the Law*.

Those three words–*in the Law*–are crucial to deciphering the context of the Covenants. Innocently, most people leave them off when asked about the greatest commandment because they just don't know *how* important it is. It's everything.

Jesus gave a Law-based answer to a Law-based question. Are Christians under the Law? No. Our only option is grace (see Romans 6:14, 10:4, 11:6, Ephesians 2:8,9). To be clear, the Law is still in effect for today but *only* to bring self-centered non-believers to their knees. Its sole usage is to cause rejec-tors of the gospel to say, "I give up on this! I need Jesus!"

This is why Paul said the Law is not of faith, the Law kills, and that it was a tutor until Christ came. Now that Jesus is here it's obsolete for children of God. Obsolete means no usage is necessary because something better and more efficient has taken its place (see Galatians 3:12,23-25, 2 Corinthians 3:6, Hebrews 8:6,13).

We don't use pay phones anymore, we have cell phones. Those who have trusted God don't use the Law anymore, we have the Spirit of Christ within us for counsel.

What most Law-pushing people won't tell you is what Jesus was asked *before* He gave His answer to the greatest commandment question:

> "Teacher, which is the great commandment in the Law?"
> (Matthew 22:36)

He's talking to a self-righteous religious person who was trying to test Him (see Matthew 22:35); someone who *thought* he could do the "best parts" of the Law to be greater than others. Unfortunately for this yahoo the Law was a package deal of 613 commandments. Do all or do none. If you fail at just *one* command, animal blood must be shed to cover that transgression, that sin, at the next annual Day of Atonement (see Deuteronomy 4:2, Galatians 3:10, James 2:10, Hebrews 9:22, 10:3,4).

Do you think this sanctimonious jerk actually loved God with all his heart, soul, and mind? Do you think he loved others as himself? I'd say nope. This is *why* Jesus answered him this way. He knew his heart. Jesus gave him two unat-tainable commandments to show him his need to turn toward faith in Him alone, by way of grace. He needed to repent of Law observance and dead works. He needed life, Christ's life (see Hebrews 6:1, John 14:6, 1 John 5:11-13).

He needed to get off the broad road of Law, which leads to destruction, and onto the narrow path of grace. Jesus was and is the gate to enter this path, and he needed to believe. 613 commandments is wide, one Man is narrow:

> *"Enter through the narrow gate. For wide is the gate and broad is the road that leads to destruction, and many enter through it. But small is the gate and narrow the road that leads to life, and only a few find it."*
> *(Matthew 7:13,14)*

> *"I am the gate; whoever enters through me will be saved. They will come in and go out, and find pasture." (John 10:9)*

Friend, as Christians, we don't need the Law. We've already entered through the gate of Christ and found lush pastures of grace. The Law is the *Old* Covenant between God and Israel. Israel is the Jewish people group whom Moses guided through the Red Sea floor after freeing them from slavery in Egypt.

If we aren't Jewish these passages about following the Law weren't written to us anyway. They'd squint their eyes and laugh if we tried to obey any of Moses' commandments–let alone the greatest. We were considered dogs and pigs, not holy enough for the Law. We were excluded from the first Covenant because of our lineage. We Gentiles, non-Jews, were not brought into the picture with any kind of covenant *until* Jesus died. Our righteousness only came by way of faith, by believing God, not by Law. Unbeknownst to a lot of Jews, that was *their* only way as well, even before Jesus came (see Matthew 7:6, Ephesians 2:12, Galatians 3:11,20,28, Romans 4:3, 5:20, James 2:23).

Sadly, even the Jews have been cut off from God *if* they refused to believe Jesus is Messiah. Their heritage means nothing, in regard to favor, now that Christ has come. Only through belief in *Him* can they be grafted back in with *us*. If they choose to harden their hearts and trample on the Holy Spirit of grace–because of unbelief–no sacrifice for their sins is left. Therefore, they'll be judged according to their Law worshiping and not the blood of Jesus (see Romans 11:1-22, Hebrews 3:15, 10:26-29).

So when Christ gave this answer, remember, He was just asked a question by a legalistic Israelite and the subject was Law. No one has *ever* loved God with all their heart, soul, and mind–ever. Only Jesus. And nobody has *ever* loved their neighbor as themselves–perfectly. Only Jesus. This is *Law* and Jesus said if you want to follow the Law you must be perfect like God, yet only *He* has accomplished this feat (see Matthew 5:48, John 14:9, Hebrews 1:3).

Has any human done this other than Him? No, not one (see Romans 3:10). Consequently, the question we should now ask is, "What's the greatest commandment according to the New Covenant?"

Jesus tells us:

> *"A <u>new</u> commandment I give you: love others as I have loved you."*
> *(John 13:34).*

This was flabbergasting to the Jews because *new* commandments were not allowed to be added to the Law. Moses gave strict instructions:

> *"<u>Do not add to</u> what I command you and do not subtract from it, but*
> *keep the commands of the Lord your God that I give you."*
> *(Deuteronomy 4:2)*

This is also why the Law-abiding citizens wanted to kill Jesus so badly. He was messing with their religion. They followed Moses, not Jesus, but Jesus said:

> *"If you really believed Moses, you would believe me, because he wrote*
> *about me." (John 5:46)*

"How dare you!" they yelled. "Crucify him!"

This new commandment in itself was blasphemous, and here He is claiming Moses wrote about *Him*?! What they didn't understand was that Jesus was about to complete the Law *in* Himself *at* the Cross! He wasn't going to do away with it, but finalize it! (See Romans 10:4, John 19:30).

Not the smallest stroke of the Law would ever go away (see Matthew 5:17,18). I don't want to be misunderstood. The Law of Moses is *still* in full force *this moment* but it *still* has the same usage as it did thousands of years ago:

> *Show the unbeliever their need for grace*–and sometimes–*to remind the believer about the grace they already have.*

So today, my friends, know this: The real greatest commandment is to love others as God has loved us in Jesus Christ. How do we do this? It's very simple but we make it more complicated than it truly is:

Allow Christ's Spirit to live *through* us, through our hands, feet, mouths, and minds. We are branches, He is the vine. Branches don't force anything. Branches never stress or strain. They just *live* in complete dependence on the vine (see John 15:5, Galatians 5:22,23).

So live. The branch life is easy. There's no pressure on you, Christian. Vines don't pressure branches. He who began this good work in you–the work of renewing your mind to His great love–will surely complete it (see Romans 12:2, Philippians 1:6, Romans 8:38,39). You are secure and you'll live out this new commandment without effort! Enjoy your life and be yourself! You've been recreated for this very reason!

A prayer for you: *Father, thank you for revealing to me the difference in the greatest commandments. The pressure which has been taken off of me has changed my life. What a relief. Keep teaching me more about the love you've placed inside of me, naturally. Right now, I lift up all who are reading this, directly to you. For those who are just beginning to walk in the truth of the New Covenant, let them know how perfectly secure they are. Ease their minds today in knowing they have all they need for life and godliness. Reveal their completeness in Christ. As they grow and mature, give them confidence in the peace which surpasses all understanding, as they enjoy your grace. In Jesus' name, amen.*

Day 5

────────⌘────────

I Want What God Wants?

*"Delight yourself in the LORD, and he will
give you the desires of your heart."*

Psalm 37:4

"Jesus didn't die so you can just do whatever you want!"

Have you ever been told that before? I sure have. It's as if those who can't stand grace–or only dabble in grace–think that *we* don't want what God wants, so we better watch out!

The truth is Jesus actually *did* die so we can do whatever we want. As believers, in our supernatural core, our desires are just like His. We are recreated spirits who've been crucified, buried, and raised back to life. We literally house Christ's Spirit and we want *exactly* what He wants (see Romans 6:3-11, 1 Corinthians 6:19, 2 Corinthians 5:20).

There's no conflict between us and God. None, whatsoever (see Romans 5:1). The only time a conflict will occur is when we forget who we are, or, when we want to "improve" our righteousness by way of Law. So yes, spiritual amnesia and legalism will cause you to *not* want what God wants but neither are *you*, Christian (see Romans 7:8, Galatians 3:1-5, 5:18, 2 Peter 1:5-9, 1 Corinthians 6:11).

The Bible says God has written His laws on our heart (see Hebrews 8:10, 10:16). The author of Hebrews deliberately changed an Old Testament passage which read *Law* to *laws*, as he (or she) wrote to the Jewish people who were *under* the Law.

This change of text matters tremendously and stood out to the Jews because they knew the author wasn't talking about the Mosaic Law. They never referred to Moses' commands as *laws* but only by *Law*. It was a package deal and could not be altered in any way (see Deuteronomy 4:2, James 2:10, Galatians 3:10).

This was huge and matters for us today too! God is not writing 613 commandments on our hearts for us to *want* to do because we would have to do *all* of them! That's what the Law says! Both, sins of omission and commission would be punishable! Just do a quick Google search of "What are the 613 commandments in the Law" and you'll be bored to tears before you finish reading half of them! AND YOU HAVE TO KEEP THEM ALL–NOT JUST TEN! *If* God was writing Law on our hearts and we messed up at just *one* of these commands, blood would have to be shed at the next annual Day of Atonement (see Hebrews 9:22, 10:1). That is, if we're Jewish–Hebrew–and if the Law was still in effect for God's people. But we're not, and it's not, because of the Cross (see Galatians 3:28, Hebrews 7:22, 8:13, 10:26-29, Romans 6:14, John 1:29, 19:30, Ephesians 2:12).

Instead of Mosaic Law, God has written His very character on our hearts, His "laws." As in, Himself. Who He is. He's rigged it by giving us a new nature, *His* nature (see 2 Peter 1:4). Nature means natural. It's who we are. It's what we want. It's Him through us–but it's us too, not just Him. It's both. It's a relationship (see John 15:5, Philippians 2:13).

Therefore, it's a *normal* thing for us to *not* sin. *When* we sin we are doing what is contrary to what we really want. Choosing to sin goes against our nature but cannot change our nature because God is unchangeable (see Hebrews 6:16-19, 2 Timothy 2:13).

Plainly stated, for us, saints, sinning is not normal at all. Instead, it's normal to express God's traits because we've been reborn *of* God (see 1 John 5:4, John 3:6-8). What do His traits look like through us? Love, joy, peace, patience, kindness, goodness, faithfulness, gentleness, and self-control; none of which can be expressed through obeying the Law (see Galatians 5:22,23). This is why Paul said the Law is not of faith and against these traits there is no law (see Galatians 3:12, 5:23).

We cannot legislate "being" our natural self yet the Law legislates everything. It says, "Do this or else!"

But the Spirit says, "You are free, child. *Be* yourself. *Trust* yourself. I've given you all you need for life and godliness." (See John 8:36, Galatians 5:1, 2 Peter 1:3, Titus 2:11,12).

Lastly, the Law also includes the Ten Commandments. Out of 613 these are *just* ten. The Jews would have laughed at us for trying to keep such a small amount of commandments. They prided themselves on keeping *all* of them. Further, Moses said do not take away from the Law nor add to it (see Deuteronomy 4:2). Who gave us the right to handpick ten like we're in a buffet line, taking what we like and leaving the rest? We don't *need* the cherry-picked "top ten"–nor any of the Law–because we have a new nature and God's Spirit in us. *He* guides us moment by moment, not tablets of stone or dead prophets (see John 14:26, 2 Corinthians 3:7-18, Hebrews 1:1,2).

Who are we to trust Jesus for His saving blood but not for His ever-counseling Spirit? Who are we to let Christ forgive us but only allow Moses to guide us? We must repent of such thinking and trust the Spirit within.

So today, my friends, know this: Yes, Jesus did die so we can do whatever we want. That's precisely why He allowed Himself to be killed. Because of the Cross and our new life which came by way of His resurrection, we want what He wants and we'll prove this one way or the other. So Christian, do what you want. Do *exactly* what you want.

A prayer for you: *God, today I want to thank you for writing your desires on my heart. I want to thank you for my new heart. It's so amazing how you've made me into a brand new creation! Right now, I lift up all who are reading this, directly to you. So many of these good people have been told they're at battle with you, but if they've placed their faith in Jesus this is wrong. Your Word says in Galatians 5:17 the flesh and your Spirit are in conflict with each other—but not us. We are not the flesh. We have a body, but the flesh is not our body. It's the power of sin attempting to come to life through us. As we walk by our identity in the Spirit, the flesh sits idle and we do what we want. YOU deal with the flesh and we are grateful. Your Word never tells us to fight the flesh, you fight it, and you win the battle each time! We truly want what you want and when we understand this fact we do amazing things by simply being ourselves! Thank you so much! Amen.*

Day 6

⬡⬡⬡

But What About... (Part 1)

"Suddenly, their eyes were opened,
and they recognized Him."

See Luke 24:31

We all have questions. God is not against us having questions, in fact, His Spirit welcomes them. Unlike those who struggle with ungraciousness and refuse to have a civil biblical conversation without A.) *attacking you* B.) *belittling you*, or, C.) *ignoring you and shutting you out of their lives*, God invites us to question everything. Why? Because the truth will always set us free.

This freedom is taught by the Holy Spirit primarily through the truth about our identity as children of God. Once we understand we're God's kids, as one-time believers, ask away with reckless abandon.

However, there are sub-categories which should be questioned in full *other* than who we already are as holy people. When we know that we have nothing to fear as coheirs with Christ, we can ask anything. If the answer leads us into fear, for us, it's a nasty lie. If the answer leads us into peace of mind, bank on it.

Legalism hates truth and the world does too because both operate on fear *rather* than truth. For the world, it's the fear of not being good enough. For religion it's basically the same except churchianity fear creates hierarchies. As in, you "need" a specific human being to "keep you right" with God. The revolving door of "Do better! Try harder! Give until it hurts and never question pastor or priest!"? It spins every Sunday with all ferocity, collecting money from selling blessings to those who don't understand they're already blessed with *every* spiritual blessing (see Ephesians 1:3).

"You don't want to miss out on God's provision do you?!" they'll shout while sweating and spitting–or even worse in my opinion, smug passive-aggressiveness. "Just be like me," they'll say but not say. Yet, some *will* say. *Their* "spiritual disciplines" is what *you* need, so hurry up and fall in line. Don't worry about Christ's spiritual discipline–that is, what *He* did to the point of sweating blood in obedience to the Father. He's just a footnote. He's not quite enough. So be radical and finish what He started.

The *truth*, however, creates easiness because it's focused on *only* Jesus and not any man or woman who isn't. And giving is never done under pressure or to earn kudos or cash from our Creator. Instead, grace is the basis for all things–life *and* giving. And our wallet should open up because we're excited about the message, not because of spilled, overflowing anxiety from a person who can't stand to rest.

God has given us an amazing gift in His Word, the Bible. As you study it, a sense of peace will encompass your life. When you experience this peace, you can respond with love and softness to those who attempt to stress you out with threats "from" God. Rule of thumb: *fear is a red flag for believers to take a step back and assess the situation.*

Christian, as you learn *fearlessly*–which is the correct way to interpret the Bible as a saint–you *will* have questions. "But what about *this,* and what about *that*?"

Good! Don't worry, just keep searching Scripture and listening to the guidance of God's loving Spirit. As you do, perfect love always rises to the top and your confidence in your true identity will grow.

Here are five *But What Abouts* I've learned the answers to from God's Spirit. Through His Holy Word, and the correct exegesis based on the New Covenant, these same truths might help you too. Friend, don't be afraid any longer:

1. **Can I walk away from God?** The answer to this But What About is very simple: *we cannot walk away from being born.* Just like you can't *physically* walk away from being born, the same applies to your spirit once it is reborn as a saint. Every Christian is a saint, equally, by way of one-time faith in Jesus' ability to forgive them. Those who are focused on "what all they do for God" this insults them greatly. I was once there and it's a dark place of misery. The gospel has nothing to do with what all we do *for* God, or how little we sin. Those are minute details after the fact. The gospel is about our supernatural death and *then* our supernatural rebirth which happens from the moment we first believe in Christ's saving ability for our sin (see Romans 6:6-11, John 1:12). This is why Jesus said to an extremely well-behaved religious man, "Don't be surprised when I say 'You must be born again.'" (see John 3:7). The gentleman He was talking to was the epitome of obeying God's commandments, so why say this if obedience is what caused a person to walk *with* God and not *away* from God? Why tell him he must be born again? Because his *spirit* was dead and needed to be brought to life! Once this happens, by grace through faith in Jesus,

it can't be undone (see Ephesians 2:8,9). Birth is final! Physically and supernaturally! Where you walk, God walks. Deal with it. I say with all love and respect.

2. **But what about when Paul said work out your salvation?** In Philippians 2:12, Paul tells the church to work *out* their salvation, yes. But—he does not say work *for* your salvation. He's advising them to let *out* what has already been worked *in*. Jesus! After all, Jesus *is* our salvation because salvation is eternal life in Christ! We can't *work* to get Jesus, but we can work Him *out* of us by expressing Him—and we should, because such is normal and healthy as a child of God (see Hebrews 7:25, Colossians 3:4, John 3:16, 14:19, Galatians 5:22,23, 2 Peter 1:3-9).

3. **But what about when Jesus said depart from me I never knew you?** In Matthew 7:21-23, Jesus explains what will happen to those who *never* knew Him, on their Judgment Day, and it is bad. However, the key word in this passage is *never*. "I *never* knew you." Those who drink from the fountain of legalanity will spit this verse out as a threat toward those who aren't "doing as much as them" (heavy on the quotations). But as you can see, Jesus *never* knew them, no matter how much *they* did. This is not a *Christian* who didn't do enough, or stopped sinning enough, but an unbeliever who had a bunch of religious actions to show and gifts constantly displayed. Read all of it and you'll see that Jesus is referring to those who find their identity in what they did *for* God, on Judgment Day, *rather* than what Jesus did for them. Friend, don't let this verse cause you fear because Jesus *does* know you. You are hidden *inside* of Him, never to be taken out. The religious unbeliever is not (see John 10:27,28, Colossians 3:3).

4. **Didn't Paul say he was the chief of sinners?** Yes, he did. But he was talking about himself *before* salvation as an example of just how big God's grace is. Don't just cherry-pick this single verse. To get

the context start at verse 12, in 1 Timothy 1, and read to verse 17. Writing to young Timothy in this pastoral letter, you'll see he uses past tense words while describing how bad of a person he *used* to be. Paul was saying his identity was horrendous as a *former* persecutor of Christians. If you truly want to know Paul's opinion of his brand new spirit, just read the rest of his epistles. He talks repeatedly about his righteousness, holiness, new self, cleansing, blamelessness, completeness, and many other positive characteristics *after* he believed in Christ. Paul is *not* a sinner—and neither are you, Christian. God cannot live in wicked, sinful places, so He created a new, *clean* place to live by way of your faith in the Cross. Your very spirit (see 2 Corinthians 5:17-21, Colossians 1:22, 2:9,10, 3:3, 1 Corinthians 6:11,17,19, Galatians 2:20, Ezekiel 36:26, Hebrews 8:10).

5. **But what about the passage that says we will all stand and give an account on Judgment Day?** 2 Corinthians 5:10 has been misconstrued to create anxiety for children of God for a long time: *"For we must all appear before the judgment seat of Christ, so that each of us may receive what is due us for the things done while in the body, whether good or bad."* The key words to focus on are *"whether good or bad."* Yes, all of humanity will stand before Christ in judgment, each person after they die, but we Christians don't have anything *bad* to be judged for. To God, what are bad things called? Sins. And what has Jesus done with our sins? He's taken them all away! (See John 1:29, 1 John 3:5). So what's left to be judged for? What's left to receive? Only good things! And honestly, Christ is our full reward and we have Him right now! So who cares what else we'll get? For me, I'm not focused on raking in the prizes when I die. I'm focused *right now* on who I already have, both in this life and the next! Jesus!

A prayer for you: *Dad, thank you so much for opening up the truth of the Scriptures to me. Your perfect love for us in Christ casts out all fear because fear has to do with punishment—but Jesus was already punished. What an amazing gift to receive, which is freedom from fear. Right now, I lift up all who are reading this, directly to you. I know that some of the things they've just read may have caused them to feel good and it should've. But so many have been taught that feeling good is bad. Teach them, Father, that as your child, feeling good is okay. It's okay to feel good stuff! And that's what the truth of the gospel does, it makes us feel good—not bad! Renew and ease their minds as you take them deeper into the knowledge of your grace, little by little, day by day. Teach them more about your perfect love and reinforce what you're teaching them through your Holy Word. In Christ's name I pray, amen.*

Day 7

Saturday Morning Hangovers, Gone

"Who has anguish? Who has sorrow? Who is always fighting? Who is always complaining? Who has unnecessary bruises? Who has bloodshot eyes?"

Proverbs 23:32

There's something about Saturday morning which is very special to me. This time of day each week makes me want to write about my past battle with the bottle. It also reminds me of the crippling hangovers. Although I'm nearly five years without a sip of alcohol, I can still remember the feeling of dread as I opened my puffy eyes on a morning such as this.

My face and fingers were always swollen from the large amount of salt consumed due to binge eating after hours of binge drinking, which was perpetually my nightcap. When I drank, devouring enormous quantities of food before bed was the norm. Some of my pants wouldn't fit any longer and denial was how I handled my waistline expanding so much.

Although I'd get drunk during other days of the week, the worst occurrences began with "TGIF!" or the like, posted on my social media. The insane cycle of alcoholism and gluttony would peak on Friday. The steps went something like this:

1. Tell myself I'm going to "control" myself and have a few beers because it's the weekend.
2. Have a few beers … in less than an hour. Truthfully, in less than a *half* hour.
3. It's still early and I've only had a few, why not keep going? Done and done.
4. Why not have a few *more*, and why not some shots too? I'm already buzzed anyway. Check.
5. Take *more* shots to increase the effectiveness of my buzz, then more beer, then tell myself I'm not really that drunk–and believe myself.
6. I'm smashed. But because I've drank so much for so often, I can play it off like I'm not. I might smell like a dive bar, but I can look as cool as a cucumber.
7. Say and do stupid crap in which I'd never say or do if I wasn't drunk.
8. Binge eat until I could hardly move.
9. Go to bed or pass out on the couch, or on the deck furniture. When I wake up a few hours later, stumble to bed. But first, chug water due to severe cottonmouth.
10. Sleep really good for a few hours because I'm completely inebriated, but afterwards, toss and turn all night, restless, as I come down from my buzz and my brain dehydrates.

My entire Saturday would then be ruined because I was hungover and bloated; bloated because of eating *whatever* at the end of the night, and lots of it.

As a result, I'd lay on the couch in the basement and feel sorry for myself all day because "I did it again." This particular moment of the week had gotten to the point of grading my hangovers from bad to worse. All along, my body kept telling me, "Hey! STOOOOOP DRINKIIIIIIIING!"

Thankfully, the whole time I did this God never left my spirit. I had been saved from the time I was a boy. My *lack* of stupid actions and attitudes didn't *keep* me saved, Jesus staying alive did (see Hebrews 7:25, 13:5, Matthew 28:20).

The only thing which could alter my perfect spiritual identity–causing me to become unsaved–was if Jesus went back in time, crawled back up on the Cross, unfinished the New Covenant, got off the Cross, became a baby, went back into Mary, and then back into God's own supernatural loin.

That will never happen.

So my dumb choices would have to change for a much different reason: I was remade to not get drunk from the moment I was saved as a child.

Drunkenness is a sin, yet I've died to sin at my core, in my spirit. I had been taken *out* of sin and placed *into* the Spirit of Jesus Christ by grace through faith. *Drinking* is not a sin. People drank in the Bible all the time including Jesus. However, finding fulfillment in drunkenness *is* a sin because such is not of faith–and that's what I kept doing (see Romans 6:1-11, 8:9, 14:23, Galatians 3:27, 5:19-21, Ephesians 2:8,9, 5:18).

I was still saved, miserable, but *still* a saint. No matter how many times I tried, getting drunk would never satisfy me permanently. And to be clear, I could have a blood transfusion of Miller Lite right now–beer coursing through my veins–yet that still wouldn't overpower what the Cross had done to me the moment I believed in the mid-80's. For this reason, it never felt right each time I cracked open a cold shooter of American Honey or was handed a frosty glass of Corona. Christ in me repeatedly said, "Matthew, that's not for you. Give it up. Trust me."

He *never* said, "I'll come and make my home in you unless you become addicted to Schlafly Pale Ale and Jameson." No. He stayed in me because His blood had satisfied the Father's wrath over my sins–*all* of my sins–not just my non-alcoholic sins (see Romans 5:1,9, 8:1).

Christ had died for my sinful drunkenness 2,000 years ago along with the rest of my transgressions. He had already paid for these terrible, licentious episodes of mine at Calvary. No more bloody sacrifice was needed, which is necessary for God to forgive sins (see Hebrews 1:3, 9:22, 10:26-29, John 19:30).

Even more, all my sins were in the future when Christ died, not just the debaucherous sins. Therefore, the moment I believed I was forgiven, all my sins were washed away, not *only* the drunken sins of my past, which I would have in the future. I had never drank a drop of booze when I was a boy, but I was already forgiven for what I would do later on in life as a man. Think about it, my future sins were banished from God's memory, by His choice, because of my one-time belief in Jesus' blood. How? Because *all* my sins were in the future when Messiah died, and so were yours, Christian (see Hebrews 8:12, Ephesians 1:7, John 1:12, 1 John 3:5).

Jesus was committed to me for eternity because of the promise He and the Father made to one another at the Cross and *me* becoming the beneficiary to that promise by faith (see Hebrews 6:16-19, 9:16-28, Galatians 3:29).

From the millisecond I knew He forgave me, I had been remade in spirit–reborn–and my tendency of alcoholism would never set right with me. Sure, I could stay in denial for 80 years–if I lived that long–but I would never be able to enjoy my perfect supernatural identity until I stopped drinking…not even a single beer.

Some people can have a drink or two and not think about it again, but for some reason the power of sin influenced me greatly when it came to overindulging. I'm not sure why, but it is what it is. I can't drink.

Now that I sit here at 6:48am on Saturday, March 23, 2019, I'm grateful. I'm grateful for this feeling I have, not hungover but energetic and content.

I'm grateful for my family, my dogs included. I'm grateful for my good health, which I would not have if I still drank. I'm grateful for this delicious coffee I can enjoy with no regrets from yesterday.

Most of all, I'm grateful for Jesus' commitment to me during my darkest hours of life. It was His commitment to me–not mine to Him–which caused me to change my choices and mature in my thinking. Why? Because He had already changed my *identity* a long, long time ago, as I sat on that cold hard pew.

Friend, if this resonates with you or maybe you're hungover right now, just ask Jesus for help. He *will* help you! He promises! He'll never turn you away! (See John 6:37). You'll never get sober and stay sober through your own efforts. If you do, you'll become arrogant or miserable because all the pressure is on you. Put that pressure on Christ. He can handle it just fine. All *you* need to do is bask in His grace, day by day, moment by moment.

I should know about sober arrogance and misery. I stopped drinking by my own efforts in 2004, white-knuckling it apart from the guidance of God's Spirit. For a year and a half I didn't drink. Eventually I shut off the world and became mad and resentful at everyone who *did* drink. That's no way to live. We are to let Christ live through us peacefully. Other people's drinking is not our business unless they're crossing our boundaries by doing so.

Just be a branch and let Christ be the vine! The branch life is good! (See John 15:5, Philippians 4:13, Galatians 5:22,23).

So today, my friends, know this: If you're a Christian and you have a problem with alcohol, you will get sober and stay sober in the most authentic way when you finally realize Jesus is committed to you forever. His commitment to us changes everything about how we live our lives, including never having to deal with Saturday morning hangovers ever again.

A prayer for you: *Father, as I breathe in deep today, this moment, I am grateful for you. I hate that it took me so long to understand your commitment to me through Jesus. Had I known this all along, I would have given up drinking decades ago, but you revealed the truth to me at the perfect time. Those dark days are now being used to help others, so I'm fine with that. Thank you again. Right now, I lift up all who are reading this, directly to you. For those who don't have a drinking problem, give them extra sympathy toward those who do. But at the same time, teach them how to set healthy boundaries for the people in their lives who struggle with this sin. For the Christian reading this who wants to quit so badly, let them know they don't have to quit. They simply need to begin; begin living the life you've already given them in your Son. He's in them. Teach them how to let Him out through their actions and attitudes, not just with drinking, but in all things. We love you. Amen.*

Day 8

Is God's Grace a License to Sin?

"For from his fullness we have all received, grace upon grace. For the Law was given through Moses; grace and truth came through Jesus Christ."

John 1:16,17

L et's establish a fact before we begin. The Jews, according to Scripture, were the world's best-behaved people group. In the Old Testament they were seen as elite in regard to how they performed with their daily choices. For the ones who obeyed, these Hebrew men, women, and children were guided by 613 commandments given by Moses after he freed them from slavery in Egypt.

Grace was not their teacher, the Law was. The word grace is only mentioned about ten times in the Old Testament, compared to the New Testament, we see it approximately 110 times. Something drastic changed at the Cross in regard to this five-letter word.

Now, let's fast-forward *to* the New Testament. Paul, a formerly devout Jew turned Christian, tells one of his most trusted colleagues turned pastor, Titus, this truth:

> For <u>the grace of God</u> has appeared that offers salvation to all people. <u>It teaches us</u> to say "No" to ungodliness and worldly passions, and to live self-controlled, upright and godly lives in this present age (Titus 2:11,12)

Do you see what Paul describes as our teacher? Grace. Do you see what instructs us to say no to ungodliness and worldly passions? Grace. Do you see what leads us to have self-controlled, upright, godly lives? *Grace.*

Don't you think if Paul was trying to *not* give people a license to sin, while explaining grace, he would've added onto this passage something like this?

> "But be careful with that grace! Never preach too much of it because people will go crazy with sinning! They will wake up each day and think of all the new ways they can sin! Never give them a license to sin by giving them grace! Don't go hyper with grace or they'll set new world records of sinning! Balance your grace teaching with Law or you'll have chaos!"

This ridiculous statement is not in the Bible for a reason. Paul–mind you, someone who had every right to brag on his Law observance before salvation–he knew that grace *teaches* people *who* they really are. Not Law. For the non-believer, grace teaches them they need Jesus, as does the Law in its purest form. For the believer, it teaches them they *have* Jesus. As a result it teaches them their holiness (see Hebrews 10:10, 1 Corinthians 6:11, Ephesians 2:8,9).

Paul was well aware that Titus' church was sinning just fine without a license, as was every body of believers. He also knew those who thought they *weren't* sinning because they were "following" the Law, they too were sinning just as badly apart from grace, if not more. From its inception the Law never made anyone holy or righteous (see Galatians 3:11, Romans 1:17). But further back, from the time of Adam and Eve, with God, He's always been concerned with one main thing, "Do you believe me?"

Such is grace.

The Law revealed this to Paul, so Paul stayed focused on grace. In fact, the author of Hebrews–more than likely Paul, but not confirmed–stated that it is good for our hearts to be strengthened by grace (see Hebrews 13:9). Not weakened, but strengthened. What the modern legalistic church is teaching, "God's grace is not a license to sin!" is foolish because God's grace is the power *against* sin. Grace *is* our strength, not a weakness.

The first questions I had, personally, when I came to understand this truth were:

1. If grace empowers me to *not* sin, what should I do *when* I sin?
2. Will God's grace ever run out *because* of my sins?

Paul addressed these exact hypotheticals in his letter written to the Roman believers. First, he wants to be clear about the heart of God, so he builds his case, "It is the kindness of God that will lead you to repentance" (see Romans 2:4). Not Law, not God's wrath, but His kindness. Other versions of the Bible say, "It is the *goodness* of God that leads us to change."

After explaining God's grace, kindness, and goodness, Paul pits grace *against* Law in chapter 5 of Romans. In regard to what self-centered people will say about grace, he beats them to their question before they can ask, in the next chapter:

"What shall we say then? Are we to continue in sin that grace may abound? By no means! How can we who died to sin still live in it?"
(Romans 6:1,2)

Notice he never said grace would run out *because* of sin but grace would actually abound? Abound means increase! The person who struggles with legalistic tendencies will spout Romans 6:1 and 2 out with spittle. That, or they'll be passive aggressive while quoting it because "they" are "more holy" than you.

Why is this? Because they find their identity in what *they* do and don't do *rather* than in what Christ has done. Such religious aggression is actually making Paul's point. Let's back up to chapter 5 for a minute and you'll see. Right before this passage in Romans 6 he *just* said that grace will *increase* when we sin–not decrease (see Romans 5:20).

So not only will God's grace *not* run out when we sin, it will overflow all over the place. More sin. More grace. That's the gospel.

This upset the sanctimonious and excited the licentious *so* much, Paul quickly pointed out the elephant in the room in Romans 6, "Why not just go ahead and sin then?"

His answer was clear.

Believers have died *to* sin so *how* can we *express* sin naturally–as in, "How can we live in it?" We can't. If we choose to sin it must be forced or we are confused. Look at it this way. If an eagle chooses to peck on the ground with chickens it would have to be forced or confused. It's not a yardbird. It's regal. We are not sinners. We are saints.

So if we *choose* to use our bodies and minds as instruments for sinning, we'll soon get a kick-back in our spirit. "Whoa! I wasn't made for this! This doesn't seem right!"

We know. Even if we're in denial.

Again, for me, I still didn't understand this because I still sinned. But then I learned something from the Spirit within which changed everything. Something I was never taught in church.

I've literally died to sin. My spirit has been taken out of sin and placed into Christ. My spirit is sinless. Not my actions and attitudes, but my identity.

Romans 8:9 tells me this, but it was most of Romans 6 which laid it out intuitively. My problem was I didn't realize Romans 6 had already happened for me, from the moment I believed as a boy. Paul writes Romans 6 in a way which keeps the door open for future believers. He knew that not everyone reading or hearing this would be a Christian. However, when you know you've *been* saved, this is a past tense section of Scripture. I'll underline what I mean shortly, but first, to set it up.

From the instant I believed Jesus forgave me my spirit was crucified on the Cross *with* Jesus, it was buried in the tomb *with* Jesus, and resurrected as a new, sinless creature *with* Jesus. WITH. With matters. Now, even after this event I *could* still choose to sin because I'm a human, just like Jesus *could* still choose to sin because *He* was a human. But did He sin? No. Why not? Because He knew He was sinless. Sinning made no sense to Him.

As a result, now that I know *I'm* sinless in spirit, sinning makes no sense to me either. Nor does it to any believer because we all house the Spirit of Christ. We are *with* Him (see 1 Corinthians 6:19).

Do you see it, friend? The world is talking about a license to sin and I'm talking about freedom to be yourself. Every Christian is sinning just fine without a license so why not tell them the truth of who they are and *then* let them work through their issues with Christ's guidance? After all, what happens when we sin as children of God? Hell? Less blessings? The silent treatment from our Dad? No. *Grace* would happen. Grace, upon grace, upon grace, upon grace, upon grace…

Grace abounds when we sin. It never runs out. If you have a problem with this don't blame me blame Jesus. There's not a single passage in the New Testament that says His grace will run out for Christians. The only time hell is threatened over sin is when the passage is directed at non-believers.

We are secure! The Cross was a huge success!

What could possibly stop such grace? Only Jesus dying again. That will never happen. No sacrifice for our sins is left to be made, only more grace to be had (see Hebrews 1:3, 6:16-19, 7:25, 10:10).

Here's what we have to deal with when we sin–not if, but when: *constant conviction of our righteousness and security in Christ.* Not loss of heavenly rewards or salvation, but God counseling us away from sinful choices and mindsets toward the truth of who we are as holy ones.

Back to Romans 6. Paul made the point of our spirit's death, burial, and resurrection, right *after* explaining the never-ending grace of God. This passage was the final blow for me in regard to getting knocked down by the truth of my Christian identity:

> *"Or don't you know that all of us who were baptized into Christ Jesus were baptized into his death? We were therefore buried with him through baptism into death in order that, just as Christ was raised from the dead through the glory of the Father, we too may live a new life. For if we have been united with him in a death like his, we will certainly also be united with him in a resurrection like his. For we know that our old self was crucified with him so that the body ruled by sin might be done away with, that we should no longer be slaves to sin–because anyone who has died has been set free from sin. Now if we died with Christ, we believe that we will also live with him. For we know that since Christ was raised from the dead,*

he cannot die again; death no longer has mastery over him. The death he died, he died to sin once for all; but the life he lives, he lives to God. In the same way, count yourselves dead to sin but alive to God in Christ Jesus. Therefore do not let sin reign in your mortal body so that you obey its evil desires. Do not offer any part of yourself to sin as an instrument of wickedness, but rather offer yourselves to God as those who have been brought from death to life; and offer every part of yourself to him as an instrument of righteousness." (Romans 6:3-13)

First of all, this has nothing to do with water baptism but spiritual baptism which _is_ salvation. Paul doesn't mention water once up until this point nor after. The word baptism simply means _to place inside of_ and that's what's happened to us, spiritually, from the instant of our one-time faith in Christ. We've been placed inside of Jesus' Spirit–baptized into Christ. We are not following Him we are _in_ Him. We've got something so much better than the disciples had before Pentecost. Christ _in_ us and us _in_ Him which is our only hope of glory (see Colossians 1:27, John 17:23).

According to Romans 6–and other New Testament passages–our old sinful spirit was killed and buried, it was then resurrected as brand new, and _then_ we were inserted into the Son of God's actual supernatural being. The Colossians, Galatians, and Corinthians are told the same:

"For you died, and your life is now hidden with Christ in God."
(Colossians 3:3)

"I have been crucified with Christ…" _(See Galatians 2:20)_

"But whoever is united with the Lord is one with him in spirit."
(1 Corinthians 6:17)

This is not figuratively speaking or later on in the sweet by-and-by. THIS IS NOW. In essence, Paul is notifying them:

"Don't you know what's happened to you? You've been remade as a being who's ready for heaven. There is no sin in heaven. There is no sin in you. Therefore, use your body in a holy manner because you are holy. Begin to see yourself how you actually are and then live authentically. Don't fake it."

So to answer my question from earlier, what should I do when I sin? Stop. Turn from it every time. I've been remade to *not* sin in my core. We all have, as Christians.

But do we turn from sin every time to be forgiven every time? No. Our forgiveness only happened *once* because we were remade and placed inside of Jesus only *once*. He won't do that again because of His grace. Grace is your security. It abounds. His grace is much more powerful than anything we can possibly do or refuse to do.

Because of this grace guarantee, our blessed assurance, rather than constantly focus on how big our sins are, we can constantly focus on how big our God's love is. We begin to mature–not change, but grow. We shift our fixation off ourselves and onto Jesus. Our minds adapt to God's grace. We go from having a sin-consciousness to enjoying a righteousness-consciousness.

Therefore, as the body of Christ, the church, we must stop focusing on a license to sin and instead focus on our license to be righteous! God's grace is the certificate of authenticity proving you *are* His child!

"Nope! I don't agree with this Matt! We need the Law and not just grace! We need a balance!"

Friend, Paul would adamantly disagree with you. But I'll give you this, for a time I would've said the same. Mainly because I couldn't see how *I* would know how to behave without the Law. However, based on the context of the Covenants, the Spirit of Christ has taught me a dab of Law is a dab of poison. We can't follow any of the Law if we are under grace, if we do, sin will master our lives.

Please, don't ignore this warning:

> *"For sin shall no longer be your master, <u>because</u> you are not under the Law, but under grace." (Romans 6:14)*

What most Law-pushers won't tell you is Paul said the Law was brought in so sin would *increase* not decrease. It serves no purpose in making people "become" better or even sinless. It only condemns those who follow it (see Romans 2:17-27, 3:19,20, 1 Timothy 1:8-11, James 2:10, Galatians 3:10, Matthew 5:48). From the time it was given the Law's only use was to show a person their need for grace:

> *"The Law was brought in so that the trespass might <u>increase</u>. But where sin increased, grace increased all the more" (Romans 5:20)*

Do you want sin to increase in your actions and attitudes? Try obeying the Law. Just try. Or do you want to enjoy being yourself and express Christ? Then consider yourself dead *to* the Law and alive in Christ.

> *"For through the Law I died to the Law so that I might live for God." (Galatians 2:19)*

Do you see its application? What the Law was meant for? To kill, spiritually. Only then could we be buried and raised with Christ. Just look at this:

"So, my brothers and sisters, you also died to the Law <u>through the body of Christ</u>, that you might belong to another, to him who was raised from the dead, in order that we might bear fruit for God."
(Romans 7:4)

How can you die to the Law's authority to convict you of 613 unique trespasses? Only *through* the body of Christ, by grace through faith (see Ephesians 2:8,9). What's more is, the only way to bear fruit for God is to never "try" to follow the Law because the fruit of the Spirit can never be legislated (see Galatians 5:22,23).

The Law includes the Ten Commandments, tithing, and 600+ other commandments from the Old Testament. Like a criminal who dies while on trial in a courtroom, you've died to the Law of Moses through the body of Christ. Even if you *weren't* given the Law, because you're not Jewish, as a Christian it has no power or influence on you.

"No freaking way, Matt! No Law at all?! How dare you?! How will people know *how* to behave without the commandments given by Moses?!"

…Friend, refocus. Relax. *Those* commandments are burdensome. Christ's are not. Jesus only has two commandments, believe and love. Both are written on our hearts as New Covenant believers, so both will happen organically. There's rest for you in *Christ's* ability to keep the Law, not *your* ability to keep a small percentage of it. Give it up, all of it. Jesus is *how* you will know *how* to behave. Not by looking back to how He acted in the Bible, but to how He's leading you today, from within (see 1 John 3:23, 5:3, Romans 6:17, Hebrews 10:16, Galatians 3:24, John 14:26, 1 Corinthians 2:16).

Are you only going to trust Jesus for His saving blood but not for His Spirit to lead you? If the Law was given through Moses, wouldn't you rather have grace through Jesus? Don't you think His Spirit will prompt you moment by moment much better than remembering words on a page? Would you consider that His *grace* will teach you how to live properly, not tablets of stone or hundreds of thou shalts? (See 2 Corinthians 3:7-18).

Don't you believe He will never lead you to sin? And don't you believe He'll always counsel you away from unnatural choices and thoughts *even* when you ignore Him sometimes? I sure do. For me, I'm going to trust Him instead of the Law. I'm going to count myself dead to the Law and alive in Christ so that I can bear good fruit. Fruit which will last and comes only from His Spirit within me.

So today, my friends, know this: Is God's grace a license to sin? Absolutely not. It's a license to be ourselves as saints. I've never met a person who finally understood this truth *not* live completely different. It's those who struggle with legalism and Law following I've witnessed fall off the deep end into licentious living, anger, and hiding. Grace is everything for us. Grace lets us stand in the light because it teaches us we *are* light. Parasites of sin are easily pointed out and picked off when we *know* we're holy. So, enjoy grace, believer. Bask in it and be yourself. Use your license of righteousness all day long.

A prayer for you: *Dad, today I'm grateful for grace. What an amazing concept! The grace you've given me has changed my life because it has EMPOWERED my life. It IS my life. Grace is Jesus in me and I'm thankful! Right now, I lift up all who are reading this, directly to you. Many of these dear readers have been taught that grace is cheap or greasy. But the truth is grace was the most expensive thing ever–for Jesus, not us. For us it's free.*

Grace isn't greasy either. The Law is. It has 613 different slippery slopes, not just ten, or nine plus tithing. Please teach them the truth. Grace is our solid foundation. Take these wonderful people into the deepest oceans of your grace and pull them under. At first, as they struggle and breath in, it will be scary. But after a few moments they'll realize grace is the life of Christ they're breathing. They can swim in your grace, forever, free. Amen.

Day 9

The Truth About Romans 7

"So now it is no longer I who do it,
but sin that dwells within me."

Romans 7:17

"**O**uch! *Smack!* stupid mosquito," a young man whispers to himself in Africa, south of the Sahara. Just bitten by this annoying bug, he knows he'll need to be checked for Malaria. The region of the world in which he lives is a hot spot for this disease. Malaria is a life-threatening, mosquito-borne parasite. It can kill a person if not treated. As an outside force that enters a host, wreaking havoc from within, Malaria is *bad*.

This internal condition does not come *from* a person but can still *infect* a person, therefore causing us harm. Same with children of God and the power of sin. It is *in* us, but *not* us. If all Christians understood this truth, Satan wouldn't get his way with us so often.

As new creations in Christ, the enemy has convinced us that *we* are sinful but we're not. It is sin within the flesh that's sinful. Honestly, our flesh *itself* is not sinful, but instead can be used as a conduit to express this nasty force. Even in our minds, through our brains, without saying or doing a thing, sin presents itself as an option to let *out* ungodly stuff through our tendencies.

This is no cop-out for unholy actions and attitudes, but instead a cornerstone of truth which allows us to decipher our *organic* actions and attitudes as saints. At our core, sin cannot enter–our spirits. God lives there and it's sealed up forever (see Ephesians 1:13, Colossians 3:3, 1 Corinthians 6:17).

The parasite of Malaria was discovered by Charles Louis Alphonse Laveran in 1880. Subsequently, he was awarded the Nobel Prize in 1907. Approximately 1,850 years prior to the discovery of this parasite, the apostle Paul discovered a parasite of his own: *the power of sin.*

To be clear, I'm not referring to the verbs of *sinning*, but instead, a force like gravity which affects everything in this physical realm. The Greek word is *hamartia.* This force entered our universal dimension the moment Adam and Eve first decided to no longer believe God. *That's* what the original sin was, not believing our Creator, which continues today with the news about Christ. Had they believed Him, about who they already were, this couple wouldn't have needed to believe Satan's legalistic opinion of "good and evil."

But sin was here to stay.

The planet was now fallen and only man could fix the fallenness because God had given us dominion over earth (see Genesis 1:26-28). A man *would* fix this–a perfect man–much later at the Cross, by taking the sin of the world upon Himself (see Matthew 28:18, 2 Corinthians 5:17-21, John 19:30).

From the opening book of the Bible, *it* is mentioned. Yes, *it*. Sin is an it.

"... sin is crouching at your door; <u>it</u> desires to have you, but you must rule over <u>it</u>." (See Genesis 4:7)

I've underlined *it* twice for emphasis. The parasite of sin is a noun. Also, you can see that it has a desire to rule over us, but we are the ones who rule over *it* (see Romans 6:12, Galatians 5:16-25). Sin is the invisible ingredient in which Satan and his army use to cook up the most diabolical plans for all of humanity.

Sin infects *flesh*, our mortal body. It does not infect a Christian's spirit *or* soul. Our spirit is final and complete, once born again (see John 1:12, 3:7, Colossians 2:9,10). Our soul is our *mind, free will, and emotions*–always changing, forever customizable (see Romans 12:2, Philippians 1:6, 4:8).

Flesh is the host of sin, flesh is the conduit, but flesh is *not* the problem. Our flesh is holy and God's idea, there's nothing wrong with our flesh (see 1 Thessalonians 5:23). But sin *through* the flesh–the parasite coming to life–is very bad. We *allow* that, or we *don't* allow that. We have free will by way of our soul, so we get to decide how we will walk at any given moment in time.

Paul, a devout religious man, believed that through his amazing behavior he'd be found righteous with God. The force of sin jumped all over this as Paul focused on obeying 613 commandments found in the Law of Moses. One of those commandments–which was one of *the* Ten Commandments–"Thou shalt not covet" became Paul's *sinful* demise.

You would think because he was focused on obeying a religious commandment, sin would stand no chance. But no, just the opposite. What did sin do when it realized Paul really didn't *want* to covet? It presented coveting galore. Paul explains in Romans 7:

"But sin, <u>taking opportunity through the commandment</u>, produced in me coveting of every kind" (See Romans 7:8)

The commandment was "Don't you dare be jealous!" and in Paul's mind he thought *"Don't be jealous. Don't be jealous. Don't be jealous."* Sin wrapped its tentacles around this idea of his *tightly* and squeezed. As Paul tried hard to *not* be jealous, jealousy was popping out everywhere like wet gremlins being fed after midnight. What caused this? One of the Ten Commandments. He says so in Romans 7:7.

So what did Paul need to do in order to defeat this power? First, he learned that he had to die to the rules of Law–all 613 which included the cherry-picked Top Ten. Then, he simply needed to trust in the Spirit of Christ to lead him *rather* than Law:

> *"But now, by dying to what once bound us, we have been released from the Law so that we serve in the new way of the Spirit, and not in the old way of the written code." (See Romans 7:6)*

The written code is the Law. The Spirit is the Spirit of Christ. This proves that the only good the Law has to offer humanity is to funnel us toward Christ. The Law excites the parasite of sin, Jesus defeats it (see Romans 7:25).

Before I go deeper into this, I want to back up to the beginning of Romans 7. Keep in mind, this was a full-length written letter to the church in Rome *from* Paul. It did not have chapters. Chapters and verses were added centuries later for easy referencing *way* after the Bible was canonized. Therefore, there's a *flow* to what Paul is writing which begins from the start of the letter.

Context of Scripture means everything, I'd say *especially* for Romans 7. Just the same as 1 John 1, 1 Timothy 1, Revelation 3 and 20, Hebrews 6-10, Matthew 5-7, 1 Corinthians 5 and 6–and more. If we *just* read a single chapter or two without context of the book or audience, Satan and the power of sin will use the Bible to destroy our lives … as well as the lives of those whom we teach.

Truth is found in context. Truth sets us free in our minds. Error is found in buffet-style scriptural exegesis. Error keeps us in bondage–*in our minds* (see John 8:32).

Paul starts the letter of Romans explaining all of humanity's problem apart from Christ–both the Jew and the Gentile (see chapters 1 through 5). He then graduates into what needs to happen to fix our issue: *we must die supernaturally, by faith in the Cross, and then be resurrected as a new sinless spirit who is connected to Christ's Spirit while temporarily still alive in this physical body* (chapter 6).

When this happens, we (we are spirits) are taken out of the flesh–which is our body controlled by the power of sin. We are then literally placed *into* Christ's Spirit, instantly. This is also called *baptism* which means "to place inside of" and has nothing to do with water. Not once does Paul mention H2O in any chapter of Romans. Water baptism is amazing and wonderful but *achieves* nothing. Like a birthday party or wedding anniversary, it's a celebration and *not* the actual event. That is, unless a person believes the moment they get wet.

We can dunk an unbeliever in a hot tub all day long and say whatever we want while doing so, they still don't have Christ.

But anyway, Romans 7 starts *out* as symbolism: a person dying to the Law of Moses *so that* they can live for Christ. He uses the example of marriage. If a woman's husband dies she is no longer legally bound to him and is free to remarry. Just the same, we've died to the Law so that we can be married to another, Christ.

Sadly, this passage has been twisted by those who struggle with *disgusting* legalism. The beginning verses of chapter 7 has been smeared into a strict law for Christian marriage. But nothing could be further from the truth. This is not marriage advice but allegory of dying to the Law so we can be released to connect to Jesus.

Of course, the power of sin will vacuum up the mind of a person who thinks this is something much different. Sin *loves* law. Mosaic, self-made, priest-made, or Momma-made.

Sin wants us to believe, by way of Romans 7:1-6, that if a Christian gets a divorce they're an adulterer if they get remarried. But tell that to the woman with broken bones and black eyes who's *forced* to stay married to a monster *because* of this passage. Tell that to the faithful, hard-working husband who's been cheated on countless times and his family's life savings blown like crazy by his frivolous wife.

Such is *trash* teaching. Don't fall for it.

Do everything you possibly can to stay married, fight *hard* for your union and always follow your heart, Christian. But be sure to know, there is no law in the Bible which makes you a second-class citizen if you painstakingly, *finally* get a divorce or get remarried thereafter. God saw your effort and you are *still* just as holy as Jesus Christ (1 John 4:17, 1 Corinthians 6:11). Do you hear me? Hey, your identity has not changed because of your marital status. You are *good*, friend.

Onward.

Paul was one of the most well-behaved religious people ever *prior* to placing his faith in Christ. As a result, the sin of the flesh *thrived* (see Philippians 3:3-7). He had really good-looking sin. His addiction wasn't drinking, doing drugs, sleeping around, partying too much or porn—it was religion. And sin ate that up with Frank's Red Hot and some ranch dressing.

From the time of his youth, Paul was instructed to obey the commandments given by Moses—the Law, the Old Covenant. He was taught to meditate on it day and night, and by doing so, it would give him great wealth and righteousness (see Joshua 1:8, Deuteronomy 30:9,10). That was correct, but only until Christ came. However, without *faith* even Law couldn't make a person right with our Creator (see Galatians 3:11, Romans 5:6, Hebrews 11).

I don't want to be misunderstood. The Law is good, holy, right, just, perfect, and unchangeable (see Romans 7:12, Matthew 5:17,18). The problem is when sin gets ahold of a person's obsession with Law, Law-*breaking* is the result—which was always its intended design. The Law's purpose was to *increase* sin, not decrease it. It was making way for *Christ's* way: free righteousness by grace through faith in Him (see Romans 5:20, 10:4, Mark 1:3, Ephesians 2:8,9, John 14:6).

Sin kills our spirit. The Law magnifies sin. Therefore, the Law kills and can never bring a person life (see Galatians 3:21, 2 Corinthians 3:6). No matter if it was the Law of Moses or modern-day church laws which came from "early church fathers"–we are *dead*. Also, the Bible says call no man *father*, by the way (see Matthew 23:9). That should tell you something.

Just look at what Paul said about our relationship with the Law:

> "For sin shall no longer be your master, <u>because you are not under Law,</u>
> but under grace." *(Romans 6:14)*

How can sin no longer be our master? *Only* because we are *not* under Law. He then describes his own past relationship with Law:

> *"Therefore did that which is good (Law) become a cause of death for me?*
> *May it never be! <u>Rather it was sin,</u> in order that it might be shown to be sin*
> *<u>by effecting my death through that which is good</u> (Law), so that through*
> *the commandment (in context, 'Thou shalt not covet') sin would become*
> *utterly sinful." (Romans 7:13, my notes added)*

This can be confusing if we are taught that *we* are sinful. We're not. Paul is referring to the Law's ability to *really* point out his sin as a Jewish man under God's Covenant made with Israel. A Christian's identity, on *this* side of the Cross, under the *New* Covenant, is not sinful. It is holy, righteous, blameless, set apart from the world, sanctified in full, and *already* seated with Jesus in heaven, supernaturally (see Colossians 1:22, 2 Corinthians 5:21, Ephesians 2:6, Hebrews 10:10,14).

I'M NOT TALKING ABOUT WHAT WE DO BUT WHO WE ARE. *Please*, separate your identity from your thoughts and choices.

So, what we must do in our minds, for Romans 7–because Paul is having such a hard time with sin–is realize he's talking about his *past* battle with *trying* to obey the Law *as* a Moses-devoted Pharisee. Romans 7 isn't Paul writing about himself in the present tense as a Christian. He no longer struggled with sin inflamed by Law *as* a Christian. Why? Christians are not under the Law. He *just* taught that in the previous chapter. Paul was *already* dead to the Law, married to Christ, and fully enjoying the New Covenant as he wrote the section we've named *Chapter 7.*

A good friend of mine, Andrew Farley, has said the sub-heading for this section of Romans should be *I Fought the Law and the Law Won.* Paul does not have two natures, as some versions of the Bible have printed. He's not fighting *himself* here but referring to his past struggle with sin as a legalist. None of us Christians have two natures. In fact, Peter tells us we have God's *divine* nature (see 2 Peter 1:4).

For the person who finds their identity in what all they do for God, rather than what all Christ has done for them, a rebuttal of rage will fly toward me, "Nope! You're *wrong*, Matt! You need to read more of God's Word! I feel sorry for you because even Paul said in verse fourteen that *he* is sold as a slave to sin!"

Friend, yes, he does. But is that the Christian life? Are we sold as slaves to sin? No, of course not. If you'll back up you'll see the context. Paul is only sold as a slave to the power of sin when *attempting* to be spiritual *through* the Law:

> *"We know that the Law is spiritual; but I am unspiritual, sold as a slave to sin." (Romans 7:14)*

That's not a Christian. Paul is telling this story about himself in the same way *we* would tell a "past-present" story, such as, "A guy walks into a bar…"

Did the guy already walk into a bar? Yes. But we are telling the story in the present. That's what Paul is doing in Romans 7. He's explaining his life as a hard-nosed, Christian-hating Pharisee who *loved* the Law, and how sin ruled every moment of his day. Paul then illustrates his death *to* the Law and how Christ saved him from sin (see Romans 7:21-25).

This is exactly why the very next chapter starts out with who he *now* is:

"Therefore, there is <u>now no condemnation</u> for those who are in Christ Jesus" (see Romans 8:1)

Do you see it? The Law isn't sinful, it's perfect. But if you put a person *under* Law, sinning will be the production. Confetti of condemnation will rain. The parasite of sin explodes like dynamite when we are focused on, "You better not, or else!"

A grace-confused person will hate this, "So Matt are you saying that when we sin it's not us? How dare you! And if we don't have to follow *any* commandments from Moses then you're just giving people a license to sin! How are we supposed to know what to do?!"

… Please, friend, try to relax. Do you see what being sin-conscious by way of Law does? It enrages the sin within the flesh. That bitterness and resentment you have toward me is *not* you–if you're a Christian. It's the parasite coming *through* you. Listen, don't worry about what to do and what not to do. Don't worry about sinning. Yes, don't worry about sinning.

The Spirit of Jesus Christ within you will never lead you into sin–ever. Trust *Him* not Moses (see Hebrews 3:3). *He* is your guide now, nothing else (see John 14:26). Demonic forces will try to lead you to sin, the power of sin itself will too–even religious people and your own unrenewed thought patterns–but He who is within you is greater than everything else (see 2 Corinthians 3, 1 John 4:4).

Nobody needs a license to sin, and all sins are willful. We do plenty of sinning *without* a license, and *without* thinking about it–Christians included. We should turn from sin every time. We've been recreated in spirit to *not* sin. But again, *when* we sin, *we* are not sinful.

Just as Paul said, it is the sin within the shell, not the shell itself:

> *"So now it is no longer I who do it, <u>but sin that dwells within me</u>."*
> *(Romans 7:17)*

If sin is within our physical members–our hands, feet, mouth, even our brain (which creates sinful thoughts out of the blue)–then what do we do? Do we *fight* sin? No. Fighting sin is pointless. Such would be an unwinnable battle because hamartia is allowed to be here until this planet is remade (see 2 Peter 3:13, Revelation 21:1,4).

Instead, we are to live our life as branches while allowing the Spirit of Jesus Christ within, to come out (see John 15:5, Galatians 5:22,23). We don't need to die to self. Those words are not in the Bible. The closest thing is our old self died, in Romans 6. We need to *live*. As *we* live, sin sits idle:

> *"Therefore do not <u>let</u> sin reign in your mortal body so that you obey <u>its</u> evil desires." (Romans 6:12)*

We don't let sin reign. *We* don't let sin reign. Sin has evil desires, not you, Christian. You have the mind of Christ! (See 1 Corinthians 2:16). Through His mind, which is your mind, we are to simply walk in a manner worthy of our calling! As we do we'll organically bear good fruit and grow in the knowledge of God! (See Colossians 1:10). The truth is we don't *want* to sin! We want exactly what God wants at all times! It is sin who wants to sin! A parasite living within our physical body–a tumor *in* us but *not* us!

So today, my friends, know this: The truth about Romans 7 is liberating. It is biblical proof that we believers are not sinful in any way. God's Spirit cannot live in sinful places so He's given us a new spirit, a *holy* spirit, and then joined our spirit. The force of sin will latch on to the gray matter in our human body, causing us to sometimes act and think sinfully–but we are not sinful. We're God's children who are no longer slaves to sin.

A prayer for you: *Father, today I want to thank you for revealing even deeper truths to me through your Word. You've taught me so much over the years, yet it feels as if I'm on the tip of the iceberg of your grace. I'm so excited about what your Spirit will reveal to me next! Right now, I lift up all who are reading this, directly to you. Dad, so many of these dear readers have been taught they are sinful, but if they're in Christ, they're supernaturally perfect. Teach them that the power of sin is very cunning. It digs its claws into our tendencies in which it knows are not proper according to you. Let them know sin can be expressed legalistically as Paul explained in Romans 7. It can manifest itself through alcoholism like it did me for so many years. It can even express itself through a Christian by way of greed, rage, self-pity, and sexual sin–both homo and hetero. You name it, if it's not coming from the faith of Christ, it's coming from sin. Sin can even thrive through giving, teaching, church attendance, mission trips, physical fitness, hobbies, and parenting–ANYTHING APART FROM CHRIST–SIN REIGNS. Teach us to walk according to who we really are as your children, as saints. We understand that no law or commandment can teach us how to walk. Only your Spirit can. We love you so much, amen.*

Day 10

What is the Church?

*"Now you are Christ's body, and individually members
of it. For even as the body is one and yet has many
members, and all the members of the body, though
they are many, are one body, so also is Christ."*

1 Corinthians 12:12

Ahhhh, church. The buildings we go to on Sunday mornings can present to us a cornucopia of feelings. Excitement, love, and empowerment may be the experience inside of our soul. But then again, guilt, fear, and pressure could be stirred up. It all depends on the message.

Here are some examples of common questions which *should* be answered clearly by church leaders:

1. ***As a believer, am I complete in Christ or not?*** The answer is yes, we *are* complete. Our identity is final from the moment we first believe.

What we do and think is not, but who we *are* is (see Colossians 2:9,10, John 1:12, Romans 12:2).

2. ***Did the Cross really work, or was it only so-so?*** Yes it worked, and we cannot add to it nor take away from it in any way. The blood of Jesus is more powerful than anything we can possibly imagine in our finite human minds (see John 19:30, Hebrews 1:3, 10:19, Colossians 1:20, Ephesians 1:7, Matthew 26:28, Romans 5:9).

3. ***At church, am I "calling down" God's Spirit into this place, like so many people over time have done, and still do, while dancing around campfires to appease fake deities?*** The answer is no. He's in *us*, in our very own spirits. We go into church buildings with Him already inside of us. Unlike those in tribal religions—who are actually summoning demonic forces—we don't need to plead, "Spirit come! Please, please, Holy Spirit come!" He doesn't show up in buildings based on begging, crying, and music. He is everywhere at all times. He is Spirit. Just the same, we don't need to invite Jesus into our hearts again and again. For Christians, our connection *with* Him is final. We are one. He is inside of us 100%, never to leave again because of the event which occurred at the Cross (see 1 John 2:2, 1 Corinthians 6:17, Colossians 3:3).

4. ***At church, do I need to "be still" so the Holy Spirit can "take control" and use me?*** No. You have full control of yourself. You're not a limp noodle or a hollow tube. You're a person. You have a personality, likes, dislikes, gifts, and talents. The Spirit is in you but you control you. You're compatible with Him and you work together as a symbiotic team. He will never cast you to the ground nor cause you to rumble in your seat. Emotions are great, but *you* are under complete control of your body at all times (Galatians 5:22,23, Philippians 2:13, 4:13, Colossians 3:23, John 15:5).

Friends, we need to be transparent about quite a few things in regard to our brick-and-mortar locations. That is, what did Jesus do *for* us, then *to* us, so that He can do *through* us? This stuff matters. When we aren't clear about who we are and what the Cross has done, it causes panic, creates concern, and increases burdens–all of which are paradoxes of what Christ came to do (see Matthew 11:28-30).

The church is us, Christian. It's you and me because Jesus' Spirit lives in us. Sure, we go to a church *building*, but there's nothing sanctified about a geographical location. Construction materials, which have been neatly compiled with a cross on top, are not holy. Strip clubs, Jehovah's Witness halls, and mosques are built with the same type of two-by-fours and concrete. *We* are the sanctified ones–not a building (see Hebrews 10:10, 1 Corinthians 6:11, Acts 7:48, 17:24). Sanctified means holy. Holy means set apart. Our spirits *are* set apart from sin, from the world, and from hell.

By calling a place "sanctified" or a "sanctuary"–or claiming that it's "holy ground"–does not make it true. No matter how out of control a person gets–hoopin' and hollering as they wipe off heavy perspiration with a hanky–Christ destroyed the need for a holy *physical* location. The same goes for the most elegant, old, traditional buildings. No place on earth is holy, *we* are holy. Nor do we *go* to places to be *more* holy, either (see John 2:19, Colossians 1:22, 2 Corinthians 5:20).

I know this will hurt some people's feelings, and I'm sorry, but *you,* Christian friend, are the true holy sanctuary. *You* are God's holy ground. *You* are sanctified in full. Yes, our actions and attitudes are *being* sanctified but *we* are not. Our identity in Christ is final from the millisecond we first believe. The Spirit of Christ cannot live in non-sanctified, unholy places–and the Scripture is clear, He lives in us! We are temples of God! Just look!

"Do you not know that <u>your bodies are temples</u> of the Holy Spirit, who is <u>in you</u>, whom you <u>have</u> received from God? You are not your own" (1 Corinthians 6:19)

The temple *used* to be a physical place for the Jews to receive forgiveness of sin. *It* was holy because God's Spirit dwelled there. At this place, bloody animal sacrifices were made to God for the Hebrew people's sins once a year at the Day of Atonement by way of Levitical priests (see Hebrews 5:1).

However, this building was but a man-made look-alike of the actual temple in heaven. Jesus, who is the final Priest, after He died and shed *His* blood, He entered into the real temple in heaven which was not made by human hands. While there, He presented His very own blood *once* for all time, for the sins of the entire world, *rather* than again and again each year for individual Jew's sins by way of animal blood (see Hebrews 4:14-16, 9:22-26).

If you are new to this teaching on blood, which is the foundation of forgiveness from God, this might help: *animal blood forgave sins year after year at the temple on earth. Jesus' blood forgave all sins for all time, at the temple in heaven.* Now, once we place our faith in His blood, we are forgiven once for all time—even future sins. How? All of our sins were in the future when Jesus presented His blood to the Father in the heavenly temple. He is not bound by our idea of time, which He created (see Hebrews 1:3, 10:10,12,14, John 3:16-18, 2 Peter 3:8).

In the temple on earth, there was a 60-foot high curtain—and very *thick* as well—only the priests could go past it to present animal blood on the altar. The very moment of Jesus' death on the Cross, that curtain was supernaturally *ripped* from top to bottom. The dividing wall between God and man was now gone—literally—both for the Jew *and* the Gentile. Before this heavy veil was torn, we non-Jews weren't included to present our best livestock for forgiveness (Ephesians 2:12).

The good news is, the requirement for temple sacrifices—or a temple whatsoever—was now obsolete because of Christ's *final* Sacrifice!

> *"At that moment the curtain of the temple was torn in two from top to bottom. The earth shook, the rocks split" (Matthew 27:51)*

The need for a building was over.

We are now the building because the Spirit of God can make His home in every person who believes in His Son. Before the Cross, He couldn't. Blood was needed to draw near to Him because of sin (see Hebrews 7:22, 9:22, 10:19, 13:12). Blood could only be poured out at the temple behind the curtain. But now, through Christ's blood, and by belief in its power to forgive us, *we* have been made holy, so *we* are now the temple. God can enter us, everywhere, all at once, by grace through faith.

Jesus explains this to the disciples; what would happen to them *after* He died and *after* Pentecost–not before:

> *"On that day you will realize that I am in my Father, and you are in me,*
> *and I am in you." (John 14:20)*

Prior to His death this wasn't possible, because of sin. That's why He said, "On that day," as in, *in the future*. Before this, the Spirit could be *with* people but not *in* them permanently. Just look at the Old Testament patriarchs, how God's Spirit came and went all the time. But on this side of the Cross He never leaves us. Ever. Why? Because of the blood of Jesus which was poured out at Golgotha and then supernaturally presented to God at the temple in heaven which took away all of our sins.

Only sins could keep God from making His home in us. But Jesus has snatched those all up and tossed them into the sea of forgetfulness (see Hebrews 8:12, Micah 7:19). Animal blood covered, or "atoned for" sins, a year at a time. Jesus, He took them all away, permanently. No sacrifice for sin is left to be made at the temple for the Jews–and for the Gentile, Jesus is not dying again and again in heaven for each of our sins we commit. It is finished (1 John 3:5, John 1:29, 19:30, Hebrews 8:6, 9:26, 10:4,26-29).

Don't get me wrong, I'm not belittling the need for church buildings. They serve great purposes! But many people are obsessed with the *place* and overlook the *Person* within their own temples. Friends, we take Jesus *to* church, we don't go to church to get Him in us again and again and again and again and again. That's worse than Judaism. "Once a year" was their deal, not 52 times a year (see Hebrews 10:3).

We must recenter how we view today's church buildings. For the Jews, God's Spirit stayed behind at the temple as they walked off. It doesn't work that way according to the New Covenant. He's infused with us forever from the moment we first believe Jesus has forgiven us. We take Him everywhere! (See 1 Corinthians 6:17, Hebrews 6:16-19, 2 Timothy 2:13).

I love church, but for many years I was taught two different Bible verses–used out of context, of course–causing me to believe that if I missed church my life would suffer greatly. Rather than teach me *I* was the church, I was led to think God would punish me for not *going* to church. Until I got my butt back in the pews and obeyed Pastor, I could expect a lot less blessings. This was false. Here are both verses used properly:

1. **Remember the Sabbath and keep it holy (see Exodus 20:8).** First of all, what is the Sabbath? The Sabbath is not Sunday morning– or Sunday at all. According to the Jews, to whom this commandment was given by Moses, it is from Friday to Saturday. This was *one* of the Ten Commandments. However, to double-up on this double-talk, unless we're Jewish, we were never *commanded* to remember the Sabbath. We are outsiders, Gentiles. The Sabbath was a day of rest for the Jews, not us. But even if you *are* Jewish, you must keep *all* of the Law, not just this one command. It's a package deal (see Galatians 3:10). Observing the Sabbath was *part* of the Law of Moses–613 commandments not just 10. From Friday

through Saturday they weren't allowed to work. *That's* the premise of "remember the Sabbath." It has nothing to do with attending a building on Sunday, or ever, for that matter. Their building was the temple and they were required to go there once a year at the Day of Atonement to receive forgiveness of sins by way of animal blood. Sadly, some grace-confused Christians want to say the Sabbath has changed to Sunday *after* the Cross, based on Acts 20:7. But the Law cannot be altered in any way so this is very wrong (see Deuteronomy 4:2). Sunday was simply a more convenient time for the early church to gather, but this gathering was not a changing of the Mosaic Law. The Jewish Christians knew full well that was impossible (see James 2:10, Romans 10:4, Colossians 2:16,17).

2. **Do not forsake the assembly of one another (see Hebrews 10:25).** Those who find their identity in church attendance will use this verse like a sword in order to cut others. But let's look at the entire passage for context, including the previous verse. *"And let us consider how we may spur one another on toward love and good deeds, not giving up meeting together, as some are in the habit of doing, but encouraging one another–and all the more as you see the Day approaching"* (Hebrews 10:24,25). I've used two different Bible translations for the same passage: A.) *"Do not forsake the assembly"* B.) *"not giving up meeting together."* Both mean the same thing. I've done this because those who struggle with legalism have been mis-taught to believe the King James Version is the only perfect version of the Bible–which is wrong. The only perfect version is the original writings which came by way of the actual *hand* of the authors. The truth is, earlier transcripts have been found since the 1600's–when the KJV was first translated. It's been updated since then, so obviously it's flawed in its rendering–as is every Bible version. To be clear, *no*

Bible translation is flawed in overall content or Spirit, but instead, in language rewording. There are certain Greek words which *cannot* be translated *perfectly* into English. No matter how many scholars might try, it can't be done. For example, Eskimos have around 50 different words for *snow*. Yet, to translate snow into English, we have *one* word. This same principle applies to Greek words. English cannot unpack this language perfectly clear. Also, rumor has it King James was not even a Christian and simply translated the Bible into English in order to become famous. *Further*, what makes us believe an *English* king who lived 1,600 years *after* the Cross is more authentic than the *first* writings? It's silly. "1611 or you ain't going to heaven" is a distraction from Satan which was meant to divide—and it has *worked*. "Do not forsake the assembly" was how English people spoke in the 17th century, but *not* now. So, this verse in Hebrews is not a law to go to church, but in context, advice for Christians to keep meeting up in groups! Why? To encourage one another! To stir up love and good deeds!

When we create a new commandment of "Thou shalt go to church!" the power of sin gets excited, the lost are repelled, and fear-factors grow in the minds of believers. Even more diabolical, the prideful egos of the religiously-devout are shot with steroids. To nip this in the bud we must understand that you and I *are* the church! Where we go, God goes—even into the buildings!

So today, my friends, know this: The church is a family. It's not a place, but us. You, me, and every believer, all throughout the world, we form the church. Like any relationship, sure, we have our ups and downs. But we're *still* a family. We are one, forever connected, in spirit!

A prayer for you: *Heavenly Father, I want to thank you for the revelation of knowing I am the church. You've taught me that you live in me permanently. As a result, a confidence has grown unlike I knew in my younger years. Your Spirit in me was being rubbed wrong when I heard sermons that taught otherwise. Rightfully so. The Cross destroyed the need for a building or middleman to be close to you! How amazing! I AM the church! Right now, I lift up all who are reading this, directly to you. So many of these dear people have been beat down by religion and it's just not fair. I've been there. I understand what it's like to be lied to about the building we call church—as if it's holy ground or your house. It's not. The church is not a building, and it never was. It's always been us. Please ease their minds today as you teach them the truth of their identity as saints. They house you in their very beings! Let them know the church building can be a great place! Being around other believers, enjoying their hugs, encouragement, and worshiping you is spectacular! But first, we must know a foundational truth: WE ARE THE CHURCH. Build on this truth, in their minds, Dad. Give them a newfound peace about the topic of church, like never before. In Christ's name I pray, amen.*

Day 11

What Should a Christian Do
When We Lose Our Cool?

"In your anger do not sin"

See Ephesians 4:26

M y daughter Grace really wants to get better at basketball. So after her
8th grade season was over I told her, "I know a great way for you to
improve your game, but it will be very difficult. You can start playing full
court pick-up games with us at the Civic Center."

I've been playing full court ball for about 20 years with other men, two or
three times a week at our local gym. It's great cardio, it's fun, and the competition is normally pretty good. Girls don't play with us–not because they're not
allowed, but they just don't. And kids definitely don't play with us.

Grace is an 8th grade girl.

These are adults, this is fast paced, and they won't go easy on her. I made
this clear, but she was excited to get to start playing with us. After all, there's

no better way to improve your skills than to play against better players. Drills are important but can only take you so far. You need to *play* to improve. So over the past few months we've gone to the Civic Center several times a week to run with the fellas for a couple hours. I really enjoy this time with Grace, not just for basketball, but the quality time we get to spend together is special.

Because I've been playing there for so long I know most of the guys very well, so they've said nothing about Grace joining us and have accepted her as just another player. Grace has a great shot and good mind for basketball, but she knows that if she plays against much higher competition–than the kids she's been playing against–she'll develop and advance in all other aspects as well.

It has worked. I've noticed Grace's skills and confidence improve by leaps and bounds. She's even hit some game-winning shots. The ride home on those nights were filled with a giddy teenager. She's having fun, feeling respected by the guys, and it's one of the highlights of her week (and mine).

Now, I'm very protective of Grace. I always have been. So I had to have a conversation with God about her playing with us before this new type of training began. Playing with men who scream, curse a lot, blame one another, and sometimes shouting matches break out–I knew I'd have to stay calm when this was eventually directed at her.

I told Grace, "Nobody's allowed to disrespect you as a female or as a person, but there will be times you get yelled at. Don't take it personally. Just listen to what they are complaining about and try to adjust your game. Help out on defense, take good shots, and don't make bad passes."

"I know Dad."

"If someone blocks you tell them 'good defense,' don't say, 'Good job blocking a girl.' Show respect and don't make excuses. Hustle, and don't overreact."

In a way, I was telling myself the same. "Don't overreact when someone fouls Grace, roughs her up, or yells at her." This happens a lot, and I've had to walk way. I've kept my cool and not played Grace's bodyguard...until last week.

The gym was packed with about 25 men playing. If you won, you got to stay on the court. If you lost, you'd be sitting a while. So nobody wanted to lose. The score was tied and next basket wins. Grace was on my team, and long story short, she should have helped on her man screening the ball better, because the game-winning shot was hit when she didn't help. This enraged the guy who got screened on our team, and I get it, but he took it too far.

As we were walking off the court he yelled about Grace not helping. That's fine. She should have helped. But he yelled again, and again. As we sat down on the bleachers, he continued to brow-beat her and I could see her feelings were really hurt.

I got mad.

"Hey. Watch how you talk to my daughter. That's enough."

"Oh shut up, she should've helped out on the screen!"

Boom.

We got into a shouting match, I got in his face, and we were pulled apart. I had no plans on touching him, but I wanted to make clear that Grace wouldn't be talked to disrespectfully, repeatedly. That's not going to work for me. She's a sweet kid and responds much better when she's respected when corrected. Barking once or twice at her was suffice. He had taken it too far.

To be clear, since she's been playing with us, Grace has seen and heard a lot of stuff I'd rather her not see or hear. I tell her all the time, "That's just ball," when people overreact because of competition. But now it was me. I had lost my cool.

This was a knee-jerk reaction to seeing how hurt Grace was, and *me* trying to protect her. Watching her head hang so low, and continuing to hear him, I reacted. Did I *over*-react? Probably. Christ in me would've wanted me to *not* react instantly. I understand that, as His Spirit has talked to me about this situation over the past few days. Not in an audible voice, but in a knowing:

"Matt, maybe you should have just went and sat by him, and said, 'Hey, can you please be a little bit more respectful to Grace?'"

But at the same time, I'm allowed to get angry. God gave me that feeling for a reason. Growing up I was taught that getting angry was sin–and *that* is where feeling-stuffing begins. Then people-pleasing. Then accepting unacceptable behavior as normal. Then codependent behavior grows. Then addictions fester to *change* those feelings. Then misery and guilt over *emotions* finally take over.

That's no way to live and I'm not doing it. Being angry is not sin. Sinning *while* angry is sin (see Ephesians 4:26).

So *when* we get angry–not if–it's best to not react immediately. But, I did. So what. I can learn from this and move forward, or not. I choose to learn and mature. The enemy wants us to believe that just because we get mad we're less of a child of God or *not* a child of God any longer. People who struggle with self-righteousness and legalism do the same thing, "No Christian would ever act like that." Don't fall for it. Happy, sad, mad, or scared, emotions don't define us. Christ's life does and His life never changes.

Afterwards, I've had some time to think about the situation better.

So what can we do when we lose our cool as holy people who house God's Spirit? First, realize we are not identified by any emotion. Emotions are a part of our soul. They ebb and flow all the time based on what's happening around us and in our minds. They are indicators, not identifiers.

Second, realize we are naturally peaceful in our spirit. Self-control and peace flow from our supernatural DNA–our heart–organically, so both will always feel right even if it takes time to agree in our head (see Galatians 5:22,23, Romans 12:2, Philippians 1:6, 2 Peter 1:5-9). Peace with others *is* our ultimate desire (see Romans 12:18). Peace with others and with ourselves. We matter too. We are not door mats. Boundaries are extremely important so we should set them and enforce them with love and respect.

Third, realize we are free and always swimming in grace (see Romans 5:20, Hebrews 13:9, Titus 2:11,12). We are free *because* of grace to just let situations be, and we are free to *reach out* to those whom we've gotten angry at *if* we decide to. For this scenario I chose to reach out and message the guy. I've known him for about a decade. He's a good dude, but like me, sometimes his passion on the court overtakes his normal actions and attitudes.

In the message I told him I was sorry for yelling at him and I should've approached him privately. Did I have to do this? No. I could have just let it go "as ball." We've all gotten into it with each other over the years. We forget about it and just keep playing, a fist-bump always confirms we're over it, "No big deal. It's fine." But as children of God, we never feel more like ourselves than when we go out of our way to make peace with others. We *are* peaceful, even when we temporarily lose our cool. That is who we are.

So today, my friends, know this: What should a Christian do when we lose our cool? Listen to the Spirit within. He'll always guide us toward peace, comfort, confidence, love, and a sound mind. I'm glad I messaged my friend because he messaged me back and said he was sorry too. He also said to tell Grace he was sorry for yelling at her. I did, and she lit up with a smile. Do you see it? Do you see how the Spirit works through us when we let Him? You never know where an apology might take you and others. So be yourself, Christian. Always be yourself.

A prayer for you: *Dad, your Word says in 2 Timothy 1:9, you saved us and called us to a holy life–not because of anything we have done but because of your own purpose and grace. This grace was given us in Christ Jesus. I believe this! I believe it's our purpose to allow Christ to gracefully*

live through us! I know you don't want us to beat ourselves up, or stay in condemnation, when we get angry. You want us to feel what we feel and then listen to your Spirit within for guidance–for how to respond. Sometimes you say, "Stand up to this with respect." But other times you say, "Just be quiet for now." Thank you for giving us your Holy Spirit to lead us each day! Right now, I lift up all who are reading this, directly to you. For those who struggle with losing their cool more often than not, teach them how to pause, pray, and proceed, when faced with frustrating situations. This has helped me greatly over the years, and I'm still learning from your Spirit. But also, teach them that if they really want relief from a blow up to just say sorry without excuses. You take care of the rest, and the person we've apologized to gets to see Christ through us. We love you and we trust you, in all things and in all situations! Amen!

Day 12

Does Obedience Keep You Close to God?

*"For you died, and your life is now
hidden with Christ in God."*

Colossians 3:3

How many times have you heard that your obedience is the determining factor keeping you close to God? For me, in my 37 years, a lot. It's as if what Jesus did at the Cross was not enough, and that I gotta do "my part."

"God helps those who help themselves!" has been belted out toward me over this subject, but those six words are not in the Bible. Those six words are actually the *opposite* of the gospel message. The reality is, God helps those who realize they *can't* help themselves.

James, who shared a mother with Jesus, quotes Old Testament Scripture to a group of people who absolutely *refused* to believe this truth:

"God opposes the proud but gives grace to the humble."
(See James 4:6, Proverbs 3:34)

Who was James directing this verse at? The unbelieving twelve tribes of Israel (see James 1:1). The Hebrew people who believed their amazing Law-*obeying* would keep them close to God. James knew those days were over because Jesus Christ had came and went. The brother he grew up with–but didn't believe in until after the Cross (see John 7:5)–replaced the notion of "I will do everything God commands!" 613 commands to be exact, not just 10, as we like to cherry-pick today (See Deuteronomy 4:2, 6:25, Hebrews 8:13). Jesus' half-brother understood that the New Covenant was here to stay and the obedience of *faith* was all that mattered (see Romans 1:5, 16:26, Galatians 5:6).

Yet, 2,000 years later we like to bark, "Be obedient to God's Word!" at sheep-like faces who just want some respite from life's difficulties. Don't get me wrong, proper outward living is good. But for Christians, we have become obedient from the *heart* which has infused proper *inward* living. Good-looking outward living is sinful when it comes from an unbeliever. Poor-looking outward living when coming from a *believer* is fake.

We are naturally obedient. Sinning is not a part of who we *are*. Sinning, for a Christian, is the same as a dog meowing or a cat barking. Could you train them to do such a weird thing? Yeah. But such will never alter their identity. Same with us Christians and sinning. It's always awkward–*always*. Even if we go a lifetime in denial. Our lives aren't that long anyway, so don't believe the lie that you enjoy sinning. You don't. You are exactly like Jesus on the inside (see 1 John 4:17).

It is a natural thing to live out the Spirit of Christ within us (see Galatians 5:22,23, John 15:5). We don't need to be yelled at, but instead, taught who we have become by our one-time faith in Jesus. Whoever we think we are, that's how we will live. Teach a Christian the truth about their obedient heart and watch how much they begin to actually *obey* God's Spirit within them. Or, teach a Christian the demonic lie of "You are a sinner!" and watch the trail of fire behind them as they peel-out like the Delorean from Back to the Future, sinning as fast as they can.

Paul tells the Romans about this supernatural epiphany in regard to their authentic identification:

"But thanks be to God, that you who were once slaves of sin <u>have become</u> <u>obedient from the heart</u> to the standard of teaching to which you were committed, and, having been set free from sin, <u>have become slaves of</u> <u>righteousness</u>" (Romans 6:17,18)

Do you see that we are obedient from the heart? That means it's a *normal* thing to obey Christ within. And do you see we've not only been set *free* from sin, but even more, we've become slaves to righteousness? That means we are locked inside of a cell of holiness, never to escape–ever! We are *slaves* to right-standing with our Creator!

How is this possible?...Because we've been supernaturally reborn as children of God. Our spiritual genetic makeup has been replaced with Christ's own perfection. This happened from the *instant* we believed we were forgiven by the Son of God (see John 1:12, 3:7, Colossians 1:22, 2 Corinthians 5:17,21). Friend, you might not have felt anything when this event occurred. We are not saved by feelings but by faith. Even better, just so you don't think you need to have a huge "amount" of faith–like the people up on stage keep shouting at you–Jesus *becomes* your faith after salvation (see Hebrews 12:2). So you can go ahead and rest. Be yourself, and relax (see Hebrews 4:11).

Unfortunately, those who find their identity in *their* behavior–individuals who struggle with an addiction to legalanity and might not know it–religious obedience for closeness to God is paramount for them. Why? Because they believe their devout actions, habits, and attitudes are on a much grander scale than the "lay Christian." The good news, for them and everyone else, is they are way off base.

The Type A personality, like myself, can easily latch on to this miserable lifestyle. Repenting until our repenter falls off can become an obsession. What does that even mean? Exactly. We don't even know *how* to repent, but we'll say we do. Overlooking sins, belittling others, and incorrectly justifying sins, all because we want to be sure we stay close to God by way of our "turning" from sins. It's a joke. Satan inflames our sin-consciousness. Grace douses it. How? By convicting us of our righteousness and *not* of our sin. Only unbelievers are convicted of their sin. *Only* unbelievers are of this world, we are not (see John 16:8, 17:16).

My own former addiction to legalism tilted my mind toward the direction of suicide quite often. Sifting through the sins of others in order to compare mine to theirs (we won't say but we think) haunted me. *"If God helps those who help themselves then I'm gonna help myself more than you! I'M BETTER THAN YOU! I'M CLOSER TO GOD!"*

Our self-righteous self-talk soon forgets about Jesus, therefore causing our thought life to fall into the disgusting gutter of religiosity. Unbeknownst to us, of course. The enemy covertly places obedience-filters over our spiritual eyes as we try and try and try and try to be good, to *stay* close to God. He and his demons will say things like:

"You *better* read your Bible!"
"You *better* not look at that porn!"
"You *better* not let them see you're in pain!"
"You *better* do mission trips!"
"You *better* not skip church!"
"You *better* not drink!"
"You *better* not act like you have a problem with alcohol!"
"You *better* _____ (fill in the blank for yourself)!"

You better, you better, you better—or *else* you're not close to God. We've swapped the Law of Moses for hellishly influenced self-made laws. These are brand new commandments and we don't know it. They have no value at all and only cause us to look *away* from the Cross therefore forgetting our one-time spiritual cleansing (see 1 Corinthians 6:11, Hebrews 10:10, 2 Corinthians 5:17).

Just think about it. If doing religious stuff keeps a person close to God—supposed "obedience"—how do we *know* if we've done enough to *be* close? We don't. The devil sure wants us to think there's a gauge—as he first did with Adam and Eve—but that's not the truth. There's no blessed assurance in quasi-grace theology. We must come to the point of jumping off the cliff of Thou Shalt and diving into the ocean body of Undiluted Grace, head first, arms stretched out. Bellyflop if you have to—but *jump*.

Friend, do you believe your closeness with Dad is continually fluctuating? Is it one day at 70%, the next 39%? Is your union with God modified when you forget to have a devotional? When you lose your temper, forget to tithe on your birthday money, or think about having sex with a person who's not your spouse, has *that* caused you to fall off to just 8%?... Or worse, 2%? And what are you going to do *exactly* to get your percentage back up?

Can you see how the enemy attacks our thoughts when we believe our actions and attitudes keep us close to God? Like a shark on a pork chop this mindset stands no chance. This idiot wants you to *think* you're not close to God so you'll live that way. *Recognize* him.

Please, listen, if you've placed your faith in Jesus you're as close to God as you can possibly get—this *moment*. You are hidden *inside* of Him. If the Omnipotent One has hidden your spirit in Himself—like a ring in a ring-box—who could possibly find you to remove you? Even *you* can't overpower God's ability to stash you away (see 2 Timothy 2:13). Who do you think you are?

I say with all love and respect but *who* do you think you are that *your* sins are more powerful than the Cross? Get over it. God knew exactly what He was getting into with you and He *still* just *had* to create you. Why? BECAUSE HE LOVES YOU.

Just look at this; how He's not only close to you, but you and He are one:

> *"For you died, and your life is now hidden with Christ in God."*
> *(Colossians 3:3)*

Christian, you are *in* God, right now, as you read this, in the spiritual realm. In *Him*. Paul informs the Corinthians of the same thing:

> *"But whoever is united with the Lord is one with Him in spirit."* (1
> *Corinthians 6:17)*

Do you see anything in either of these passages about Paul shouting, "*Stay* obedient to *stay* in God!" or "*Continue* in obedience to *continue* to be one with Him in spirit!"? Of course not. Because any part of our identity which is not obedient has died (see Galatians 2:20, Romans 6:6, Colossians 3:3). We are now obedient from the heart! We have an obedient *identity*! *And* we're currently seated with Christ in heaven at this exact moment! Our spirits, that is (see Ephesians 2:6).

We are always in one of two places, spiritually. In Adam, which is in sin. Or in Christ, which is in perfection. Once we are in Christ we can never go back to being in the supernatural loin of our original sinful forefather. We've *died* to sin–to Adam–then crucified *with* Jesus on the Cross, and *then* supernaturally resurrected as sinless. We are now literally *in* Jesus Christ (see Romans 5:12-19, 6:6-11, Ephesians 1:3). Yes, literally.

So if we are organically obedient and in no need to do anything to be close to God, what do we do when we sin? Stop it. Turn from it. Sin is not natural to you, Christian. Likewise, if we are as close to God as we can possibly be right now, why should we do any good works? Because good works is *natural*. Like a Labrador Retriever chasing a tennis ball, you *want* to do good works. Good works is organically fulfilling to you on a very deep level.

Loving others, forgiving people, doing the right things and being patient? All of this stuff doesn't *cause* our closeness to God, but *grows* from our closeness to God. Do you see it? Believer, you *are* close so live *out* your closeness! You *are* a branch so let the vine live *through* you! (See John 15:5).

So today, my friends, know this: We don't get closer to God by obeying commandments, a pastor, or by straining to live out seven steps from a motivational author. We get closer to God by death. Spiritual death, and spiritual resurrection. We get *hidden* in Him *by* Him afterwards—never to be found again. Not by Satan, sin, nor death. We don't need our ears tickled through being told to do more, be more, or to do our part. Our part was to believe Jesus was obedient to the point of death on the Cross; and we did that, Christian. We are now obedient from the heart and as close to God as we can possibly get!

A prayer for you: *Dad, today I'd like to give you thanks for causing me to become obedient from the heart. What an awesome concept. You've rigged this thing to where I can't get away from it! By my one-time faith in Jesus, you've made me a slave to righteousness! How awesome! Right now, I lift up all who are reading this, directly to you. So many of these dear readers*

just want some rest, they want the pressure to go away. They want rest from religion. They want rest from sinning. They want rest in their minds. Please remind them that Jesus IS their rest. Remind them that Jesus was the one who was truly obedient, and our faith in Him is all you require to be close to you. What a graceful gift. Teach us more, Father, about what He's done and what you've done to us, through Him. In His name, amen.

Day 13

What Is the True Meaning of Repent?

"The Lord is not slow in keeping his promise,
as some understand slowness. Instead he is
patient with you, not wanting anyone to perish,
but everyone to come to repentance."

2 Peter 3:9

"Without repentance there is no forgiveness!"

Have you ever heard someone yell this? Boy, I sure have. Sometimes in a venomous way. What this individual doesn't realize is both repentance *and* forgiveness happen at the same time, evenly and instantly, for everyone who places their faith in Jesus Christ. What they see as *their* righteousness–which isn't Christ alone but Christ plus what they stop–*this* is causing repentance and forgiveness to be separate. Only for them though. Not for us saints.

Jesus chastised a group of jerks with this same mindset in Matthew 7:15-23. They were fixated on their repentant *behavior* and *not* on their repentant *faith* which is the only way to be saved. Ultimately this lot was sent to hell because *He* never knew *them* personally, although they claimed *they* knew Him. They didn't. They only knew what they did *for* Him. Satan was happy to give godless signs, wonders, and miracles. This continues today.

When the word repent is contorted the enemy loves it very much because this takes our attention off the finished work of the Cross. He adores the fact that although Christ came to free people, "Repent!" has been turned into a law for Christians.

From the mouths of overbearing, self-centered religious relatives and public figures, to furious preachers who are mean as the dickens; to those who spit and grit their teeth, to the soft-spoken and passive-aggressive, this word has been used as a dagger to stab the souls of countless men, women, and children.

"You never *truly* repented! You're not saved! Just look at you!" Maliciousness oozing from people claiming to know Jesus, "Repent you nasty sinner!" has ruined lives and caused many to not give Christ a chance.

Sure, repent is a biblical word used quite often in Scripture, but it has *two* meanings:

1. Change of belief.
2. Change of actions and attitudes.

Grace-confused people have mashed the two into one in order to back up their pharisaical doctrine. The truth is the majority of scriptural references for repent is number one, change of belief. By repenting from not believing Christ has forgiven you to believing He has, this causes a person to be reborn instantly in their spirit (see John 3:7,8). Tragically, the person who struggles with the sinful tendency of legalism incorrectly thinks number one doesn't exist. For them, each and every mention of repent is about what a person doesn't do any longer.

"Are you saying repentance doesn't matter?!"

"Yeah, but you gotta repent!"

These are some favorite quotes of theirs.

If we look at the Greek definitions of both words for repent, which are used in the original biblical manuscripts–yes, two different words–it becomes obvious they're not the same. They're quite the opposite.

I'll explain the differences shortly, but first what we must do for each instance of repent in the Bible is look to the context. *Who* is saying repent or repentance, *why* are they saying it, *who* is the audience, and most importantly, was it before or after the Cross? Context is always our friend. It allows believers to enjoy a calming peace.

Those who are addicted to legalism hate context. This is why it seems as if they're never peaceful. They're either stressing out about their own sin, having an, "I'm a dirty worm, I'm not worthy," false humility syndrome; or they're continually furious over the sin of others because they don't sin "like them" and "they" need to start living right.

Let's look to John the Baptist's usage of repent. He preached a Law-based repentance which is the opposite of what we Christians believe. John's theology was, "Don't turn away from the Law but back toward it. Do a better job at obeying the 613 commandments." John wasn't referring to just our modern day, cherry-picked top ten plus tithing–but the *whole* Law.

Nothing John said was directed at Christians. We are New Covenant believers and our Covenant hadn't yet happened when John was still teaching. His ministry was only directed toward those who were under the Law. He was preaching to the Jews and his message was, "Start obeying Moses better! Repent toward the Law you promised to keep!"

Do Christians need to do this? No, of course not. Although we were never given the Law we've still died *to* the Law *so that* we can live for Christ (see Romans 6:14, 7:4, 10:4, Galatians 2:19).

When John preached, "Repent of your sins!" he was telling the hypocritical Jews to stop acting like they were obeying the 613 commandments perfectly. When he baptized these repentant Law-lovers that *water* did nothing special. It simply gave them a clear conscience to give Moses' commandments a better shot (see Matthew 3:1-12).

What the modern church has confused *our* forgiveness with–that is, how to be forgiven–John's water baptism and repentance hounding did *not* forgive his followers. He had no power to forgive nor did the water he used. Only blood forgave and they all knew it (see Hebrews 9:22, John 1:29).

Instead, this was the Jewish version of "rededicating themselves."

"I'm really going to commit myself to God this time! Watch me and you'll see!"

Sound familiar? This happens in today's churches all the time. Patrons are called up to the front, or to stand, or to raise their hand and be acknowledged for their past week or months worth of screw-ups.

"Are you finally going to sell out?! Then prove it! Be like me and commit yourself this time and *stop* sinning! Don't be ashamed to admit your many, *many* sins! If you're not ashamed then God won't be ashamed of you! Recommit your life to God!"

Jesus said something similar to some non-believers in Luke 9:26 and Mark 8:38, before the Cross. Yet the New Covenant has never been about *our* commitment to God but about the Father and Son's commitment to each other (see Hebrews 6:16-19, 2 Timothy 2:13).

We don't need to make a show in church to get right–we *are* right, because of them. For believers, this happened once and it won't happen again. We have nothing to be ashamed of. What could possibly bring us shame? Only sins, but the Cross has banished those as far as the east is from the west (see Psalm 103:12, Hebrews 10:17, Romans 8:1).

It's useless for Christians to be recommitting themselves all the time like the Jews whom John guilted in the wilderness. We simply need to have our minds renewed to who we already are, and then mature (see Romans 12:2, Philippians 1:6).

John the Baptist was still pushing Law repentance in Matthew 3 because Christ had not yet established the New Covenant by shedding His blood on the Cross (see Hebrews 9:5,15, Matthew 26:28, 1 John 2:2, Romans 3:25). John *knew* the promised Messiah would bring in a better way, a better *kingdom* than that which was already in force through the Old Covenant patriarchs (see Matthew 3:2,11,12).

This is why *Christians* can't look to how John the Baptist used the word repent and then apply it to us. Contextually, we will never be repenting toward the Law. It's been fulfilled in Christ:

> *"For Christ has already accomplished the purpose for which the Law*
> *was given. As a result, all who believe in him are made right with God."*
> *(Romans 10:4)*

Further, in Matthew 3, "fruit producing through repentance" is mentioned and the context isn't about Christians changing our behavior to produce more fruit. John is informing these whitewashed tombs to repent back toward Law observance and show fruit from *that*. From the *Law*.

Here it is. Pay close attention to what I've underlined. We children of God are *not* being scorn in this firm rebuke:

> But when he saw many of <u>the Pharisees and Sadducees</u> coming to where he was baptizing, he said to them: "You brood of vipers! Who warned you to flee from the coming wrath? <u>Produce fruit in keeping with repentance.</u> And do not think you can say to yourselves, 'We have Abraham as our father.' I tell you that out of these stones God can raise up children for Abraham. The ax is already at the root of the trees, and <u>every tree that</u>

does not produce good fruit will be cut down and thrown into the fire."
(Matthew 3:7-10)

Do you see who he's aiming at? Mosaic Law-abiding citizens, not us. And do you see the standard he places on them? Produce fruit in keeping up with the Law or else be cut down and thrown into the fire. Wow, sounds pretty harsh, but the Law is nothing *but* harsh (see 2 Corinthians 3:7, Matthew 5:48).

What's more is, Christians are not trees, we are branches. Nowhere in the Bible is a Christian referred to as a tree because trees are self-sufficient, not relying on anything outside of themselves. Jesus, however, explains where *we* get our life and sustenance:

"I am the vine; you are the branches. If you remain in me and I in you,
you will bear much fruit; apart from me you can do nothing."
(John 15:5)

Do you see where *our* fruit comes from? The fruit mentioned in Galatians 5:22 and 23? *Love, joy, peace, patience, kindness, goodness, faithfulness, gentleness and self-control*? Not from ourselves but from Jesus.

The vine, *then* the branch, *then* the fruit.

Yet even this beautiful passage will be ripped apart by those who don't understand God's grace nor our relationship to Him through His Son.

"Yeah Matt, *if* you remain! Jesus said *if* you remain in me!"

Well, do we? Yes. Yes, we do, as Christians. Birth is final, spiritually, just like birth is final, physically. Does our physical DNA remain once we are born? Yes. Are we working to abide in the physical DNA we were born with? No. Now apply the same to your spirit.

When we were reborn we inherited God's supernatural DNA. We don't work to sustain this. We don't work to abide, or live, in Him. His seed remains in us and us in His seed (see 1 John 3:9, John 17:23). John 15:5 *has* happened and we are *in*. Paul said that God has hidden us inside of Himself with Christ and we are now one spirit (see Colossians 3:3, 1 Corinthians 6:17).

Like so many badgered passages, John 15:5 is descriptive of a believer and not *pre*-scriptive. This isn't a threat by Jesus but an explanation of what happens *as* we live our lives.

Unlike John the Baptist, whose ministry of Law had to decrease so Jesus' ministry of grace could increase (see John 1:15-17, 3:30), Christ mainly preached repentance of unbelief. As in, turn from confidence in the Law, or yourself, toward me.

By exposing the true standards of the Law–perfection or bust (see Matthew 5:48)–He brought people to the end of themselves so their need for grace would be exposed in even greater ways (see Romans 5:20). Why? So they would finally believe God (see Genesis 15:6, John 6:29, Romans 3:20, Galatians 2:16, 3:11).

"Repent toward *me*. I am enough," was the Spirit behind everything Jesus said. "You don't need the Law, you need me."

The word repent has become a fighting word for a lot of English speaking people. I believe it's because our translation of the original Greek *words* for repent cannot express *both* words properly. There are two, but English speakers only have one. Our six-letter spelling can't unpack both Greek words accurately in how *we* communicate in our native tongue. This is where the crap has hit the fan.

Just like so many other Greek-to-English-non-translatable-words, we've lumped *metanoeo* and *metanoia* into one word, *repent*, and said, "Voila!"

As a result, a law has been created out of what should be two *different* Greek words:

1. Metanoeo – Change of belief
2. Metanoia – Change of actions and attitudes

Two words, two completely different meanings, yet we have, "REPENT!" Here are the examples:

1. Metanoeo – "I am turning from *not* believing that Jesus has forgiven me to believing He *has*."
2. Metanoia – "I am going to *stop* that behavior and I'm going to *change* my attitude."

Only number one can save. Number two can be conducted by a believer *or* a non-believer. Number two can be used by any motivational speaker or pastor who doesn't understand the New Covenant. But the truth is clear, to be saved we must repent of our unbelief in Christ as our Savior–once (see Hebrews 10:10, 1 Peter 3:18, John 3:16-18, 5:24).

Jesus snapped at the Pharisees and Sadducees all the time but not so much about their behavior. It was mostly due to their absolute *refusal* to believe He was there to forgive them. When we see repent coming from the mouth of Christ, repentance from unbelief is His core message. The basis of His repent pleading was, "Believe me. Repent from belief in the Law and Moses and turn toward belief in me alone. I'm the only way. Animal blood atonement will no longer work."

This overall theme is everywhere in Matthew, Mark, Luke and John, yet many still assert, "Only faith *and* repentance saves!"

Do you see the hang-up in this trick statement? Once we understand the two kinds of repentance–metanoeo and metanoia–we realize Christians *have* repented by faith. Faith and repentance is a two-sided coin of metanoeo.

The "faith and repentance" people are focused on mixing both Greek words of repentance *together*, metanoeo *and* metanoia. They're saying, "Faith repentance and action/attitude repentance, combined, is the only way to be saved."

Thankfully, this isn't found in Scripture but the opposite *is*.

Metanoia is based on works and thoughts and can be conducted by any human. The unbelieving Jews had plenty of metanoia in their lives but they lacked metanoeo. Hence, the repentance and faith camp is wrong. In fact, if there's a hint of metanoia mixed in with *any* metanoeo, such is no longer based on grace. Therefore it's no longer the gospel.

Legalistic-acting people love to boast on their "amazing repentance" but the Bible has much to say in conflict:

> *"For it is by grace you have been saved, through faith–and this is not from
> yourselves, it is the gift of God–not by works, so that no one can boast."*
> *(Ephesians 2:8,9)*

> *"And if by grace, then it cannot be based on works; if it were, grace would
> no longer be grace." (Romans 11:6)*

Let's look at ten repentance lies to make the true meaning of repent even more clear:

1. **"God will only forgive you if you repent *and* you're sorry."** I know a lot of people who believe this and they're miserable. If sorrow completes God's forgiveness what if you're not sorry enough and how can you tell? Even unbelievers have sorrow for their mistakes at times. That doesn't make them forgiven. People on stage will guilt us, laying it on thick, "Come forward! *Show* your repentance! Express remorse!" This is *not* how God forgives. Be sorry all you like, He only forgives because of faith in blood, which is true repentance. Even Old Covenant forgiveness had nothing to do with remorse but animal blood. The Jews were sorry they broke Moses' commandments

but they still had to wait until the next annual Day of Atonement to hand off an animal to be sacrificed by a Levitical priest at the temple (see Hebrews 7:11-28, 9:11-28, Colossians 1:20, Ephesians 1:7, Luke 22:20). Being remorseful because of our poor choices and bad attitudes is normal and healthy for us saints, but no amount of self-pity can cause us to be more forgiven than we are at this exact moment in time–which is perfectly (see Hebrews 10:14). We learn, mature, and grow from the understanding that God *forgave* us by the power of Jesus' blood, not by putting on a show of sorrow, privately or publicly. Always recognize your mistakes and move forward in confidence knowing that you *have been* forgiven. Never allow religious people nor the enemy to convince you to spend days, months, and even years trying to be sorry enough to be repeatedly forgiven. That's trash. That's anti-grace. Jesus was already sorry enough *for* you.

2. **"When you sin, God will turn away from you until you repent."** Hold up. I thought He would never leave me nor forsake me? Which one is it, Mr. Double-Talk? And what if I don't repent on a level suffice to get Him to come back? And how can I be absolutely sure I *did* repent? A self-righteous person will be more than happy to answer these questions because this is where they find their identity. BEHAVIOR REPENTANCE. METANOIA. Who else had this obsession? The people who killed Jesus. Fortunately this lie is based on what *I* repeatedly do, yet the gospel is based on what Jesus Christ *has* done. As His beloved children, God never turns away from us, especially when we sin. The only way He would do this is if Christ died again, and stayed dead. We are brand new creations and He's always well-pleased with who we are (see Hebrews 7:25, 13:5, Galatians 2:20,21, Matthew 28:20, 2 Corinthians 5:17).

3. **"If you die with unrepentant sin in your life you will be judged for them on Judgment Day."** For unbelievers, yes, but not for us. For this

lie, if it were true, we'd all be shocked when we meet Jesus face to face because we *all* will have unrepentant sin on our Judgment Day. Unrepentant metanoia galore. Each of us will die while still struggling with some sort of sin. We're human. If we say we *don't* have any sin struggle, that's a lie, so there you have your unrepentant sin. The good news is, Jesus has already been judged guilty for all of our unrepentant sins. The punishment was death for each one. He died, once, for all of them (see Hebrews 10:10). The author of Hebrews explained this to the Jews who wanted to keep getting forgiveness by way of repeated animal sacrifices at the temple, "No sacrifice for sin is left." Jesus was the final sacrifice, not *our* repentant choices and thinking (see Hebrews 10:26-29, John 5:24, Romans 6:10,23).

4. **"You must repent of *each* sin *every* time you sin."** C'mon. If we're being honest we don't even know *how* we're going to sin, so how can we be absolutely sure we've repented properly, let alone each time? "Only willing sins count, Matt!" one might scoff. Friend, all sins are willful. Our wills are involved every time. We are not pre-programmed sin-bots. We did it, we said it, we thought it. "Well if I forget about my sins, God forgets them too!" No, sorry, He's God. His memory is perfect. That's a farce. Do you see what we're doing here? FOCUSING ON SIN. This is a sin-consciousness way of thinking. God wants us to graduate into a righteousness-consciousness thought life (see 2 Corinthians 5:21, 2 Peter 1:3-9, Philippians 4:8,9). He knows we will live out who we think we are, as does Satan. Don't worry about sinning, just be yourself. Live your life and trust your righteous identity (see Romans 14:23, Galatians 5:13-25, Proverbs 23:7).

5. **"True belief will show repentance!"** This very statement causes many to leave their church. Some give up on being who God recreated them

to be altogether because of such nastiness. This is a Mosaic mentality and not grace-based at all. This is a *law*. Laws don't work for us. The only thing a law will do is stir up sin and excite the flesh. Shows of repentance to prove belief is exactly what the Pharisees wanted to give. This is why Jesus told them to go show off in a closet and not let anyone know about their deeds (see Matthew 6:1,6, 1 Corinthians 15:56, Romans 6:14, 7:8,11).

6. **"You gotta repent *and* believe!"** This can be lumped into the "repentance and faith" group I mentioned before this list. Remember the two Greek definitions of repent? Apply the differences to this semi-truth. When you repent–metanoeo–you *have* believed. This isn't a process but an instance of faith. It's *one* coin with *two* sides.

7. **"You must perform deeds to keep up with your repentance."** Unlike John the Baptist's instructions to the legalists, this is from Acts 26:20. Luke is recording Paul's journey and right *before* this statement, Paul said, "Repent and turn to God." So you can see it is faith repentance *first*. If this weren't true, that is, if Paul wasn't saying they were already saved, then how many deeds would be necessary to keep up with repentance? The person who struggles with the insanity of legalanity will tell you, but the saint will not. You are free, Christian. This freedom will inspire you to perform all your deeds. There is no number. Numbers are laws and you've died to those.

8. **"Repentance is something we must do daily."** This statement isn't so bad, just murky. I would remove the word *must* because must is a punishable word. King-Jamesers use the word *shalt* and others use *should*. Must, shalt, and should have to go away for us to enjoy our freedom. I would also be clear about the proper definition of repent. We're not repenting of unbelief daily, but instead, of our choices and coping mechanisms.

9. **"You're only forgiven as long as you truly repent of *that* particular sin, and don't do it again."** *That* can be anything. This might be the worst lie of all. If this were true then why did Christ die? This lie can also be said as, "You're only forgiven of your sins if you stop sinning." This makes no sense. This means the New Covenant is more difficult than the Old Covenant. Before Jesus, the Jews didn't stop sinning to be forgiven, they gave their best bull, goat, or lamb to the priest at the temple once a year. This lie causes the Law of Moses to be more appealing than the Cross of Christ. Repent, yes, every single time you sin, but not to be forgiven. Instead, to be your true self and to enjoy your heaven-ready identity.

10. **"Believers are only forgiven if they *continually* repent."** So we're only forgiven until salvation and then the Cross is useless? This theology is demonic. It negates the power of Jesus' blood and puts the spotlight on ourselves. Yes, again, we should repent–metanoia–each time we sin but *never* to be forgiven. To be forgiven again would mean Jesus would have to die again. He isn't in heaven getting up and down repeatedly, on and off the Cross, each time we sin. This would be the only way *continual* forgiveness could happen. He's resting just fine after finishing our sin problem once and for all time (see Hebrews 1:3, 9:26, 10:10, John 19:30).

When someone says, "I repent of my sins," what does that mean? For the Jews, they needed to repent from the dead works of the Law and believe in the Christ (see Hebrews 6:1). For us Gentiles it's the same except we're repenting from thinking we don't *need* Jesus to forgive us to knowing that He has (see Romans 1:18-20).

God has been kind to all of humanity, patiently waiting for His creation to turn from not believing Him to *back* to believing Him (see 2 Peter 3:9,

Romans 2:4). Unbelief was the first sin. Had Adam and Eve believed God about who they already were–perfect–they wouldn't have eaten from that tree, seeking satanic knowledge about what is right and wrong.

So today, my friends, know this: Don't be afraid or angry over the word repent. Repenting of unbelief caused us to become children of God! When we were reborn, babes in Christ, God didn't hold us in His arms and yell, "Now you *better* repent, or else!" He speaks to us softly, "I'm so happy to have you as my child. We're going to do amazing things together. I can't wait to teach you more and more. I love you *so* much."

A prayer for you: *Father, thank you for teaching me the difference in belief repentance and behavior and attitude repentance. It's helped me greatly. I've heard some people say repent means to agree with you, and I like that because it's true. Right now, I lift up all who are reading this, directly to you. Many want to know what would happen if we don't repent? Through your Spirit you've revealed if we don't repent of unbelief we'll be eternally separated from you. But as your child, if we don't repent of our sinful choices and mindsets, we won't be punished by you. Jesus was punished enough for us. We might have to face earthly punishments but not heavenly. We're very grateful for this and we don't want to grieve you, so keep teaching us more about who we are and counsel us moment by moment. In Jesus' name I pray, amen.*

Day 14

Can Christians Have Tattoos?

*And on His robe and on His thigh He
has a name written, "KING OF KINGS,
AND LORD OF LORDS."*

Revelation 19:16

Pardon me while I barf a little, as I quote some judgmental phrases about tattoos:

"How *dare* you get a tattoo! Heathen! That clearly goes against the holy Word of God! How are you going to repent of *this* sin?! I feel sorry for you on your Day of Judgment!"

"A *true* Christian would never mark up their body! You're proving to God and everyone else you're not really saved!"

"Now doesn't that look trashy. You should be absolutely *ashamed* of yourself. A genuine man or woman of God would *never* ruin their body with disgusting tattoos. I don't even want to be *seen* with you."

This type of vindictive, mean, teeth-gritting trash talk makes me want to toss my cookies. Each time I use sanctimonious sayings in my devotionals to make a point, I feel like I need to take a bath. But I *must* use cantankerous examples in order to bring to light just *how* nasty some people can act.

As I'm sure many of you can attest, there are supposed believers who dig their claws deep into the souls of others as they judge them for getting tattoos. It's no wonder we have such a bad reputation. When we say such hate-filled stupid stuff, people rarely get to see Jesus through us.

Now, from the get-go, I want to be very clear about Christians putting ink into our skin: there is *no* biblical commandment for us to *not* get tattooed.

I'll get to the single passage from Leviticus the grace-confused folk use, but when it comes to getting inked, remember this as your guide: think long and hard about it. Take some time, and then think long and hard about it again.

Getting tattooed is a permanent thing so we must use godly wisdom and ponder greatly about this choice. It will be there for life, and whatever reason you're getting it now, your mood might change later. What's popular today won't necessarily be popular in ten years–or in twenty or thirty years (just think of the mullet, side-spike, and parachute pants). Plus, more than likely you'll have a career, people will constantly be looking at it–and asking you about it–and *you* will also have to see it everyday. So be absolutely positively *sure* it's what you want.

If you're not happy with it afterwards, what are the alternatives?

1. Cover it up.
2. Remove it with laser treatments.

Unfortunately, cover-ups are not always great because there's only so much a tattoo artist can do with it. And if you want to have it removed, the laser process is very painful, expensive, and takes years. I should know. I got a tattoo when I was very young. From the moment I got it I didn't like it. So a few years later I had it covered up. To make matters worse, I didn't like the cover-up. Other people said they liked it, but I didn't. If I *did* like it, I would've been glad to keep it, but over the past two years, I've spent thousands of dollars to have it removed. Nearly fifteen sessions of laser treatments later, I still need at least several more. It's been annoyingly tedious, like peeling an onion one layer every eight to ten weeks. To add to my vexation, the commute to the tattoo removal office is an hour away from my house.

Oh but wait, there's more!

Have you ever been lasered? And I'm not talking about the funny "lasered" like Dr. Evil said in air-quotes. I'm talking scream-your-head-off torture. I'm referring to ask-the-lady-to-stop-so-you-can-catch-your-breath *lasered*. Unless you've felt it, you have no clue how painful being zapped and burned for thirty minutes at a time actually is. The smell of toasted skin is awful and the agony is ten times worse than getting the tattoo.

I brought my wife to one of the treatments, just to sit in and witness it. Afterwards she said, "That was very hard to watch. I hated to see you in so much pain." I'm considering taking Grace to a future session so she'll think long and hard about getting a tattoo when the time comes.

My point is, contemplate deeply about your choice, then proceed, or don't. If you're drunk, high, or emotional, you definitely don't want to do it. Just wait.

However, on the flip side, there's a lot of amazing tattoos out there, and you're free to do whatever you like. You're free to *get* a tattoo or *not* get a tattoo. It was for freedom that Christ set us free! (See Galatians 5:1).

But for the person who struggles with judgmentalism, here's the passage they'll handpick from the Old Covenant to claim we aren't "allowed" to get a tattoo:

"Do not cut your bodies for the dead or put tattoo marks on yourselves. I am the Lord." (Leviticus 19:28)

First of all, you can see this is for the Jews who were cutting their body and tattooing themselves *for their dead relatives and friends.* I'm not sure why. There's no other scriptural reference on this subject. Maybe it was to honor them, or maybe they did this out of grief? Either way it doesn't matter because this is *one* commandment out of 613, and *Christians* don't live by a single commandment given by Moses.

I can already hear the rebuttal from someone who's been taught to mix the Covenants. "What?! Matt, are you saying the commandments given through Moses don't matter?!"

Friend, no, that's not what I'm saying at all. The commandments given to the people group of Israel from Moses *do* matter–a lot. In fact, they matter *so* much to me I hold them to their highest standards according to Christ and the apostles:

OBEY ALL 613 PERFECTLY, OR NONE.

(See Matthew 5:48, James 2:10, Galatians 3:10)

If I *didn't* respect the commandments from Moses I'd pick and choose what I liked and ignore the rest. Further, if we want to follow this tattoo commandment authentically, first, we must be Jewish. We Gentiles were never given the Law from Moses, we were outsiders (see Ephesians 2:12). Only those whom he just freed from Egypt were chosen by God *to* obey them and they agreed—never forced (see Exodus 19:8). *They* entered the first Covenant with Yahweh, not us. The Jews would laugh in our faces if we made the claim we're not getting a tattoo because we're following the Law.

Secondly, to follow the Law we must obey all 613 perfectly. I repeat, Law observance is perfection or bust. As a Jew, if you break a single command you must get forgiveness through animal blood at the next annual Day of Atonement, at the temple, by way of a priest from the Tribe of Levi (see Hebrews 9:22, 13:11,12).

Will you be doing that? Nope. The Twelve Tribes of Israel have been scattered, the priests were replaced by *the* Priest, and the temple is no more (see James 1:1, Hebrews chapters 4-7, in 70 AD the temple was destroyed).

Like a single beer in a 6-pack which is sold at your local convenience store, this single commandment is part of a 613-pack. Buy the whole case or get out. Moses reveals the true standard of the Book of the Law:

> *"Do not <u>add to</u> what I command you and <u>do not subtract from it</u>, but*
> *<u>keep the commands</u> of the Lord your God that I give you."*
> *(Deuteronomy 4:2)*

No adjustments or modifications can be made whatsoever. The dietary laws, moral laws, wardrobe laws, ceremonial laws—*all* of the Torah must be executed wholly if you want to be righteous by obeying it. James, the half-brother of Jesus, reminds his Jewish friends of this truth:

> *"For whoever keeps the whole Law and yet stumbles <u>at just one point</u> is*
> *guilty of breaking <u>all</u> of it." (James 2:10)*

Paul said the same thing when he wrote to the foolish Law-loving Galatians who were trying to mix the Covenants together for "extra" righteousness. He went so far as to *quote* Moses *from* Deuteronomy:

> For all who <u>rely on the works of the Law are under a curse,</u> as it is written: "Cursed is everyone who does not <u>continue to do everything written</u> in the Book of the Law." (*Galatians 3:10*)

What does this have to do with Christians getting tattoos? Everything! The very commandment which has been cherry-picked *from* the Law–Leviticus 19:28–the modern church has turned *into* a law *for* Christians. There's not a single verse in any New Testament epistle which advises us to not get a tattoo, and we're not Jewish.

But even if we were, as a Jewish person we'd have to do all 613 entirely because there are no more sacrifices being made for sins at the temple through animal blood. Jesus was the final Lamb, but to some, that did not matter (see John 1:29, 11:53). The Moses followers were informed about the consequences for rejecting faith in Messiah:

> "If we deliberately keep on sinning <u>after we have received the knowledge of the truth, no sacrifice for sins is left,</u> but only a fearful expectation of judgment and of raging fire that will consume the enemies of God." (*Hebrews 10:26,27*)

Self-centered people like to use this passage from Hebrews as a threat for Christians. But this is actually directed toward the unbelieving Jews who had *heard* about Jesus' final sacrifice yet still wanted to present *animal* sacrifices for forgiveness at the temple. Do you see it?

If we read all of Hebrews 10 we discover the requirements of the Law of Moses is the context and standing firm in faith in Christ *alone* is the message. We Christians were not given the Law, so we don't have to turn from believing in it. Therefore, this section is not directed at us.

Why am I making such a big deal out of the Law? Because the tattoo commandment used today by hypercritical people is *in* the Law, yet we Christians have no relationship *with* the Law. The Law is the Old Covenant between God and Israel. The Law was *replaced* with the New Covenant for all who believe in Jesus (see Romans 10:4).

When Christ shed His blood He finished the righteous requirements of the Law *in* His own physical body. He did what no human ever could. Because God had given dominion over this planet to man, a man had to fulfill the Law perfectly. Jesus did just that, so He *finished* the Law *in* Himself (John 19:30, Romans 8:3,4, 2 Corinthians 5:21, Galatians 3:13, 4:4,5, Matthew 5:48).

This is why animal sacrifices are no longer required by God for forgiveness for breaking the Law, and why the Jewish people were looking forward to Messiah. The annual trek to receive forgiveness of sins was getting old. Plus they wanted to keep their prized goat.

The New Covenant began when Christ offered His own blood for the sin of the whole world! (See Romans 6:23, Hebrews 1:3, 9:24). It didn't begin at the birth of Jesus but at the death of Jesus! Why was the bloody Cross the very *moment* in which the New Covenant came to pass? Because only blood can bring in a Covenant with our Creator. Even the first Covenant had to be sprinkled with blood by the *first* mediator, who was Moses, in order to bring *it* into effect. That is, the 613, ten of which were *the* Ten Commandments–also known as the moral part of the Law (see Exodus 24:8).

Jesus' blood, however, *replaced* the Old Covenant because only *one* Covenant can be in effect with God at a time (see Hebrews 8:13). The author of Hebrews painstakingly pens these truths to the unbelieving Jewish people who were stuck on Moses:

> *"Jesus has been found worthy of greater honor than Moses, just as the builder of a house has greater honor than the house itself."*
> *(Hebrews 3:3)*

> *"But in fact the ministry Jesus has received is as superior to theirs as the covenant of which he is mediator is superior to the old one, since the new covenant is established on better promises." (Hebrews 8:6)*

What are the better promises in the New Covenant? Simple. The Father's promise to the Son at the Cross to remember our sins no more–and vice versa–the Son's promise to die *for* those sins *once* and for all time (see Hebrews 6:16-19, 7:25, 8:12, 10:10). We are now the beneficiaries to *their* promise by a one-time graceful faith in Jesus' death for our sins (see Ephesians 2:8,9, John 3:16-18, Hebrews 9:16-18).

Beneficiaries *do* nothing to receive an inheritance. They don't *make* promises, they don't reach out and *take* promises, nor do they name and *claim* promises–or beg, fast, hope and *plead* for promises. Beneficiaries sit still and bequest assets after a death. Someone dies and *they* benefit *from* that death, without doing anything at all. We believed Jesus and became children of God who've inherited His righteousness (see John 1:12, Colossians 3:24, 2 Corinthians 5:21).

Do you see why the event at Golgotha was so amazing?!

I want to be clear. Was there anything wrong with the Old Covenant? Not at all. In fact, the fault was found in the people's inability to live up to their end of the bargain. So God in all of His brilliance *removed* the people and then *replaced* the Covenant. He then inserted *Himself* in mankind's stead–which was His plan before the foundation of the earth! (See Hebrews 8:8,9, Revelation 13:8).

But let's back up for a minute. Has the Law gone away? No. It's still in full effect for *today* just as it was during Jesus' time. However, what most Christians don't understand is that the Law's use is just the same in 2019 as it was back then: expose the severe hypocrisy of the most self-righteous people on the planet so they will turn toward faith in Christ alone (see 1 Timothy 1:7-11, Matthew 7:13-23, Galatians 3:2).

This is why Jesus said He did not come to abolish the Law but to fulfill it– to show it off for everything it's worth! (See Matthew 5:17). What's it worth? Absolute perfection or absolute failure! Jesus even *raised* the standard of the Law in the Sermon on the Mount in order to bring *additional* pressure to the legalists who believed they were righteous through the Law. Some heard His message and immediately repented from legalism, yet others wanted to kill Him over such talk.

So when we handpick the tattoo commandment out of Leviticus, we are doing exactly what Jesus said we *can't* do by *not* getting a tattoo:

"Be <u>perfect</u>, therefore, <u>as your heavenly Father is perfect</u>."
(Matthew 5:48)

Mosaic Law observance–according to Jesus, not our modern church– must be accomplished *just* as perfectly as God in the flesh accomplished it. He doesn't "grade us" based on performance. That's Old Covenant Judaism, pre-Cross theology. Christianity is pass or fail. Life or death. 100% righteous or 100% sinful.

For this reason, Paul said the Law is *not* of faith and that we must die *to* the Law *so that* we can live for God (see Galatians 2:19, 3:12, Romans 6:14). He never said the Law has died but that *he* died *to* the Law. It–all

613–had no authority over his actions and attitudes because the Spirit of God *within him* would never *lead* him into sin. The Holy Spirit replaces the Law's guidance for all who believe in Jesus (see Romans 10:4, Galatians 3:24,25). Even more, Paul claimed the Law is a ministry of death and that sin *increases*–not decreases–when we "try" to obey it (see 2 Corinthians 3:7-10, Romans 5:20, 7:8-11).

This proves if we want to follow the tattoo commandment we must also follow these too:

- *"Do not eat any meat with the blood still in it"* (see Leviticus 19:26). So much for that rare steak which many Christians enjoy.
- *"Do not cut the hair at the sides of your head or clip off the edges of your beard"* (Leviticus 19:27). If your barber gives you a nice fade and trims your beard, sorry, you're out.
- *"Stand up in the presence of the aged, show respect for the elderly"* (see Leviticus 19:32). Every time a senior citizen walks by, if you don't stand up, you've just broken this commandment.

I could continue with many more commandments from the Law, but as you can see, it is very burdensome. It was meant to be, so we would lean toward God's grace.

We have no relationship with the Law as New Covenant believers. We don't look to the Law for anything, not even for morality. Remember, it's all or nothing. Don't worry though, the Spirit will never lead you into any type of immorality. Satan and his demons will, the power of sin will, and our old ways of coping will (unrenewed mindsets), but the Spirit inside of us will never lead us into anything that is not of faith (see Romans 14:23, Galatians 5:22,23).

So if you want a tattoo, get a tattoo. Just think about it, pray about it, and do your research on the style, the artist, the pain involved, and placement on your body. Ask God for wisdom about it (see James 1:5). But be sure to know, as a Christian, no amount of ink in your skin can alter Christ being in your heart. Once He's there, He's there forever. Tattoo ink is not more powerful than Jesus' blood. Truth be told, biblically, even Jesus has a tattoo... on His thigh:

> *And on His robe and on His thigh He has a name written, "KING OF KINGS, AND LORD OF LORDS." (Revelation 19:16)*

That's a pretty cool tattoo if you ask me! Who else could pull that off but our Savior?!

I know, I *know*, legalistic demons are going bat crap crazy right about now, pestering those who struggle with legalanity. But the Bible is clear: Jesus is tatted up with some sweet ink!

So today, my friends, know this: God would rather you have a tattoo on every square inch of your skin, and He live in your heart, than you have *no* ink, and yet refuse to allow Him to *join* your heart. Samuel said it best:

> *"The Lord does not look at the things people look at. People look at the outward appearance, but the Lord looks at the heart"*
> *(see 1 Samuel 16:7).*

Your heart is what matters, which is your spirit. Not your skin, but the real you. The everlasting you. Enjoy your freedom, Christian, and make wise choices which are always led by Christ within you.

A prayer for you: *Father, thank you for the New Covenant. What a great idea you had. This Covenant seems so new to many of these dear readers, but it's actually as old as Jesus' death. For those who are coming out of the harsh, double-talk teachings of Moses plus Jesus, Law plus grace, death plus life—ease their minds today. Assure them with your Spirit, that, although yes, they'll need their thoughts renewed to the freedom found in the New Covenant, they're already 100% righteous because of it. Give them a sense of peace and help them to unlearn the lies of Covenant mixture. Teach them to make the Cross their main focus. As Jesus lives through them, they'll enjoy His wisdom in regard to tattoos, forgiveness, finances, confidence, boundaries, sex, parenting, and everything else they can think of. He is our one true Counselor. Amen.*

Day 15

Water Baptism, Tongues, and Prophecy

"I thank God that I did not baptize any of you…"

See 1 Corinthians 1:14

" **W**ho were *you* baptized by? Because I was baptized by Peter!"

"Oh yeah, so what! John was closer to Jesus, he said so himself, and *I* got baptized by John!"

"Ha! Peter and John are not as great as Paul! *Paul* is coming to town, and *he* will be the one to baptize me!"

The early church bickered over something as silly as "Who baptized whom?" The people in Corinth actually believed it mattered who dunked them in water. For this reason, Paul had some sharp rebukes:

> *"I thank God that I did <u>not</u> baptize any of you except Crispus and Gaius" (1 Corinthians 1:14)*

"For Christ <u>did not send me to baptize</u>, but to preach the gospel"
(See 1 Corinthians 1:17)

Now don't you think if water baptism saved a person, Paul would have never penned these words? He would've been crystal clear: "You need to be submerged in water to become a Christian." Yet he never said such a thing. In fact, he said we receive the Spirit *by hearing with faith*, not once, but *twice* in his letters:

"<u>So faith comes from hearing</u>, and hearing by the word of Christ."
(Romans 10:17)

"This is the only thing I want to find out from you: did you <u>receive the
Spirit</u> by the works of the Law, <u>or by hearing with faith</u>?"
(Galatians 3:2)

Paul understood that going under water was a symbolic action of our spiritual death, and that it didn't *cause* our spiritual death–which is required to be saved (see Romans 6:6, Colossians 3:3, Galatians 2:20). He knew that being placed *into* water was an expression of what actually happened to our *spirit*–which was placed *into* Christ's Spirit, the millisecond we first believed He forgave us. Paul also recognized that coming up *out* of the water was a celebration of our new spirit being birthed to life!

Water baptism is a wonderful thing! Just the same as throwing a birthday party is a wonderful thing! But we are not being born again and again each year when we celebrate our physical birth, just the same as we are not being born again and again *spiritually* when we get in the hot tub at church or submerged in the river. These are beautiful events, but they aren't causing anything supernatural to happen.

In 1 Corinthians 1:14, Paul thanks God that he *didn't* baptize anyone except for two people. He said Christ didn't send him *to* baptize, but to preach the gospel (see 1 Corinthians 1:17). So obviously, as Paul said to the Romans and Galatians, it is *hearing* the gospel which allows people the opportunity to be saved, not water submersion.

Regardless of this New Covenant truth, there's a group of individuals who make the claim that if a person doesn't get water baptized then they're not a true Christian. As a result, some of their patrons get baptized multiple times in an attempt to someday *feel* something, but they never do. "This time I hope it works."

Others have been led to believe that if they'd *just* been baptized "properly" they'd never sin again; or they need to be baptized again and again to wash away more sins. This is called "water baptism righteousness" and such a quasi-grace theology can never be retrofit into the gospel for a reason: *it's not the truth.*

I don't want to be misunderstood, I highly recommend all believers celebrate their new birth with a water baptism. I was saved since the 1980's but did not get baptized in water until 2015. It's never too late to throw this birthday party. But be sure to know something paramount to this wet festivity:

No amount of liquid in all the universe could ever wash away our sins.
Only our one-time realization of knowing Christ has forgiven us can
accomplish this feat.

Water baptism is a celebration! Again, it's like a birthday party! It's a day of honor of looking back on *when* we were born, but it's not the actual day we *were* born unless our day of water baptism was the day we first believed!

Hopefully you've not had to deal with water baptism legalists, but sadly many have. Grace-confused church leaders accuse people of being sub-Christians, or *not* Christians, if they aren't publicly bathed in *their* holy water. So where is this confusion coming from? Like most legalism fungus on our planet, it grows from overlooking Scripture in context. A majority of poor scriptural exegesis can be blamed on contextual disorientation. This is why when we study our Bibles we should ask ourselves some simple questions to establish a frame of reference for *each* book:

"Who is this written to and why?"

"Who is the author, where is the author, and why?"

"Is the Old Covenant being referenced or the New? Or is this a comparison of both?"

"Is this passage written to a believer or non-believer–or Jews, Gentiles, or both?"

"Is this book recording the actions of the apostles and patriarchs, or is this doctrine according to the New Covenant?"

"What was going on in this particular church at this point in time in history?"

"Was Jesus bringing to light the hypocrisy of the Mosaic legalists, or comforting those who saw Him as Messiah?"

"Is this symbolism, Law, or advice for godly living?"

"Was Jesus just asked a Law-based question, or a grace-based question?"

And for this devotional:

"Is this referring to <u>water baptism</u> or <u>spiritual baptism</u>?"

Just the same as confusing Moses' commandments with Jesus' commandments–that is, each time we see the word *commandment* in the Bible–we can easily do the same with the word *baptize*. Water is not always the context. Sometimes the passage is about the actual Spirit of God.

But first, let's back up and define baptism. The word baptize means: *to place inside of*. With the true comprehension we can decipher whether each passage in the Bible is describing a person's *physical* being or *spiritual* being:

1. **Physical baptism** – This baptism in Scripture is always referring to a person's body of matter, their physical flesh, so water *is* correct. Plus, you can't get a spirit wet because it is not of this realm. Before the Cross, anytime a Jew was baptized in water they first admitted to breaking Mosaic Law, then they confessed to repent from breaking it again. These were *not* random sins as our modern church has made up, such as drinking, smoking, sleeping around, or cursing, but *only* infractions according to the Law. There were 613 different ways to break it. Gentiles were never baptized before the Cross because we were never given the Law. But for the people group of Israel, after confessing to repent, only *then* were they dipped in water as an expression–or symbol–of "being clean" in their conscience (see Matthew 3:6,11, Mark 1:5,8). However, this pre-Cross water baptism did not make them forgiven, as only the blood of animals could do such, which happened annually at the Day of Atonement (see Hebrews 9:22, 10:1-14). Why do you think John the Baptist was named John *the Baptist* if he was at work *before* Jesus began His own ministry? It was because John baptized people according to the Old Covenant commandments for a renewed frame of mind. After the Cross of Christ brought in the *New* Covenant, water baptism became a symbol of what has happened to a person's spirit, which is being placed into *Jesus'* Spirit. This is why Peter said in Acts 2:38, "Repent, and each of you be baptized in the name of Jesus Christ for the forgiveness of your sins; and you will receive the gift of the Holy Spirit." They had to repent of unbelief in Jesus' forgiveness in order to receive

His Spirit into theirs–*spiritual baptism*–which I'll get to next. But the truth about Acts 2:38 is this had *nothing* to do with repenting of sinful actions and attitudes because that was baptism *according to the Law*. John the Baptist preached *that* type of repentance–the apostles did not. Instead, they taught repentance of *faith* in Christ as Savior.

2. ***Spiritual baptism*** – This baptism happens *once* from the moment we believe Jesus has forgiven us. At that exact moment, our spirit is literally placed *in* Christ's Spirit like cereal being placed in milk. The milk is in the cereal and the cereal is in the milk–they become one, yet still separate. We may or may not have felt anything, that doesn't matter. Remember, Paul told the Romans and Galatians we receive His Spirit by *hearing* and *not* by a feeling. We aren't saved by our emotions but by our admittance *in our heart* that Christ forgives us. When we do, our old sinful spirit dies on the Cross with Jesus–literally–it is buried in the tomb with Jesus–literally–and then our new sinless spirit is resurrected with Jesus–yes, literally. This is not symbolism at all nor "in the future"–but now! We actually become one *with* Jesus in spirit, like a letter being placed in an envelope which is then put into a shredder! That shred pile is one, yet the letter and envelope are still separate! If you're reading this as a Christian, Jesus is reading this with you! You are together forever, infused, intertwined, united, *inside of* and baptized *into*! After we believed Jesus saved us–that instant of faith–our spiritual baptism happened! Paul goes into great detail about spiritual baptism in Romans 6 and not once does he mention water (see Romans 6:3-11, Galatians 2:20, Colossians 3:3, 1 Corinthians 6:17).

Unfortunately Satan has added even more confusion to baptism in our churches. Some divisions–*ahem* I mean, some *denominations* make the claim that spiritual baptism happens twice; as if God couldn't get it right the first time, or that we must speak in tongues to "achieve it." Yet Paul said, "Not all speak in tongues, do they?" (See 1 Corinthians 12:30).

Don't you think that if Paul believed this spiritual gift was required for every Christian he would have written an entire epistle on *just* tongues? I sure do. But instead, he downplays speaking in tongues, even saying prophecy is much greater of a gift (see 1 Corinthians 14:5). So why isn't this group of people teaching that *prophecy* is required for a supposed "second baptism" *rather* than tongues? …That rhetorical question answers itself.

Has tongues and prophecy gone away? No. None of the gifts have disappeared, they've simply been mistaught as to what they really are. I'll explain, but first, to test whether or not a person finds their identity in Christ alone—rather than a gift—simply question them over the subject of tongues and/or prophecy. Most who find their worth in spiritual gifts and church status will become enraged. Some will even threaten you with hell, as if they have the power to send you there. That, or they'll revert to insults and belittlements. *Some* will even laugh at you because they have no true defense based on Scripture being read in context. Yet others choose a passive-aggressive demeanor or the country club silent treatment because *they* are "more holy" than you and their gifts "prove" that.

"So be gone. You're not welcomed here." They'll say with a chuckle. "I'm not having a Bible conversation with *you*. Don't you know who I am? I'm *chosen* and the elders have verified that."

But this is exactly what adding to the gospel does. Our egos get punched in the mouth and our feelings get hurt, so we revert into defense-mode. Saltiness is then the flavor of choice, as we don't know what to say or do. When the Cross is presented as all that's needed, legalistic demons go haywire, pestering the most eccentrically-minded men and women of our churches. I say this with kindness: a supposed *first* baptism and then *second* baptism makes no sense at all *according to the Bible*. Paul told the Romans that if they don't *have* the Spirit of Christ then they don't even *belong* to Him. Once is enough, just look:

"And if anyone does not have the Spirit of Christ, they do not belong to Christ." (See Romans 8:9)

Is this not clear? How are we going to be saved once *without* His Spirit? C'mon. God is not giving us His Spirit in portions, we *receive* His Spirit instantaneously *in full* from the moment of belief in Christ's ability to forgive us. We don't *achieve* His Spirit by way of foreign language speaking, which is exactly what tongues is, according to Acts 2:6-11. Biblical exposition of this gift easily reveals the truth of tongues: *speaking a language from a country in which we do not naturally know.* Why? So foreign people can *hear* the gospel in their *native tongue* and then *believe* in Jesus so they can be saved.

This gift doesn't *cause* the Spirit to join us, but instead is a sign He *has* joined us. That is, if you've received this particular gift of foreign language speaking–but not *all* do (see 1 Corinthians 12:30). What gift do we all receive evenly? *Love* (see 1 Corinthians 13:13, Romans 5:5). Expressing this love in many different facets is the true will of God (see John 15:17, Galatians 5:22,23). Not tongues, not prophecy–nor other gifts which are many and diverse but *love*.

Further, foreign language speaking–tongues–is a sign to the unbeliever and *not* the believer (see 1 Corinthians 14:22). This is why it's not necessary for salvation or a "second baptism" of the Spirit. Just think about it. For those who *hear* tongues–so that they *can* be saved by hearing–some of them don't even *have* a tongue or a voice-box. Will God not give His Spirit to them if they believe, even though they *can't* speak? Of course He will! The tongues law has got to go!

So where are certain people getting this theology? A second baptism by way of tongues? Unfortunately, through poor interpretation of biblical text. Let's look at the passage they're using. Luke records an event in the book of Acts, chapter 19, which involves baptism *and* speaking in tongues. Please pay close attention to what I've underlined for context:

While Apollos was at Corinth, Paul took the road through the interior and arrived at Ephesus. There <u>he found some disciples</u> and asked them, "Did you receive the Holy Spirit when you believed?"

They answered, "No, we have not even <u>heard</u> that there is a Holy Spirit."

So Paul asked, "Then what baptism did you receive?"

"<u>John's baptism</u>," they replied. (Acts 19:1-3)

Let's stop right there for a moment. *Whose* disciples were these? John the Baptist's *not* Jesus'. Do you see it? They had no clue who Jesus was, so they had no clue who the *Holy Spirit* was. John's baptism was according to the Law, Jesus' was according to the Spirit. They had not even *heard* about Messiah and were following John (remember, Paul said it is by hearing with faith we receive Him).

These disciples of John had *only* been taught Mosaic Law, which was John the Baptist's entire ministry and *not* Jesus' (see Mark 1:4, John 3:30). These people were not Christians–yet. John preached 613 Thou Shalts, which were handed down from Moses, including the Ten Commandments (see Deuteronomy 4:2). Jesus preached *two* commandments, believe and love (see John 13:34,35, 1 John 3:23).

Now, if you see these people as *Christians*–rather than followers of John the Baptist–the error of a second baptism definitely seems plausible. However, they were *about* to hear of the Christ whom John prophesied about, *then* they'd believe, *then* a celebration of water baptism happens. Let's continue:

Paul said, "<u>John's baptism was a baptism of repentance</u>. He told the people to <u>believe in the one coming after him, that is, in Jesus</u>." On <u>hearing</u> this, *they were baptized in the name of the Lord Jesus. When Paul placed his hands on them, the Holy Spirit came on them, and they spoke in tongues and prophesied. (Acts 19:4-6)*

Don't forget, John's water baptism *before* the Cross was a symbol of behavior and attitude repentance–*according to Moses' Law infractions*–which is the *exact* baptism they had heard of and *not* the baptism of the Spirit. They were now being informed about Pentecost, about the Spirit's baptism which was available for everyone. This is why Paul asked this very question and *then* went on to explain they have to believe in Jesus now and Moses no more. They had to repent of unbelief in Christ in order to receive His very Spirit. Once they did–which was *believe* first–they were baptized in water to celebrate *after*.

I understand some questions might be posed to what I'm saying, "Matt, but what about the part of this passage when Paul placed his hands on them? Why would he do such a thing? And do I need to lay my hands on people so they can receive the Spirit?"

To answer that, I'll ask some questions too. What if–and this sounds a little stupid–what if Paul didn't *have* hands? Or arms? Would they *not* have received the Holy Spirit? If Paul's two hands had some magical power, why didn't he just go down the city street touching people and turning them into Christians?

Do you see the sillly rationale of *touching* someone so they can "take possession of" the Spirit of Jesus Christ? Maybe–and I'm still being facetious here–after having hands laid on them, they'd fly across the room and squiggle on the floor in order to "get" the most of Him. Or *maybe*, week after week they'd need to go find Paul so he can zap them *again* so they can receive the Spirit *again* because they lost fellowship? With such super powers, why doesn't Paul touch a tree and make it born again, and their family dog too while he's at it?

I jest, but this is a real demonic rabbit trail our minds can go down when we witness non-gospel stuff passed down from our relatives, or *assume* a recorded event in Acts is doctrine for salvation. Truth be told, if we're going to do that, why stop at tongues as proof of salvation? Why not require someone to have a flame above their heads too? (See Acts 2:3). I mean, this happened to the apostles, so why not teach someone "how" to do this at flame school? Maybe have an online course or go deeper into training by way of a cell group? But no, we cherry-pick a *single* gift and then run off with it like a madman while lying to people about it.

Even more, if Acts *is* doctrine *rather* than recorded actions, why aren't churches littered with dead bodies when the plate gets passed around for tithing on Sunday? Lying about money should be causing people to drop dead (see Acts 5:1-11).

We have many *epistles* loaded with doctrine. Acts is just that: "Acts of the apostles."

Just like with the Law of Moses, *we,* as New Covenant believers, like to use Acts as a doctrine buffet line. We take what we like and leave what we don't, then we get mad when we're called out on stuff. The reality is, the apostles were getting their theology in order all throughout this book, just the same as *we* do, when we first begin to understand the power of the Cross. I *still* email and text my colleagues, in regard to the New Covenant, as I read through Scripture. Like the apostles were doing, I want to be sure we're all on the same page about the message. Every single one of us is learning and growing, it's a process in our minds. As the original group of Christians went through the same maturing phase as you and I, Luke wrote it down in Acts as Paul informed him of what had happened. These are *recorded* events, a history book–very valuable, but not doctrine. Should it be in the Bible? Yes! But again, we must read it in context for what it is.

If we want to know what the apostles truly figured out after Acts, we have many letters to subsequently go by. James, John, Peter, Paul, Jude–read what they wrote to the churches for what the Spirit taught them over time. Looking to Acts for doctrine would be the same as looking to brand new Christians for doctrine. Maturation phases are vital to expressing the truth of the New Covenant clearly.

Let's go back to tongues for a moment. I need to emphasize that tongues is an *evangelistic* gift of speaking foreign languages so unbelievers can hear and believe. Why do you think the gospel was able to spread so quickly? Paul was an apostle to foreign language speaking people–we Gentiles–this is why he spoke in tongues more than anyone else (see 1 Corinthians 14:18). He went from town to town preaching in the local language about Jesus.

If we look up tongues in Acts 2:6-11, it's easy to see that *human* dialect in which we do not naturally know is the context. Tongues is not repeated syllable babble or tick-tock-bing-bock talk meant to make us look cool. Even more, God doesn't need to hear us *pray* in tongues because He knows *all* languages; and not once are New Covenant believers instructed to pray in tongues privately. Tongues is actual words spoken in Spanish, German, Russian, English, Vietnamese–any language of this planet. Paul had to put a reign on the latest episode of *Tongues Gone Wild* in 1 Corinthians 14 as he said:

> *"Unless you speak <u>intelligible words with your tongue,</u> how will anyone know what you are saying? You will just be speaking into the air."*
> *(See 1 Corinthians 14:9)*

If you read this entire chapter, even back then, this spiritual gift was being misconstrued in church. Yes, speaking in tongues *is* a real supernatural gift, but it is *only* for non-native-language-speaking guests to hear *their* language. When brother Bob randomly barks nonsensical stuff in the middle of service, that isn't tongues. Even more, someone supposedly *interpreting* brother Bob's chatter, that isn't *interpretations* of tongues.

With all due respect to brother Bob and his interpreter, this is a generational, passed-down incorrect *learned* behavior, based on bad Bible studies. Those who speak tongues speak foreign languages they've never known. Those who interpret tongues, speak that *actual* foreign language, or they have the gift of translating it into *your* language so *you* can understand it. Read all of 1 Corinthians 14 and this is simple to see. For an even deeper look into the gift of tongues, check out *The Truth About Speaking in Tongues* from my book *60 Days for Jesus, Volume 3*.

I want to touch up on one more thing about laying hands on others. Laying our hands on someone is simply laying our hands on someone. That's it. Nothing more, nothing less. I know that when *I* lay my hands on someone and pray for them, or hug them, or put my hand on their shoulder, it's a comforting thing. It's not me transferring any power. Instead, I'm relaying without words, "I'm here with you."

What about prophecy? These men in Acts 19 also prophesied after receiving the Spirit of Christ. Great! But what *is* prophecy? Old Covenant prophecy foretold the future–the future about the coming Messiah. Now that Christ is here, future-telling is not necessary from anyone because Jesus coming to earth *has been* completed. His first trip, anyway.

The author of Hebrews explains how we no longer need people to prophesy as they did according to the Old Covenant:

> "In the past God spoke to our ancestors <u>through the prophets</u> at many times and in various ways, <u>but in these last days he has spoken to us by his Son,</u> whom he appointed heir of all things, and through whom also he made the universe." (Hebrews 1:1,2)

New Covenant prophecy is not crystal-ball reading or scanning the crowd and pointing people out. It's simply edification, encouragement, and consolation. It is building others up with our words!

The Corinthians were educated on this topic by Paul:

"But the one who prophesies speaks to people for their <u>strengthening</u>, <u>encouraging</u> and <u>comfort</u>." (1 Corinthians 14:3)

Encouraging people is a gift! Being a shoulder to cry on is a gift! Empathy is a gift! *This* is New Covenant prophecy! I understand these words will chop off the legs of legalistic gift demons galore, and that is my intent. Like a 50-cal on the battlefield, the armies of hell stand no chance when we begin to decipher what supernatural gifts actually are. The forces of hell want us to define ourselves by our gifts, but God wants us to define ourselves as His children.

Many will stand up and walk out on these truths of tongues and prophecy while absolutely *fuming* because my words threaten who they *think* they are. They've been admired *way* too many times over these gifts, so how dare *I* inform them that these gifts don't define them? But once they burn out on how amazing their gift is they too will fall off into the chasm of God's bottomless grace. Hopefully, anyway.

Friend, I speak from experience as I too used to see my gifts of writing and communication as my true identity. When someone's opinion threatened this I became enraged or depressed. Now I see opinions as simply opinions *rather* than a hazard to who I really am. It's fine what others think, I think stuff too. As a result of having my worth now centered on Christ alone I can actually respond to poor opinions of me with gentleness and respect, or not say anything at all because I'm still secure.

This is exactly why Jesus wants to teach us who we truly are. Nobody can threaten our identity when we *know* our identity.

This brings us around the horn to understanding how baptism saves us, and also, how we can comprehend the gifts *some* of us receive *after* spiritual baptism. Not everyone receives the same gifts and that's okay. Receiving the

Spirit is what's most important. So get water baptized if you haven't and celebrate your supernatural birthday! But don't get baptized in water to earn anything from God. That's impossible.

I want to look at two last rebuttals in regard to water baptism for salvation because I know someone will email me if I leave this out. In John 3, Jesus explains to a religious man how we are born *first* by way of the water sac in our mother, and then *second* our spirits are *re*born by *the* Spirit. Some will attempt to use this passage as evidence of Jesus saying we need to be water baptized but that's not the context at all.

When Jesus was speaking of being born of water *and* spirit, Nicodemus couldn't fathom such a thought. This is why he asked how a person could possibly be born from their *mother* a second time. Mom. Momma. *Mother.* This is the water Jesus was talking about being born from—her womb. He wasn't referring to our bodies being dunked in a water hole or an oversized bathtub behind glass at church.

For water *and* spirit, Christ is explaining our one-time *physical* birth and then our *second* spiritual birth:

> Jesus answered, "Very truly I tell you, no one can enter the kingdom of God unless they are born of water <u>and</u> the Spirit. <u>Flesh gives birth to flesh, but the Spirit gives birth to spirit</u>. You should not be surprised at my saying, 'You must be born again.' The wind blows wherever it pleases. You hear its sound, but you cannot tell where it comes from or where it is going. <u>So it is with everyone born of the Spirit</u>." (John 3:5-8)

Do you see the difference? Flesh is water—the embryonic pouch we live in for nine months. When we come out of Mom this *has* happened (Flesh gives birth to flesh). Our second birth is a supernatural birth which comes by way of believing Jesus for forgiveness. Like wind blowing, you can't see this when it happens (Spirit gives birth to spirit).

This information authenticates that water baptism is not necessary for salvation, but instead, being reborn in spirit by faith *is* necessary. I understand this will anger some because of what they've been taught–this is *not* my intent. Yet, I'll still hear, "Matt, you are lying! You will answer for this and rightly burn in hell!"

This person's rude quote I'm presenting is no exaggerating straw-man. Those actual words have been messaged to me many times over this subject. Do you see how infuriating such a matter can be for those who don't understand the power of the Cross? *Very.* Like uncaged birds, scruples and stability fly out the window as they yell, "Even Jesus Himself was baptized! It is *required* for the forgiveness of sins!"

Friend, I'm sorry, but Jesus had no sin to be forgiven of. He was perfect in every way. The contextual reason for Jesus being baptized was because it was foretold about in Scripture as a part of the Law needing to be fulfilled. Sure, His baptism was a shadow of what was to come for all of us after the Cross; but, He said it was "fitting" that His own baptism be done in order to fulfill all Jewish prophecies pointing to His righteousness:

> But Jesus answered him, "Let it be so now, for thus *it is fitting for us to fulfill all righteousness.*" (See Matthew 3:15)

"But wasn't Jesus already righteous?" you might ask. Absolutely, I'd answer. Therefore, He was fulfilling the righteous requirements *of the Law* for those *under* the Law, Israel. The Jewish race. He *had* to do this *before* He went to the Cross so He could redeem those under the curse of the Law (see Galatians 3:10,13, 4:4,5).

Let's look at one last passage about water baptism in which some will say is biblical data for salvation requirement, 1 Peter 3:20 and 21:

"to those who were disobedient long ago when God waited patiently in the days of Noah while the ark was being built. In it only a few people, eight in all, were saved through water, and this water <u>symbolizes baptism</u> that now saves you also–<u>not the removal of dirt from the body</u> but the pledge of a clear conscience toward God. <u>It saves you by the resurrection of Jesus Christ</u>"

Peter uses the example–the symbolism–of the water which flooded the earth in the time of Noah as the symbol of the Holy Spirit flooding the earth *after* the Cross. *It* saved Noah and his family because they were safe in the ark, just the same as the Spirit now saves *us* because we are safe in Christ. Do you see that? However, Peter quickly attempts to clear up what he's just penned. He informs his audience that he *isn't* referring to being *outwardly* cleaned by water *for* salvation–as in water baptism. Interrupting his own sentence to emphatically insert, "not the removal of dirt from the body," making sure they understand salvation comes only "by the resurrection of Jesus Christ."

Peter knew full well that he could dunk an unbeliever in water for twelve straight hours while yelling, "I baptize you in the name of the Father, Son, and Holy Spirit!" and such a person would *never* receive the Spirit of Jesus. It is by grace we are saved, through faith. There's nothing we can do, or *not* do, to earn our saving. It's a free gift:

"For it is by grace you have been saved, through faith–and this is not from yourselves, it is the gift of God–not by works, so that no one can boast."
(Ephesians 2:8,9)

So today, my friends, know this: There is currently a person in heaven who lived a horrendous life of crime, yet he never confessed a single sin to a priest, he never took communion, nor paid alms. This person was never prayed over by church leaders and doused with oil, he never spoke in tongues, he never prophesied nor cast out a single demon. This individual also did *not* walk an isle. He didn't lay anything at the altar. He never raised his hand in the crowd while others had their heads bowed and eyes closed. Nor did he do mission trips or tithe to the penny in order to be blessed by God more abundantly. Lastly, this person was *never* baptized into water, but right now, this moment, he's enjoying paradise with Jesus. The thief who hung on his own cross next to *the* Cross, what did he do to be saved?

He became obedient from the heart.

He was reborn in spirit by a one-time faith.

He believed Jesus was innocent and that *he* was not.

This is what saves.

If you've not done so, please believe today. Be saved my friend. Believe Jesus. (See Luke 23:39-43, Romans 6:17, Hebrews 7:25, 10:10)

A prayer for you: *Hi Dad. I've really enjoyed writing this devotional over the past few mornings. As I've sat here for hours, it's felt like minutes. This special time of the day in which I spend writing is such a wonderful gift you've given me to enjoy. I really DO enjoy it! Thank you so much! And thank you for opening up my mind to the truth of water baptism, tongues, and prophecy. Thank you for this relief in my mind. Please teach me more about how to express these truths in an easy, graceful way. I don't want to come across as insensitive to those who are stuck in this type of legalism, so please do this through me. I know you will. Right now, I lift up all who are reading this, directly to you. For some, what they've just read has helped them. But for others, it might have angered them. For*

the latter, please teach them that faith always comes first, before anything else, to be saved. In regard to water baptism, there's an account in Acts 8:36 about an eunuch who had just believed in Jesus and then came upon some water. He was so excited AFTER believing, he said to Philip, "What prevents me from being baptized?" and then Philip did just that! Nothing prevented him because he was saved! He wanted to celebrate! Baptism, both physically and spiritually, is a wonderful thing to commemorate! We thank you for both! In Jesus' name I pray, amen.

Day 16

Is Homosexuality Sin?

*"And that is what some of you were. But
you were washed, you were sanctified, you
were justified in the name of the Lord Jesus
Christ and by the Spirit of our God."*

1 Corinthians 6:11

Yes. The answer to the title of this devotional is yes. Based on the words in the Bible, even in the New Testament, homosexuality is sin. Even if you look at the original Greek text, homosexuality is the context. There's no getting around it.

The problem is, we've made a witch-hunt out of this single sin while downplaying other sins. The very same passages which claim homosexuality is not okay, also says drunkenness is not okay, greed is not okay, disobedience to parents is not okay, the love of money, lying, trading slaves–and many other sins–is not okay.

So why are we not holding *all* sins to the same standard? Mainly because of traditional poor teaching which focuses on behavior rather than on identity. But also, the neglected half of the gospel which is rarely taught: *it wasn't just Christ who died, we died too; it wasn't just Jesus who came back to life, we came back to life too* (see Galatians 2:20, Romans 6:6-11, Colossians 3:3). What that moment of faith in the Cross does *to* a person–which is makes them sinless in their spirit, which is the only way God can make His home in *our* spirit–*this* is what's missing from the majority of sermons (see Colossians 1:22, 2:9,10, 1 Corinthians 6:17,19, John 14:20,23).

We focus on this single sin as "one of the worst" because when we don't understand the New Covenant, we don't understand what God has done to our spirits: *washed them clean by making them brand new* (see 1 Corinthians 6:11, 2 Corinthians 5:17).

I was scrolling through Facebook recently when a clip from American Idol popped up, so I stopped to hear this person's voice. Before singing, he said he'd recently came out, to Katy Perry. "You inspired me to come out."

Her response was, "I approve of you," with a nice, warm smile.

This was very genuine on her part. It was sweet and heartfelt. The man blushed and went on to sing amazingly. But for a moment let's picture this *same* scenario, only with a different type of sin, rather than homosexuality.

"Katy, you inspired me to cheat on my wife. All these years, from the time I was young, I've wanted to sleep with many different women and I've finally taken the steps to do so. Thank you for your inspiration to commit adultery, multiple times, over and over. I finally feel like I'm being my true self and not withholding my sexuality. I'm never going back to being committed to one woman. Thank you."

I understand the first rebuttal to this idea would be, "No Matt, that's different. He wasn't born to cheat on his wife."

How would you know that? After all, this is what he *feels* about himself. What if he told you, "I've always wanted to have sex with tons of women. From the time I was a young boy, I could feel it. My attraction to many different females, my desire to have sex with them, has always been undeniable. Even my mom knew. She said she could always tell. I should have never gotten married to a *single* woman because I've always wanted to sleep with many of them. I can't fight this feeling. I need to live it out so I can be myself. I don't care about anyone's opinion of me. I'm going to have sex with many women, and not my wife."

If you interviewed an honest person who battles feelings of pedophilia, they would say the same thing, "I can't help it. I'm attracted to children. This is who I am." Do you think Katy would have replied, "I approve of you," had he said *this* instead of, "I'm gay."? I doubt she would have.

Nobody is born with a pedophile gene, or an *I-must-have-sex-with-a-lot-of-women* gene. Nor has there ever been a gay gene found. Instead, it is the *influence* of the power of sin in each person's mind which causes sinful desires. Specific sinful tendencies impact humans in many different ways. These tendencies come from the *force* of sin, *hamartia*, which entered our realm when Adam decided to no longer believe God (see Genesis 4:7, Romans 5:12, 6:11).

We can hand-pick the sin of homosexuality if we like. We can say a gay lifestyle is worse than all other sins. We can even try to mix the Covenants together–which is impossible–and say God sees homosexual sins as worse than most. But that's not true. The truth is, on this side of the Cross, anything that is not of faith is sin (see Romans 14:23).

So why does the sin of homosexuality influence some people and not others? To answer that, we could ask some other questions. Why does the sin of alcoholism and drug addiction affect some and not others? Why does the sin of gluttony affect some and not others? Why does the sin of gossip affect some and not others? Why does the sin of legalism and hyper-criticism affect some and not others?

Pornography, greed, jealousy, Mosaic Law observance, adultery (emotionally and physically)—or while we're at it—*opposite* sex attraction sins, such as fornication and rape? Same sex attraction, or SSA, would be our modern-day Scarlet Letters if it were up to some devout churchgoers.

They'll spew, "Don't defile your body! That's what the Bible says!" as they go through the line at Burger King for the fifth time this week. They'll have a third helping of fried chicken, clogging up their arteries—their temple—bite by bite. But the gay people are "worse sinners" and "better repent before it's too late." *This* is the trash that causes us Christians to be hated. *This* is the trash Jesus would not stand for, and flip a table or two over. He said we will be known by our love, not by our nasty judging of all who don't sin like us (see Matthew 7:1, 13:35).

We must stop pointing out—*judging*—and start pointing *to* the solution: *new life in Christ.*

An unbelieving person who struggles with homosexuality doesn't need to be yelled at, "Repent! Or else you will not inherit the kingdom of God!" No. Not at all. They can stop acting on their sexual urges all they like, that still won't save them. They need new life, Christ's life (see John 3:16-18, Colossians 3:4, Hebrews 7:25). They need a supernatural death, burial, and resurrection *with* Christ (see Romans 6:6-11, Galatians 2:20, 2 Corinthians 5:21). This happens from the moment they believe Jesus has forgiven them—not just from gay sins, but from all sins.

"Nope! They still gotta stop practicing sin! That's what the Bible says!"

Friend, no Christian can practice sin. That's the whole point behind this word in the New Testament. It's impossible because we have a new *natural* practice, which is holiness. Re-read every passage which talks about "practicing sin" with the lens of the New Covenant on. It's never talking about a Christian because Christians can't do such a thing *because* we've been born *of* God. We have God's own nature. His nature is sinless. This is why we are called His children (see 1 John 3:9, 2 Peter 1:4, John 1:12).

Think about it. A practice is an ongoing thing to get better at something. What does a lawyer do? Practices law. What does a doctor do? Practices medicine, ongoing, to improve at it. Even if they practice for fifty years, they never *complete* their practice. They'll always say, "I practice law," or "I practice medicine." Not, "I do law," or "I do medicine." It's a *keep on keeping on* thing. Do more of to improve at.

Christians cannot practice sin, as in, *do repeatedly to get better at.* We cannot get better at sinning by doing more of it, it's not our practice. From salvation, sinning is no longer natural to us. To unbelievers? Yes, they *love* sin, naturally. But *we* have literally died to the power of sin—hamartia, not the verbs of sinning—and made alive *in* Christ. We've been taken *out* of hamartia and placed *into* the Spirit of Jesus, which is spiritual baptism (see Romans 6:3,11, 8:9, Galatians 3:27).

We *have* inherited the kingdom of God! It is in us *as* we live and breath! (See Mark 1:15, Ephesians 2:6, 1 Corinthians 6:19).

When salvation happens for a person who struggles with the sin of homosexuality—or anyone—they receive a brand new, perfectly cleansed forever, spirit. Did they get a new brain? No. A new soul? No. They will still have old flesh patterns to overcome by way of the new Spirit within them combined with *their* new spirit. Their thoughts will be renewed to new truths day by day, moment by moment, from God, *"You are my child. You were not recreated to act on gay tendencies. You've died to this sin. You are holy."*

It's not about equality, it's about new life within.

"Yeah, but Matt, if they still act on those gay tendencies, they are sinning."

Sure, you are right. But *they* are not sinful, just like *you* are not sinful when *you* act on sin in non-homosexual ways. You were washed. You were justified. You were raised and seated with Christ in heavenly realms—and so were they.

"No way, Matt! They gotta turn from that sinful lifestyle or burn in hell! If they keep sinning they never really got saved!"

Friend, if that's your theology then nobody has *ever* really been saved–including you. This makes no sense for a reason: *all of us sin after salvation, a lot.* Even more, all sins are willful and we repeat our willful sins every day. Our will is involved with each sin we commit. We're not zombies.

"So are you saying they can still be gay?!"

I'm saying they *aren't* gay. I'm saying they are holy saints who struggle with the sin of same sex attraction. Just like I'm not an alcoholic. I'm a holy saint who struggles with the tendency of wanting to get drunk. Although I have over five years of sobriety, give me a 12-pack and watch what happens if I chose to drink it. Sinning. I'll get drunk. Drunkenness is sin. When it comes to alcohol, the power of sin influences me much differently than others who *don't* struggle with drinking way too much, way too often.

However *alcoholic* is not my identity and *gay* is not any Christian's identity. We are all holy children of God who struggle with _____ (insert your sinful tendency here), but we are *not* sinful. Good, bad, or indifferent, we are not what we do! We are who we are by birth! This is why Jesus said, "Don't be surprised when I say, 'You must be born again.'" (John 3:7).

I could still be getting drunk all the time to this day. Would that make me not saved? No. I'd still be saved. Yes, I'd be getting some flash-in-the-pan fleshy thrills from my drinking, but after each episode, drinking would never set right with me. Why? Because it's not of faith. It's not authentic. No matter how hardcore my denial is.

Same with homosexuality. A Christian could act on this, even get married and say because they're married it's okay, but this *still* would never set right with them *permanently*. They have a brand new heart, a spirit which is one with God. God is not okay with homosexuality–nor any sin. Even if they went 45 years living this way, in denial of their holiness by saying it's not sin, they *know* it's wrong. The Spirit bears witness to their spirit (see John 14:26).

The Bible says we've become obedient from the heart, that we've become slaves to righteousness (see Romans 6:17,18). This means we can't get away from it. Homosexuality is not righteous according to Holy-Spirit-inspired Scripture. So an inner battle will continue in a person's mind until they repent—just like any sin. If they continue, their salvation isn't lost, Christ would have to die for that to happen (see Hebrews 1:3, 7:25, John 14:19). But instead, their peace and purposefulness will be (see Romans 12:2, Ephesians 2:10, Galatians 5:22,23).

Hebrews also tells us God's laws have been written on our hearts and minds—not Law, as in the Mosaic Law—but laws, lowercase, as in His character and desires (see Hebrews 10:16). We literally want what our Creator wants, and we'll prove this one way or the other.

A person who struggles with this particular sin can move to an area where it's socially acceptable, they can follow all the celebrities in Hollywood who claim it's not sin, they can even watch the shows on TV and Netflix which act as if it's fine. But we can't ignore God's Word backed up by His Spirit within us. He's got a better plan for all of us, one which isn't centered around any type of sin.

So today, my friends, know this: Love and respect everyone, no matter their sin. I know this topic is sensitive in our society today, but nobody will care anything about what we have to say if we aren't loving and respecting them while doing so. Be gentle. Be patient. Be kind. Don't react to hate when you speak the truth with love. Instead, *respond* peacefully. Don't make threats, and don't tell people what to do. Tell them about what Christ has done *for* them, because He loves them. The opportunity at being made new through faith in Jesus is available to all who will believe!

A prayer for you: *Heavenly Father, this is an extremely touchy subject with the culture we live in; I understand that, and I hope these dear readers felt my sensitivity for them as they read this devotional. For a time, you know that even I questioned your Word about homosexuality. I thought, there's too many people who claim to be gay for this to be right. But your Spirit has revealed that your Word is right, and I was wrong. My friends who struggle with this sin are very important to you, and I know this. Just the same as I'm important to you, even when I struggle with my flavor of sin. Countless amounts of Christians have been so darned rude over this, treating people like it's a disease, we've gotten a bad rap. From the pulpits, angry, grace-confused preachers have not told the truth. They've said people must repent of their homosexuality to inherit the kingdom of God, but then lie each week about their own sins which they never repent of. Your Word does not say repentance of behaviors and attitudes saves us, but only repentance of unbelief in Christ as our Savior. When this happens, you give us a new, sinless spirit, and you make your home in us permanently. From then on out, no matter the sin, your Spirit will always counsel us into all truth. But no matter what, you never leave us nor forsake us—even if we struggle with a particular sin for the rest of our lives. We'll be miserable, but our sinful choices can never override the power of the Cross. We have peace with you forever. Right now, I lift up all who are reading this, directly to you. Those who are fighting homosexuality, give them peace in knowing they're spotless because of their one-time faith in Christ's forgiveness. And for the person struggling with legalism, those who see homosexuality as worse than their own sinful choices, give them peace too. Let them know because of their faith in the Cross, they too will not be judged for their sins, because Christ was already judged. In His name I pray, amen.*

Day 17

⸺⊶⊷⊶⸺

What I've Learned After
Five Years of Sobriety

*"Let perseverance finish its work so that you may
be mature and complete, not lacking anything."*

James 1:4

There are moments in our lives when we decide to stop or start a certain behavior, or willingly change an attitude we've held onto for a long time. For me, today marks an anniversary of such a change. Five years ago, May 8th, 2014, was a day like any other. Except now, I would never drink another drop of alcohol for the rest of my life.

Many people believe those who struggle with alcoholism are weak. If you said that to me five years ago, I'd reply, "You are wrong." From outward appearances, I was anything but weak. I had built an extremely successful business, I had a family, a nice home, I stayed in shape, I enjoyed fun hobbies and ate good meals. I even had a very large social media ministry. But underneath, when it came to my life without drinking, oh yeah, I *was* weak.

I simply could not picture myself *enjoying* myself without consuming my favorite beers or shots. Each time my unrenewed, immature mind thought about quitting, anxiety would hit me. The buzz from alcoholic beverages "made everything better." Life would not be that great if I couldn't experience being tipsy any longer. Even though tipsy times were mostly drunk times–not just tipsy–my main problem was this:

How do I perceive myself?

Now *this* is what makes everything better! Not drinking, but knowing our identity! When we struggle with *thinking* we need to drink, we have an identity issue. Not that our drinking causes our identity to change; as a Christian, that's impossible. No amount of drunkenness, which *is* sin, can override the blood of Jesus. That perfect red liquid is much stronger than my Miller Lite and American Honey.

But I didn't fully understand the gospel, yet, so I didn't fully understand my identity, yet. As a result, I didn't really know how to perceive myself. So I kept drinking.

When we know who we are–like, *honestly* know what the Cross has *truly* done to us–that's it, game over. Our perception about ourselves changes our entire lifestyle. The legalist is focused on *not* sinning, but the saint is focused on expressing their righteousness. The legalist will yell, "You can't just do whatever you want!" but the saint says, "Yes I can, because I want what God wants." We *actually* believe this and live it out!

It's clear to us when we don't live it out because the Spirit bears witness to our spirit when we're faking our identity. When we sin, we are being phonies. Frauds. We have literally died to sin. We have literally been taken out of sin and placed into the Spirit of Christ (see Romans 6:3-11, 8:9-11, Galatians 3:27, Colossians 3:3, 1 Corinthians 6:17).

Yes, literally–not figuratively–and I'm going to use that word again shortly. I am talking about your spirit, friend.

What's more is *all* Christians are saints, equally. Saint simply means holy one, and that is what the Cross has caused us to become by grace through faith (see Colossians 1:22, Hebrews 10:10, Ephesians 2:8,9). When we know we've been recreated to *not* sin, to *not* get drunk, enjoying sobriety is an amazing thing! You're not missing the booze because you know that's like putting sugar in your gas tank. Yeah, some people can drink normally, but we can't, and we know it. So we don't. The power of sin influences us differently over this issue, and we're at peace with that.

When our perception of who we are changes, anything that is not of faith won't work for us. Getting drunk is not of faith. Not *just* getting drunk, but refusing to forgive others, flirting on social media as a married person, watching porn, constantly trying to prove your worth to others, cherry-picking "less than" sins, trying to follow the Law of Moses, codependency, people-pleasing, looking to church attendance for kudos from God, pastoral worship–even tithing to be blessed, as if God is a loan shark–all of this stuff was being purged up and out of my thought life by the Spirit within.

Today marks the five-year anniversary of a new beginning in my *thinking* about who I *am*. Thoughts are what cause us to drink. Change our thoughts, change our lives. It's so simple it's hard to fathom.

To be clear, when we stop drinking *we* don't change. As believers we've *been* changed, once. Born again, once. Yes, our actions and attitudes change but not us–not our identity. Good, bad, or indifferent, we are not what we do or don't do. Instead, we mature and grow into who we already are–into our sainthood. A sapling oak tree is an oak tree, just immature. It never changes, it grows. We are members of heaven, children of God, just very immature from the time of our supernatural rebirth. We are *not* changing but growing. As we grow, we break free from the sinful choices and attitudes which entangle us but we are not those sins. The Bible says the old *has* gone and the new *is* here! Even better, our full maturation will not be complete until we shed this shell of flesh, so go easy on yourself! (See Hebrews 12:1,2, 2 Corinthians 5:17, Philippians 1:6).

Many self-centered people will say we weren't truly saved until we stopped drinking. But such is folly in the fullest and spits on the work of the Cross. We don't stop sinning to get saved, so we don't stay stopped sinning to stay saved. If this were the case, every human being would be doomed because all of us die with sin we still struggle with. If we say we don't struggle with any sin, that's sin in itself compounded with lying–which is sinning. A healthy amount of repentance would do a person good with this kind of mindset.

Others will claim, "You got delivered from a spirit of alcoholism!" No. Sorry. That didn't happen either. No demonic spirit has had permission to touch me since the time I was saved as a young boy. The Bible is clear that no demon can have any contact with my body or spirit, all they can do is accuse me in my mind of not being who I am (see 1 John 5:18, Revelation 12:10). We have to stop giving the devil so much credit. He was de-clawed, de-toothed, and disarmed at the Cross.

The only thing the demonic realm can do to me is lie to me about my holiness, they can't possess me. I'm *literally* possessed by the Spirit of Jesus Christ. He'll never share me with a demon. So "deliverance from alcoholic spirits" makes no sense for a Christian. For an unbeliever? Yes, and those spirits after being cast out will come back with more evil spirits (see Luke 11:24-26). But we believers don't need to worry about that. We simply need our minds renewed to who already indwells us–God. There's not a single passage in the Bible about a believer having demon cast out of them–even a spirit of addiction. We are sealed up with the Holy Spirit forever and He guards the door! (See Ephesians 1:13).

I've learned a lot in the past five years, most of the common alcoholic phrases have been deciphered through the Spirit within me. I wish I knew then what I know now, but that's okay. God takes us from glory to glory as we learn more about who we are as His kids. Here's what I'd say to myself if I was sitting across from myself, on this day, five years ago, when I was 32:

"Hi buddy. I know you're scared and anxious. I know you've tried a thousand times to quit, but this time you won't just quit. You'll begin living the life you were meant to live all along! Be aware, the bad thoughts will come, the temptations will come, and the pain *will* come too. Feel your pain. Feel it. Feel it, and lean into the comfort of Christ. Scream. Cry. Hurt. Feeeeeel! You *must* feel. When you do, you *will* become weak. But this is where your strength will come from–through your pain, through your weakness. Soon enough you'll feel weaker than you ever have before, but that weakness will be the greatest thing you've *ever* felt before. Your mind is about to be renewed to the truth of who you are, which will be very painful to your old thoughts. Over time this will make more sense, so be patient as the Spirit guides you. Your weakness is where His grace will rest the most as He teaches you new thoughts to have about yourself, Him, and others. Weakness is good. The Spirit is your friend who holds nothing against you. Let Him love you and don't fight it.

Please remember that on your very worst day of pain you'll still be able to say, 'But I didn't drink.' Imagine that! I'm so proud of you! If you could only see five years down the road! You are about to do more than you've ever done before–and for the right reasons! You'll begin to do absolutely *everything* from a state of rest! I know you don't understand that yet, but you will! You'll write those books! Five of them so far! Bestsellers! You'll reach millions each week through your social media platforms! You'll learn how to have the deepest, most fulfilling marriage with Jennifer! She'll see you completely different than she does right now! Grace will get the best of you! She is such an awesome 14-year-old! You'll enjoy the little things you keep overlooking! But more than anything, you'll learn about the New Covenant. Oh if you only knew now! *Your* perception of who *you* are is about to change! False humility is going to be an afterthought–you'll never talk bad about yourself again! Stressing out about spreading the gospel and saving the world will be no more! You'll enjoy being a branch and you'll stop trying to be the Vine! Religious headstones will be kicked over left and right by you! Legalistic people will be mad, but you'll learn how to show them love and respect! *This* is what will change their hearts toward the truth! Gentleness! Who would've thought?! THE JOURNEY YOU'RE ABOUT TO EMBARK ON, SOBER, WILL BLOW YOUR MIND! Who you truly are is about to be revealed to you on levels you could've never imagined before. So don't worry, don't be afraid, this is just the beginning."

A prayer for you: *Heavenly Father, look at what we've done! You and me together is an amazing force! Thank you for helping me make it this far! I'm so grateful for your strength and for teaching me who I am! Right now, I lift up all who are reading this, directly to you. For those who are stuck in an addiction, set them free in their minds. Guide their perception about themselves into the right direction. Teach them about the power of Jesus Christ. Reveal the New Covenant in even greater ways. In His name I pray, amen.*

Day 18

God Is Not Breaking You Down

*"I have come that they may have
life, and have it to the full."*

See John 10:10

Our Creator has received a pretty bad rap by way of humanity's incorrect opinion. From the beginning of time, the enemy has somehow convinced us God *isn't* good and He's holding us back from enjoying our lives.

He's whispered, "God's design for you is pain, so you'll snap! GOD IS BREAKING YOU DOWN! He *wants* you broken so you'll have to worship and serve Him because He's so full of Himself! Why would you want anything to do with such a monster?!"

Unfortunately, lots of people have believed this liar and as a result we've blamed God for many things which are not His fault.

Jennifer and I were recently watching the new movie *Unbroken: Path to Redemption*. It's the follow up film about war hero, Louis Zamperini. The focus of the flick is his battle with unemployment after the war, severe alcoholism, and PTSD due to a two year stint as a POW.

To make matters worse, prior to prison camp in Japan, for 47 days he drifted at sea. His plane crashed into the ocean in 1943, during World War II. On a side note, he held the United States high school record for the fastest mile in track and *also* ran in the Olympics. To say the least, this man's life *was* a movie. But Path to Redemption centered around Louis blaming God for all his problems—and I mean *all* of them.

Ironically, he was furious and salty toward a God he didn't even believe in. Louis had the following accusations against our Creator:

1. God caused the plane crash.
2. God caused him to be lost at sea on a raft for a month and a half.
3. God caused the Japanese army to find him and imprison him.
4. God caused the Japanese army to torture him for two years.
5. Once he was back at home, God caused him to not be able to find a job.
6. God caused his self-pity and extreme loathing of life.
7. God caused his devoted wife to *not* let him blow money.
8. God caused him to drink.
9. God caused his wife to be a nagging Christian who wanted him to *stop* drinking.
10. God caused everyone to pick on him.

As you can see, none of this stuff was God's fault; and contrary to popular belief, God wasn't *causing* these things to happen in order to "break him" so that he would turn to faith in Jesus. God doesn't work that way. Islam works that way (the word Islam literally means *submission*) and other world religions do too. But the God of the Bible is *good*.

Paul tells us in Romans it's the goodness of God which leads us to repentance, not the pounding away of God (see Romans 2:4). Painful situations always come *at* us, but God is always working *in* us and *through* us. He's not trying to increase our problems. His desire is to help us with them by way of His Holy Spirit. Even for those who don't yet believe, He's steadily pursuing their hearts and wooing them—*not* carrying a lasso and a billy-club. God is a gentleman *offering* Himself to us, never pushing Himself *on* us (see 1 Corinthians 13:4-8, Galatians 5:22,23, Matthew 11:29).

Just the same as we can't blame Bill Gates for the problems on our computer—because he invented Windows—we can't blame God for the problems we have on earth, because He invented the universe. *We* flubbed it up, not Him. His plan of action to take care of our original ancestors' mistake was redemption through His own Son, not piling on the heartache.

Even more, God is not causing havoc in our lives and then comforting us at the same time. Do you realize how many churches teach this "two-headed monster god"? A lot. Countless pastors articulate our Father as being a troublemaker and a comforter both at the same time; as if He's here to hurt us and then swoop around and heal us. This theology is highly incorrect.

Sure, there are some religious *people* like that—some even church *leaders*—but the God of all comfort is nothing like that. Mental and physical abuse—and sometimes *sexual* in the name of God—may come from nasty legalists, but not from our Creator. God's goal is to build us up, not break us down; and He definitely isn't breaking us down *to* build us up. That's not the gospel of grace, which is what Paul called this good news (see Acts 20:24).

God isn't trying to "improve" us either. From our first moment of faith in Christ, He literally kills us on the Cross *with* Christ, in the supernatural realm. He then *remakes us* brand spanking new! We are not better versions of ourselves but whole new creations *learning* who we now are! As we do this we take the veil off of self improvement from our mind's eyes and go from glory to glory in our thought life! (See Romans 6:6-10, 12:2, 1 Corinthians 6:17, 2 Corinthians 3:16-18, 5:17,21, Galatians 2:20, Colossians 3:3).

I understand many struggle with the incorrect idea of God harming us *so that* He can help us. I've been there. But what an absolute ogre and psychopath would our God be if this were the truth. Can you see why this notion is from hell? It is Satan who's pit us against our doting Dad with vile and septic lies about His true character.

I'll tell you what the main problem is: *human* ogres and psychopaths running churches and "Christian cults" acting as if they're representing our Father while spitting profusely in their sermons and gritting their teeth. Countless sheep believe them just because they're up on stage.

But it's not simply the fact that many of these charlatans misrepresent God's love–but also, we've mistaken the word discipline with punishment. There's not a single passage in any New Testament letter that says a Christian will be punished by God. Punishment is reserved *only* for those who reject faith in Messiah; and there's only *one* verse which mentions discipline:

> *"For the moment all discipline seems painful rather than pleasant, but later it yields the peaceful fruit of righteousness to those who have been trained by it." (Hebrews 12:11)*

First of all, do you see what happens through discipline? The fruit of the Spirit happens. So discipline is a good thing. Many Christians believe discipline is God laying down the hammer or whopping us with a belt. It's not. He has already laid the hammer down in full, on Jesus, and whooped Him plenty at the Cross. Do you not realize *your* punishment was put on Him completely and it's finished? Do you not *know* that Jesus' body was pummeled for every single screw-up you and I would ever commit? Past, present, and future?

Yes, even in the future. Even the sins we've not yet committed. God is not bound by time! A day is like a thousand years to Him, and a thousand years is like a day! (See 2 Peter 3:8). He created *time* for us! The 24-hour rotations of the earth. The sun in which we get our seasons. These created *things* are for us to live *out* our temporary physical life as time creatures. Then we enter into eternity with or without God based on whether or not we've believed on Jesus, once. He resides in a realm with no time—at least as we know it. So He's taken away all of our sins *once* and for *all* time! (See Hebrews 10:10, 1 John 3:5).

If you really think about it, how many of our sins were in the future when Jesus was punished for them? All of them. This is why we have no right to say behavior repentance and/or confession cleans us off daily. God requires blood and death for every single one of our sins! (See Hebrews 9:22, Romans 6:23). So if you've placed your faith in Jesus' sacrifice, you've been perfectly cleansed forever. By *one* offering, Jesus took on *your* sin punishment at *that* exact time in human history! (See Hebrews 10:14, 1 Corinthians 6:11).

Discipline, according to God, is not the same as punishment. YOU DO NOT WANT GOD TO PUNISH YOU. TRUST ME. His punishment is not taking away your Christmas bonus or causing your car to break down. IT IS DEATH (see 2 Corinthians 5:15, 1 Peter 3:18). This is why God's discipline doesn't break you down. It encourages you into the truth of who you are, as well as who He is.

Discipline from God is not punishment, but discipleship. The very word discipline comes from the word *disciple.* So if you look to how Jesus treated His disciples in Matthew, Mark, Luke, and John, you'll see how God disciplines *us*, which is always with love and respect. Jesus and the Father are one. They aren't playing "good-cop bad-cop" (see John 14:9).

Yes, sometimes Jesus corrected them with a firm rebuke, but He never *punished* any of His disciples, even when they said and did stupid stuff. His side of the relationship was always expressed with hope and caring guidance even while explaining harsh truths. Jesus *is* God. So this is how God treats *you*, today, Christian. Just look:

> *"Jesus Christ is <u>the same</u> yesterday and today and forever."*
> *(Hebrews 13:8)*

I want to repeat myself for emphasis: *discipline is not the same as punishment.* This is crucial to understand because punishment from God only happens because of sin. But as believers, Jesus died and took those all away (see John 1:29, 1 John 3:5, Hebrews 10:4). The Cross was a huge success!

If I thought it wasn't, and that *I* have to add to it to make it better–or sustain it through what *I* do and *I* don't do–I'd be an idiot! I should doubt my salvation every day! But even more, who in the *heck* do I think I am, if *I*, a created thing, can actually *do* what only the blood of Jesus can do? Do you see the logic? There isn't any in such a semi-grace doctrine! My blessed assurance isn't so great!

God is not reactionary to ours sins. Again, His reaction would be our death. Therefore He counsels us *away* from sin, with love, *because* He has recreated us in spirit to *not* sin (John 14:26, 2 Corinthians 5:17, Romans 6:2,11, 1 John 3:9).

Let's go back to Louis' story. Even though he was blaming God, these painful circumstances weren't coming from God. Instead, one or more of these five factors were the culprits:

1. **The world, planet earth** – This place is fallen. It is broken. Death, destruction, weather and literal storms, seasons, flawed DNA, human bodies that need food and water to survive; people living here who are influenced by demonic forces, unbelievers who do not house the Spirit of God–and more–is *in* this world. What was once perfect is now a harsh place to have life. But–the world is *not* God.

2. **The power of sin** – Not to be confused with the verbs of *sinning*, but the Greek word *hamartia*, it is a noun. It's an actual force on this planet like gravity, which entered our physical realm when Adam and Eve no longer took God by His word. *It* is a dirty film *on* and *in* everything physically created. From the opening book of the Bible it's mentioned (see Genesis 4:7). Paul talks about hamartia in Romans 5, 6, and 7, in great detail. But–God is *not* sin, obviously.

3. **Demonic armies from hell** – An infantry of demons are allowed to roam this planet for now. Jesus said Satan–who is their director–only has three main goals for his pathetic existence: *steal, kill, destroy* (see John 10:10). Accusations in our minds is their primary M.O.–but again, this is not God.

4. **Unrenewed human mindsets** – This might be the most overlooked issue when it comes to people blaming God for their problems. Paul constantly talked about changing our minds for a reason (see Romans 12:2, Philippians 4:8, Colossians 3:2). Our old thought patterns and methods of coping cause us to remain stuck in the same situations day after day. Yet we blame our Creator for how *we* are thinking. The truth is we have our own minds and He doesn't control them. Again, not God.

5. **Our decisions** – There's no easy way to say this but just because God isn't punishing Christians that doesn't mean our own choices aren't causing earthly punishments. In heaven, we reap what Jesus has sown. But on earth, we reap what *we* have sown (see Galatians 6:7,8, James 3:18). As you can see, this isn't God either. It's us.

None of these things are from our Creator. He's for us not against us. He's here to help us without overriding our free will.

A person who struggles with self-righteousness and overlooks the Cross might exclaim, "Matt, are you saying that Moses, Job, Jonah, Joseph, and people from the Old Testament didn't get punished by God?! How dare you!"

Friend, these Patriarchs, in regard to their suffering, *none* of it was caused by God. Instead, He *allowed* painful situations to happen *so that* Israel would be protected *so that* the line of Judah could produce Jesus Christ with His exact human DNA. It's always been about Jesus, from the very foundation of this vast universe. Allowing is much different than causing.

God didn't *cause* Israel to become enslaved. The Egyptians did that.
God didn't *cause* Job to suffer. Satan did that.
God didn't *cause* Jonah to be swallowed. A sea creature did that.
God didn't *cause* Joseph to be sold into slavery. His jealous brothers did that.

God didn't cause these tragedies to happen in order to break these people down so they'd surrender. He allowed certain circumstances in order to protect the seed of Abraham–Jesus–so that Christ could take away our sins and give us life! (See Genesis 17:4, Colossians 3:4, Galatians 3:16, Romans 5:1, John 1:29, Hebrews 9:11-28).

Any type of *punishment* He was handing out before the Cross was rightly deserved because His wrath over sin was not yet satisfied (see Romans 5:1,9, 2 Corinthians 5:21). There's a big difference in His vengeance being dealt to His enemies, and Him *allowing* difficult circumstances for those who believed in Him to achieve a greater good.

Now that Christ has come and paid the final price for *all* sins, what is it that breaks a person down? The world, the power of sin, accusations of Satan and his demons, our unrenewed mindsets and bad decisions–but not God.

So today, my friends, know this: God isn't breaking you down, He's building you up. What kind of good father would abuse their children so they would then surrender, get on their knees, and crawl toward him? A good father *wouldn't* do that. A good father runs to their children when in distress,

157

hugs them, and comforts them. He encourages them. He tells them the truth about their identity, their true strength, and reminds them of who they are.

Even while disciplining us with healthy boundaries for our own benefit, God cares deeply. That's our Father. Our Father is *good* (see Matthew 7:9-11). For the unbeliever, God is not dealing with them in a harsh way either, but in a kind way, so they'll turn toward Him and believe in Jesus (see Romans 2:4, John 3:17,18). Their own choices are punishment enough. The world, Satan, hamartia, and their thoughts? *Those* are punishment enough. God is not vindictive or mean as the dickens like some of our religious relatives and acquaintances. God is gentle, patient, loving, and kind. He's humble in heart and you are too, Christian. You are good like God is good. You've inherited all of His traits.

A prayer for you: *Dad, thank you for being my Dad. Because of the lies I was taught about you–brainwashing, really–I thought you were really unpleasant. Thankfully you're not. I thought you were rightly punishing me each day for my dumb choices. But you were not. Your Spirit has revealed your true character to me. I trust you so much, and I love you so much. Thank you for being a wonderful Father to me. Right now, I lift up all who are reading this, directly to you. So many of these dear readers have had a bad relationship with their earthly father, they believe you're the same. Reveal to them you're not. As your children, you're always on their side. You defend them, go to bat for them, show them favor, and you protect them. Even in their darkest hours you are hard at work in their lives. Your gentle care and guiding discipline is better than they can comprehend. I pray their minds become renewed to the truth of who you are. You don't*

cause bad things to happen to us but you're there with us, in the midst of all of it, using pain for eternal purposes. You never leave us. Teach these wonderful people all about your goodness through your Holy Spirit. Thank you for building us up each day, rather than breaking us down. In the name of Jesus I pray, amen.

Day 19

Does God Spit Christians out of His Mouth?

"So, because you are lukewarm—neither hot nor cold—I am about to spit you out of my mouth."

Revelation 3:16

"**M**an, it is *hot* out here. Son, would you please open up that cooler and hand me an ice-cold bottle of water?"

"Sure Dad. Here you go."

It's mid-August in Oklahoma. The sun is at its highest peak for the day, beating down on a father and son as they bale hay in the fields of their family farm. The dad gasps, "Thank you—" desperate for breath after chugging the cold, refreshing drink. "That really hit the spot."

Now just imagine if this dad had asked his son to crawl into the cab of the truck to get his hot coffee, or even a lukewarm bottle of water. Neither the hot coffee nor the lukewarm water would've served the proper purpose, which was to cool him off. It was *hot* outside so he needed a *cold* drink. Cold was very good.

Let's fast-forward to the middle of December that same year.

"Dad, I'm freezing!" the young man exclaims as they hunt in their snow-covered woods. "I can't wait to get back home for some hot chocolate!"

"You and me both, buddy. That sure sounds nice. And maybe a dip in the hot tub too. I might fire it up."

Would it make any sense to you if the boy said, "I can't wait to drink a frozen lemonade when we get back to the house!"? No, not at all. It would be nonsensical to drink a cold beverage in such a situation because he's *cold*. It would serve *no purpose*. Neither would a lukewarm drink. He needed something hot. Hot was very good.

Purposefulness, I repeat, *purposefulness* is the proper context behind one of the most fear-mongering, religiously abused passages in the Bible, Revelation 3:16:

> *"So, because you are lukewarm—neither hot nor cold—I am about to spit you out of my mouth."*

From the pulpits, street corners, and internet, those who struggle greatly with self-centeredness will scream, "God won't stand for lukewarm Christians! He will spit you out of His mouth on Judgement Day! You better get to work and do *more* before it's too late!"

Friend, don't worry. The good news is, as Christians, we're not in God's mouth. We're in *Him*. Paul explains:

> *"For you died, and your life is now hidden with Christ <u>in</u> God."*
> *(Colossians 3:3)*

> *"But whoever is united with the Lord <u>is one with Him in spirit</u>."*
> *(1 Corinthians 6:17)*

For a moment, allow me to digress into the wrong outlook of Revelation 3:16. Even if we *were* in God's mouth and even if He *did* spit us out, because of the Cross and our faith in it, He would slurp us right back up. But God is not spitting Christians, slurping Christians, spitting Christians, slurping Christians–based on our performance. We are His beloved children, we are one with Him forever, and nobody can snatch us out of His hand. Jesus assures us:

> "My Father, who has given them to me, is greater than all; <u>no one can snatch them out of my Father's hand.</u>" (John 10:29)

God is no liar and His hand is strong. So why do so many people use Revelation 3:16 as a threat of losing salvation for not doing enough? Several reasons, and all of them lie in the mind of the individual making such false accusations. Here are two of them:

1. **This person finds their identity in what *they* are doing "for" God.** Because of their Judaism-lite mentality, he or she is very afraid–but won't admit it. They think *they're* not doing enough, so they want others to be afraid too. As a result, they'll compare their deeds to yours and mine, and theirs are always "better." But deep down they know they fail daily, and sadly, fear of failure is often expressed in severe anger or passive-aggressiveness. By creating fear in others through twisted Scripture, they get a false sense of security. Albeit, short lived each time because this is error.

2. **Cherry-picked, out-of-context Scripture.** Just like the slogan for real estate is "Location, location, location," for Scripture, "Context, context, context" is key. We can believe the lies of many modern-day "Christian Pharisees" when we don't keep the audience of a book–and

162

the entire letter—in context as we read. Anyone can handpick a passage to make their point, that doesn't mean they're teaching it in its true context. Authentic biblical exegesis only comes by way of rightly dividing the Word into *Old Covenant* and *New Covenant*. Without the Cross being the dividing line and focus, we are wrong, always.

Over the centuries many sanctimonious men and women have tried to unravel the mysterious writings in Revelation, some with diagrams and "detailed" timelines. But we would be lunatics to think we can accurately decipher this vision John had while banished to Greece's version of Alcatraz, Patmos Island. Rather the third chapter—in regard to the verse in question—or the twentieth, the entire book of Revelation is symbolism. So when we begin to create graphs and chart out a man's dream into principles and itineraries, we're just asking for egg on our faces. God spitting out Christians is no different.

I understand this will infuriate the most well-educated, but I don't care. Some theologians and professors are too book smart for their own supernatural good. Unlike the other letters written to the churches by John, Paul, Peter, James, Jude, and the author of Hebrews (more than likely, Paul), Revelation is *not* meant to be read the same. It's a great painting of what *will* happen to Creation, a panned out picture of what's yet to come.

This revelation penned by John as he was exiled is dramatic, metaphoric, *symbolism*. It's all true, but the bottom line behind the book is this:

THE DEVIL LOSES. WE WIN.

Just read the last page. Other than that, if we believe we're experts on the things John wrote, it's only a matter of time before we get embarrassed in a severe way.

Disastrously, grace-confused people will sandwich Revelation 3:16–"God will spew you out of His mouth!"–with something Jesus said in Matthew 7:21-23:

> *Not everyone who says to me, "Lord, Lord," will enter the kingdom of heaven, but he who does the will of my Father who is in heaven will enter. Many will say to me on that day, "Lord, Lord, did we not prophesy in your name, and in your name cast out demons, and in your name perform many miracles?" And then I will declare to them, "I never knew you; depart from me, you who practice lawlessness."*

Don't let this worry you either. It was not written to Christians. Jesus is speaking to some unbelieving Jews *before* the Cross; those who wanted to practice the Law of Moses to earn righteousness with God *rather* than believe He was Messiah. This is why He said, "you who practice *lawlessness.*" Lawlessness was breaking Mosaic Law. Christians were never invited to obey the Law of Moses because the Law is not of faith (see Galatians 3:12, Romans 6:14, 10:14).

These Hebrew people wanted to brag on their "amazing feats" in order to earn their way into heaven–even doing them in Christ's very name. Satan was more than happy to give them results which were *not* from God, although it looked like they were, as they cast out demons and performed miracles.

The problem was this: Jesus *never* knew them, personally. Never means never, that's why He said it.

If I say, "I know Donald Trump," and then I do a bunch of things while attempting to represent him, then I *meet* Donald Trump and act like we're friends, he'd look at me like I'm crazy. We have *no* personal relationship. Same with these Law-lovers and Jesus Christ.

Therefore, this passage is not for Christians who don't do enough works to get into heaven, but for legalistic yahoos who thought they were "on fire" for God. "Lord, Lord, look at what all *I've* done for you!"

Do you see it? That's not the gospel. The gospel is, "Lord, Lord, thank you for what all *you've* done for me." They knew exactly who Jesus was but He never knew *them* in a personal way. For us saints, He *does* know us.

"I am the good shepherd; <u>I know my sheep and my sheep know me</u>"
(John 10:14)

I can already hear it, "Yeah right, Matt! You're just telling people they can be lazy! You're just telling people they can sin away! *You* will be one of the false prophets God spews out of His mouth! Jesus said only he who does the will of my Father will enter heaven!"

Friend, breathe. There is rest in Christ. At no point in my books do I ever say we can be lazy. I say we are motivated from within and *that's* where our true fulfillment comes from. Is Christ lazy? No, and He lives in us and works *through* us. Neither do I say, ever, we can sin away. We are free *from* sin, not free *to* sin. Even deeper, the truth is we don't *want* to sin. Try sinning and you'll see. If you're saved, there's no permanent life in sinning. It's always a dead end street. So, *don't* sin. Is that clear? You'll regret sinning every single time eventually if not instantly.

And yes, Jesus does say only those who do the will of my Father will enter heaven in Matthew 7, but what is the will of the Father? Like the Pharisees, it sounds to me like you're turning the word *will* into *work*, and you know what? That's a great idea because Jesus said *this* to the legalists who wanted to be told to do more stuff:

"The work of God is this: <u>to believe in the one he has sent</u>." (John 6:29)

Believing, to God, is the greatest work we could ever do. Believing Jesus can, and will, forgive. This is why Revelation 3:16 cannot be combined with Matthew 7:21-23. If you have this mindset, dump it. It's demonic, out of context, and anti-Cross because it puts the focus on what *we* do rather than on what Christ *has* done.

The entire chapter of Revelation 3 is a call to the symbolic churches in Sardis, Philadelphia, and Laodicea, to repent of turning away from the simplicity of the gospel. Read the entire chapter and you'll soon see that these churches had become fat and lazy. This section of the body of Christ had turned lukewarm—neither hot *nor* cold. They had lost their purposefulness *not* their salvation. Losing salvation is absolutely impossible because Jesus would have to die permanently. Losing salvation is absolutely impossible because the promise the Father and Son made to each other at the Cross would have to be broken. That will never, ever, *ever* happen! (See John 1:12, 3:16-18, 14:19, Colossians 3:4, 2 Timothy 2:13, Hebrews 1:3, 6:16-19, 7:25, 9:26, 10:10,14).

Further, there's nothing wrong with being cold! Cold serves a wonderful purpose! For those who want to tell you, "You're not on fire for God! You're going to be spit out!" they really need to read the passage *before* Revelation 3:16. John said we should be hot *or* cold, not just hot. It's lukewarm that's the problem. Lukewarm does nothing and serves no purpose. Pond water is lukewarm, stagnant and idle.

> *"I know your deeds, that you are <u>neither</u> cold nor hot. I wish you <u>were</u> either one <u>or</u> the other!" (Revelation 3:15)*

I hate that this will hurt the feelings of the *on fire* Christians, and I'm sorry. But to God, cold is good too. The people being addressed in this passage were not having their salvation threatened, but their purposefulness being brought to light. Their usefulness. Their actions and attitudes were lukewarm and that's no place for a child of God to be. There's plenty to do while we're still here, and while we still have the ability. So we should get to work! We've been recreated in Christ to do good things—*but* getting to work and doing good things doesn't save us nor keep us saved. Only Christ's life does.

So today, my friends, know this: God would never spit us out. He holds us close. He's never disappointed in our lack of works, either. To Him, disappointments are called sins and Jesus took those all away at the Cross. Instead of shaking His head in disgust, He's always smiling warmly and encouraging us with the truth. When we lose sight of our first love, the one who saved us, Jesus, His Holy Spirit guides us back *into* the truth…gently, with grace. You are safe. You are secure. You are loved. Don't be afraid.

A prayer for you: *Heavenly Father, what an amazing gift you gave us at the Cross. The promise of eternal life with you forever. Satan has done diabolical things in the minds of Christians by making them believe they can be spit out by you for not doing enough. Set them free today, in their thinking. Let them know Jesus did enough! So many of these dear readers are still afraid that they're lukewarm, cold, or not hot enough. Reveal the true context of Revelation 3. Teach them they have nothing to fear because fear has to do with punishment—and you already punished Jesus in full. Both our sins of omission and commission were dealt with at Golgotha! It's been finished! Give them freedom in their minds today as they learn the truth of the gospel of grace! Amen.*

Day 20

The Cross Was the Final Altar

When he had received the drink, Jesus
said, "It is finished." With that, he bowed
his head and gave up his spirit.

John 19:30

Blood. God has always required blood to forgive sins. The words *ask for forgiveness* are not in the Bible for a reason: ask all you want, blood must be shed to settle up with your Creator.

The author of Hebrews explains:

> *"Without the shedding of blood there is no forgiveness of sins."*
> *(See Hebrews 9:22)*

Before the Cross–to make forgiveness even more difficult–God wouldn't even accept your bloody sacrifice if you weren't Jewish. But let's digress for a moment and say we were. We would've still needed a middleman, a priest from the tribe of Levi, to present our animal blood to God in the temple. Behind the curtain in this place, where only Levitical priests were allowed to go, there was a platform called *the altar*.

At the annual Day of Atonement, animal blood was poured out *on* this altar to atone for, or "cover up," a person's sins for the past year. Jesus, however, took away sins forever. He didn't simply cover them up until the next Day of Atonement.

Animal blood *paid off* sins once a year. It put you back in the black. Jesus *banished* all of your sins *once* and for all time (see Hebrews 8:12, 10:10). They called Him *Messiah* because only *He* could do such a thing. This prophetic Person would deal with sins permanently, not year after year. The blood of bulls and goats *reminded* Jews of their sins—no permanent forgiveness. Yet still, afterwards they felt relief because they knew God had forgiven them until the next annual trek (see Isaiah 53, Hebrews 10:3).

According to the Bible, one type of blood was used in the Old Covenant (animal blood), and the other (Messiah's) in the New Covenant. One liquid had very little power, the other had unlimited power. Here's the contrast:

> *"It is impossible for the blood of bulls and goats to take away sins."*
> *(Hebrews 10:4)*

> *"The next day John saw Jesus coming toward him and said, 'Look, the Lamb of God, who takes away the sin of the world!'" (John 1:29)*

This was so important to the Jews! Messiah would take away sins permanently, not just atone for them, but throw them into oblivion! After the Cross they didn't have to keep getting forgiveness at the temple through animal blood! This was huge!

According to the Law of Moses—which is 613 commandments, ten of which are the Ten Commandments—blood had to be shed for each commandment they broke. When this happened, these were called transgressions, or sins. The Law defined sin for the Jewish race, not for us Gentiles. After the 613 commandments were given by Moses, Israel (another name for the Jewish people) was not allowed to add to them nor take away from them. The whole Law had to be kept perfectly, unmodified (see Deuteronomy 4:2, James 2:10, Galatians 3:10).

What most pastors won't tell you today, either because they don't know or they're afraid, is only the Jews were allowed to keep these commandments. So when we read the Old Testament and act as if it's directed at us, commandment wise, we are wrong. We Gentiles, non-Jews, were not part of the Old Covenant–the 613–nor our cherry-picked top 10.

Paul explains our former plight which was *before* we were included in the New Covenant through Jesus' blood:

> *"remember that at that time <u>you were separate from Christ, excluded</u> <u>from citizenship in Israel</u> and <u>foreigners to the covenants of the promise,</u> without hope and without God in the world." (Ephesians 2:12)*

Separate? Excluded? Foreigners? But somehow we want to say the Old Covenant is for us. It isn't. Yes, all of the Bible is right and true. However, we Gentiles have no relationship with the Law but *only* with the Spirit of Jesus Christ, through believing in Him:

> *"Christ is <u>the end of the Law</u> so that there may be righteousness for <u>everyone who believes.</u>" (Romans 10:4)*

We are not believing in the Law–none of it. We're not allowed. We are believing in *Him*. Therefore in His *blood*. Why? Blood forgives. All unbelievers have a sin problem and must be forgiven (see Romans 3:10,23).

So if only blood forgives, and we weren't included in the former Covenant, how can we be forgiven as Gentiles? Because the middlemen–the priests from the tribe of Levi–were replaced by Jesus! They had to find a new job due to God outsourcing their employment to Messiah!

Even more, the temple–the building where blood was offered up at the altar–it would also be replaced! With what? With us! Actual human bodies where the Spirit of God would now dwell by faith, not by walls! (See Hebrews 7:16,24, 1 Corinthians 6:19, Acts 2:1-4).

Even the Jews had to turn from the Law and believe in Jesus' blood. They were cut off from access to God and had to be grafted back in through faith in Christ alone. Paul pleads with his countrymen to repent of their unbelief:

"And if the people of Israel turn from their unbelief, they will be grafted in
again, for God has the power to graft them back into the tree."
(Romans 11:23)

Jesus, who descended from the tribe of Judah, not Levi, became our final priest. The Jews no longer have any way to receive forgiveness by blood after He came and went. This is a good thing! All of humanity needed a priest–not just them–one who would never die! (See Hebrews 7:25). The entire *world* needed a great high priest who would present His own blood to God for the forgiveness of sin once and for all time! Therefore, since the tribe changed (Levi to Judah) and new blood was presented (perfect blood from the final Lamb), the priesthood changed and so did the Covenant! (See Hebrews chapters 7-10).

The New Covenant began at the Cross, the final altar. Blood was poured out for everyone's sins all across the globe, not just for the Jews (John 3:16-18, 19:30, 1 John 2:2, Romans 3:25, Galatians 3:28).

This is why we don't need altars in our churches today. Jesus will never present His blood for sins ever again. It's finished. The Levitical priests have been replaced, the dividing curtain between us and the Most Holy Place has been torn, the temple is gone, and the altar is obsolete (see Matthew 27:51, Ephesians 2:14, Hebrews 8:13, 9:3). No more bloody sacrifices are necessary to forgive sins.

Today's Jews who don't believe in Jesus are in a state of limbo. While rocking back and forth, wailing at an ancient wall, they can't present animal blood to receive forgiveness. They beg God, "Hurry up and send a Messiah!" but the tribes are no more, so *priests* are no more either. The one true priest already died and rose back to life. *They* are now without hope, not us. They refuse to believe the world's sin issue has been dealt with by one sacrifice (see Hebrews 10:10,14, 1 John 2:12).

Since only a priest with blood can reconcile us to God–because God can have nothing to do with sin–Jesus *had* to do this. Now, we must accept this reconciliation *to* God, by grace through faith in His Son's deity (see 2 Corinthians 5:20, Ephesians 2:8,9, John 1:12).

There's a passage in Hebrews 10 which is often used by the grace-confused community to incite fear of loss of salvation *because* of sinning. But in fact, this portion of Scripture is explaining the uselessness of bloody animal sacrifices at the temple altar. As you read this, please know that the text has nothing to do with Christians whatsoever. This is directed toward Jewish people who followed Moses and refused to believe in Christ as Messiah. The Messiah, prophesied about in the Jews' very own book of Isaiah–the final, once for all, bloody sacrifice–*He* is the context, *He* is the truth, and the "sinning" referenced is breaking the Law of Moses in one or more of 613 different ways. This is cyclical, because "sinning" is also unbelief in Jesus:

> *"If we deliberately keep on sinning after we have received the knowledge of the truth, no sacrifice for sins is left, but only a fearful expectation of judgment and of raging fire that will consume the enemies of God. Anyone who rejected the Law of Moses died without mercy on the testimony of two or three witnesses. How much more severely do you think someone*

deserves to be punished who has trampled the Son of God underfoot, who has treated as an unholy thing the blood of the covenant that sanctified them, and who has insulted the Spirit of grace?" (Hebrews 10:26-29)

Do you see the context? Hebrew people who refused to believe Jesus has forgiven them by grace. That's why the name of the book is *Hebrews*. It's not *Gentiles*. These Jews, in this part of the letter, are enemies of God. *We* are His family (see John 1:12). They were trampling on Him by speaking ill of Him, "He's not the promised Messiah!" therefore, blaspheming. They rejected His Holy Spirit into *their* spirit, which is the only unforgivable sin (see Matthew 12:30-32, Hebrews 3:15).

These people thought they could continue to receive forgiveness each year at the temple by way of animal blood. They absolutely *refused* to accept the truth that Jesus was the last sacrifice. No sacrifice for sin is left! They had *received* the knowledge of Jesus and stonewalled at believing in His power to forgive.

Again, this is *not* written to Christians because the Law of Moses is mentioned. God never commanded us to obey Moses but to accept His grace by listening to Jesus (see Matthew 17:5, Hebrews 12:15). We have a better deal. We were given the two commandments of Christ–believe and love–neither of which can be legislated (see John 3:16-18, 13:34, 1 John 3:23, Hebrews 7:18,19, 8:13).

To them, the altar was more important than the Cross. Disastrously, many of our churches do the same thing today as their main focus is on a carpet-covered set of stairs or man-made platform up front. The altars in our churches need to go because what they represent is not of God.

"Nope! This is wrong, Matt! I left a church because they didn't have altar calls each week!"

Friend, I hear you. I used to think the same, as if someone couldn't be saved unless they went to the front. That, or their saving didn't stick because they kept on sinning, so a second, third, fourth–and so on–altar visitation was needed. But what I've learned is there's no verse in the Bible which states we have to walk to the front of a church building to be saved. Nor do we have to raise our hand in the crowd to be acknowledged by a pastor. This is 100% absent from the Old and New Testament.

We've adopted this practice because in the early 1900's "altar calls" became popular at tent revivals. However, this behavior is non-existent from all biblical text. Why? Because this is a *work*. Anything *we* do or *don't* do–in order to achieve righteousness–physically or mentally, is a work. If it's a work, it's against grace. If it's against grace, it's not of faith. The gospel can only be entered into by grace *through* faith. Paul educates the Romans:

"And if by grace, <u>then it cannot be based on works</u>; if it were, <u>grace would no longer be grace</u>." (Romans 11:6)

So if we aren't saved by altar calls then how are we saved? In the most graceful way possible: *by hearing or reading with faith.*

Paul said this very thing to the Christians in Galatia when they tried to add Judaism into the gospel message. Judaism had an altar. Judaism is Moses. Moses is all works-righteousness. After calling them *fools* with an exclamation point, Paul asks a simple, rhetorical question:

"This is the only thing I want to find out from you: did you receive the Spirit by the <u>works</u> of the Law, <u>or by hearing with faith</u>?" (Galatians 3:2)

HEARING. WITH. FAITH. This is *how* we receive the Holy Spirit into our own. A legalist will shout, "Even the demons believe!" and that's true, but they aren't believing in Jesus to forgive them. They're already damned to hell, we aren't. Non-Christians have a chance to benefit from Jesus' sacrifice if they will believe in His forgiveness while still on earth. Even though demons are well aware of who Jesus is, they can't do that (see James 2:19).

In Galatians 3:2, it's obvious Paul is pitting Mosaic Law *against* faith. This is very important to know because he also said the Law is not *of* faith in the same chapter (see Galatians 3:12). To add to this, in Romans, he pronounced the only way to be set free from sin is to be set free from Moses! (See Romans 6:14). This flies in the face of the sanctimonious who "try" to follow the Law on *this* side of the Cross. Romans 6:14 sinks that ship immediately:

"For sin shall no longer be your master, <u>because</u> you are not under Law, but under grace."

Another rebuttal someone might throw at me to validate there's more to salvation than simply hearing with faith, is Romans 10:9:

"If you confess with your mouth, 'Jesus is Lord,' and believe in your heart that God raised him from the dead, you will be saved."

"See, Matt?! Confess with your mouth! You gotta say the words to *prove* yourself!"

Friend, what about the people who don't *have* a tongue *to* confess? What about those who are born mute or have no voice box? What about the persecuted people who've had their tongues cut out? Do you think God won't save them if they believe Jesus has forgiven them *just* because they can't say words? Of course He will! We are saved by hearing and believing! Nothing else!

We can confess with our mouth all day long, "Jesus is Lord!" but if faith didn't come first those confessions mean nothing. Plus, if we look at the context of the book of Romans, where this passage came from, these Christians were supposed to say that *Cesar* is lord because they lived in Rome. Saying otherwise meant certain death. For this reason, Paul points out they must confess that their *real* Lord is Jesus, but *only* by faith first. By believing with the heart.

We are not saved by our words but by our one-time faith in Jesus' words. We make Him fully Lord *and* Savior, both, evenly, obviously, the moment we believe this truth. This is why Lordship salvation is a joke. It's demonic and puts un-necessary pressure on us saints. If you're stuck in it, run for the hills. Break free.

So if we don't need to be saved at the altar, do we need to be "cleansed" each week by physically moving our body to the front of a church? No, we do not.

"No way, Matt! Even Jesus made Peter *let* Him wash his feet!" (See John 13:1-17).

You are right, He did. But this was not a symbol of Jesus needing to cleanse us daily, or weekly, or whenever—and there's no altar, so forgiveness cleansing is not the context at all. This was Jesus teaching the disciples how to rest and let *Him* work, and then, to do the same for one another. Remember, only blood forgives, not feet washing. This was cultural at the time. Jesus doesn't cleanse our feet. He kills us, buries us, and resurrects us as brand new creations who are forever connected to Him (see Romans 6:6-11, Colossians 3:3, Galatians 2:20, 2 Corinthians 5:17, 1 Corinthians 6:17).

The truth is we've *been* cleansed, we've *been* washed, *once* and for all time by *one* bloody sacrifice—our spirits have. Look at what the Bible says about our identity subsequent to faith in the Cross:

> *"But you were washed, you were sanctified, you were justified in the name*
> *of the Lord Jesus Christ and by the Spirit of our God."*
> *(See 1 Corinthians 6:11).*

> *"And by that will, we have been made holy through the sacrifice of the*
> *body of Jesus Christ once for all." (Hebrews 10:10)*

Past tense. One body. Once for all. You are completely forgiven forever, Christian. So we'll have to turn from our sinful actions and attitudes for a much different reason than to get re-forgiven countless times. The Jews didn't turn from sins to be forgiven, they gave blood once a year. So what makes us think we can achieve forgiveness through what we start or stop?

We turn from sin because sinning is not natural to us. We've been made holy. Sinning will never set right with us permanently, no matter how many times we do it. So it's best to just not do it (see Ephesians 2:10, Colossians 1:22, Philippians 1:6).

Turn from sin every time, repenting is a good thing. But God will never forgive us again because Christ will never die again. Once for all means *once for all*. It's finished means *it's finished*. You've died to sin means *you've died to sin*.

Our sins are not more powerful than Jesus' blood. He's resting just fine. Look at this:

> *"After he had provided purification for sins, he sat down at the right hand of the Majesty in heaven." (See Hebrews 1:3)*

Unlike the Levitical priests who presented animal blood at the altar for forgiveness–who weren't allowed to sit down and rest–Jesus sat. He completed the work. He's the final priest. According to the New Covenant, human priests are now fake. First, because they are not from the tribe of Levi, second, because they aren't the Messiah. In fact, Peter said we believers are *all* a part of a royal priesthood (see 1 Peter 2:9). Therefore, hierarchies are antiquated. We are equally holy by our new birth, by our new identity, *not* by votes, our sex, marital status, or robes. We have a priest, not from Levi, but one who descended from Judah in the likeness of Melchizedek (Melchizedek was an Old Testament priest with no beginning or end, possibly an early appearance of Christ). Our priest, Jesus, has perfect blood which was presented at the real temple altar in heaven *rather* than the man-made shadow of that altar on earth (see Genesis 14:18-20, Hebrews 7:1-3,14-17,24,25, 9:23-28).

The pressure which is put on countless congregations to "go up front to the altar" to receive repeated forgiveness and cleansing is not okay. It's a mockery of the Cross and an insult to the blood of Jesus.

When I came to understand the New Covenant, plainly laid out in Hebrews, it became blatantly clear that altars have no place in our churches. If anything we should have a symbolic location called *The Empty Tomb* where people can kneel down and pray but not *the altar*.

No more sacrifice is needed. No more blood. No more altars.

Sadly, due to incorrect interpretation of Scripture—as well as severe emotionalism being taught and shown—certain churches have a call for patrons to come to the front, to their quasi-altars, and "lay stuff down." The problem is, for them, this is not just symbolism. It's doctrine. It's literal. It's *needed*.

I'm not saying *don't* go up front for some prayer. I'm saying don't see "up front" as special. You are just moving your body.

Many believe a needed location is required to get right with God again and again…and again. That place is at their altar, even though Christ destroyed the need of such a geographical spot. Here's how it works. While standing in the pews a person next to you gives an elbow nudge and a head-bob toward the stage, as if to say, "You've sinned a lot this week. You have to go up front."

Shamed and victimized, I've been coerced to do this many times myself. "Excuse me," I'd quietly announce, as I made my way to the isle. Causing a scene while slowly walking up front, displaying such "amazing humility" as the "good Christians" stayed in their seats watching with disgust. Some might shout gibberish, acting as if it's tongues, like I'm being scolded through the supernatural realm by way of their "gift." Sweating and shaking as I arrived at my destination, a self-righteous look from the person by the altar quickly informed me of my pathetic situation and how badly I "needed" them. Multiple hands were then laid on me for being less-than, *again*, in order to, "Pray my nasty sinnin' away!"

"I hope this deliverance sticks this time and I never sin again! Help me, God! *Please*, help me!"

After hearing loud shouts while witnessing other "sinners" get blasted to the ground around me, then weeping profusely and wiggling, I'd fall over too. Chasing dramatic feelings "to prove my remorse" was the name of the game.

Madness, all madness. This is insanity not Christianity. And we wonder why non-believers think we're crazy. It's because of this type of lunacy. The Spirit will always exude self-control *through* us. That should say something as to how authentic these actions truly are (see Galatians 5:22,23).

Such pastor-led charades are worse than Judaism. This *never* happened in the Bible–ever. So why are we doing it now? The Levitical priests didn't run around perspiring and yelling, calling people to the front of the temple and placing hands on them with a Star-Wars-like-Force as they shot Jews across the room. Come *on*.

The priest simply walked up to the man or woman, took their animal, went to the back behind the curtain, killed the animal, and used the blood at the altar to receive forgiveness for that person's sins. And they got forgiveness for a *year* at a time. That seems pretty simple, and dare I say, *peaceful*, compared to what we see today.

This neurotic, weekly-get-right trash is nearly demonic because when we do this we're crucifying Christ again and again in our minds. We're ignoring what His blood did *once*. We're also depending on a building and a human, therefore diluting the grace of God by not accepting the blood's full power.

Who's really having their ears tickled? Who's truly *not* rightly dividing God's Word into the Old and New Covenants, but mixing them?Jesus said this isn't allowed, as did Paul (see Mark 2:22, 3:25, Galatians 5:9).

We don't get forgiven nor "lay stuff down"–sins, fears, addictions, whatever–at any place or through any human. This does nothing except create more anxiety. It causes us to believe we have to hurry up and get to the church on Sunday *before* we can release ourselves from our mistakes.

The enemy then gets to work, "You might as well go wild until then. What's one more sin? You can't do anything about it until you see Pastor anyway."

Altar calls lead us to become dependent on a preacher and stage rather than on Christ within us. We've looked to a fake altar rather than realize all of our failures were already put on the Cross, the *final* altar. Our bawling, jiggling, hopping and twisting around, cannot cause us to become more forgiven or more holy than we are at this exact moment in time as believers.

I'm all for remorse over the sins we commit, but no amount of pleading on the floor will cause Jesus to die again which is necessary for the forgiveness of sin. WE ARE FORGIVEN, ONCE, BY FAITH IN THE BLOOD OF JESUS. This cannot be improved upon nor sustained by us.

Because of the love of Christ, God's wrath over your sins–even future sins–is gone. All of our sins were in the future when Jesus gave His blood for them. Accordingly, believers *have* accessed peace with God:

"Therefore, since we have been justified through faith, <u>we have peace with God through our Lord Jesus Christ</u>" (Romans 5:1)

"Since <u>we have now been justified by his blood</u>, how much more shall we be <u>saved from God's wrath through him</u>!" (Romans 5:9)

Notice Paul doesn't put a question mark at the end of Romans 5:9? Even though this *is* a question, he's making a *declaration* about Jesus' blood!

Confession doesn't repeatedly forgive Christians either, and why not? First of all, the Levites never had a confession booth in the temple, they had a knife. Also, what if we *forget* to confess a sin? God doesn't forget just because we forget. God doesn't overlook sins just because we overlook sins. Confess all you want, blood at the altar is required, not words. Jesus gave that blood *for* us.

1 John 1:9, the "confession for continual forgiveness" verse, is a staple-food passage for Cross-belittlers. In context, the first chapter of 1 John is an invitation to unbelievers to confess they *need* forgiveness, which is Christianity 101. Chapter 2 is then addressed to believers. The rest of the letter is a contrast of what a believer and unbeliever looks like by nature, by identity. Many have used this book as a way to view the *outside* of a person to prove their salvation, but John is talking about hearts the whole time.

If going to the front of a church or confession forgives me, then I'd rather be part of the Old Covenant rather than the New. Annual forgiveness sounds much better. I would prefer to hand over my best goat to a priest and then go home until next year. The author of Hebrews had to make the same case I'm making, that Christ would have to continue to die if once for all forgiveness was not true:

> "Otherwise <u>Christ would have had to suffer many times</u> since the creation of the world. But he has appeared <u>once for all</u> at the culmination of the ages <u>to do away with sin by the sacrifice of himself.</u>" (Hebrews 9:26)

This is now, not later! This type of forgiveness is available to everyone who will believe! Jesus accomplished everything for us at the Cross with His blood and He will never suffer for our sins again!

A prayer for you: *Heavenly Father, I know this devotional will upset some people, as it would have me a decade ago. You and I both know that's not my intention, please help them to understand this. Set people free in their thinking, from anything added to the Cross. It's not needed because Christ was enough. Right now, I lift up all who are reading this, directly to you. For those who have been taught they need an altar, a pastor, a weekly trip to the front of the church–or confession–give them relief in their souls. Reveal the true power of the blood of Jesus in even greater ways! If they want to go up front they are free to do so but that trip will not forgive them any more than they are right now–which is completely if they've believed! Amen and amen!*

Day 21

Christians Don't Have a Sinful Nature

"Through these he has given us his very great
and precious promises, so that through them
you may participate in the divine nature"

See 2 Peter 1:4

Your body was God's idea. It is perfect in every way. Although *you* might not think it's perfect, God still does. Your flesh is His most amazing creation. Your body is His masterpiece of all created things. God designed the entire universe for the purpose of your flesh to have the ability to live out its life in time. Your flesh, your body, is a marvel unlike anything else in His vast system of stars, planets, and galaxies.

A recent study was done on the monetary value of the human body, the physical flesh which houses our spirit. The appraisal was calculated based on selling individual components such as our bone marrow, lungs, kidneys, heart, and each separate part of us which God has made.

Our estimated worth is approximately 45 million dollars.

We are a phenomenon unlike anything else! Not only that, but the intricacies of our body's systems all working *together* is miraculous! The symphony of our circulatory, skeletal, digestive, nervous, musculatory, reproductive–and more–all in sync as you read this sentence cannot be recreated by any man! Man has tried, but failed!

Nor did random happenstance cause this harmonious shell of life to appear out of nothing, or *evolve* from nothing. God did this. God made *you*–your flesh, your body.

Look at your hand. Go ahead. Stop reading for a few seconds and hold your hand up in front of your face…move your fingers around…twist your wrist and forearm…it's perfect. The Creator's imagination is on full display in front of and *through* your eyes. He thought that up.

If the Master Designer had a body–and He did in Christ–you are exactly what He would want to look like. Human. What an absolute honor it is to be one of His ideas! (See John 1:14, Colossians 1:19).

Paul wrote to the Christians in Thessalonica informing them that not only is their spirit and soul blameless, but so is their body (see 1 Thessalonians 5:23). Unfortunately, many Christians believe they're at war with their body, saying such things as, "I just gotta fight my flesh each day! My flesh is cursed! I need to crucify my flesh! My flesh is the problem!"

The good news is, this is incorrect according to Scripture. Our flesh, our *body*, is not the problem at all. It is but a tool for our spirit to use. It's an instrument for our soul to be able to express itself at any given time. It's a wondrous thing!

Instead, *the* flesh is the problem. Not flesh–not the body–but the flesh. When we put that t.h.e. in front of the word *flesh*, it becomes something altogether different than the human body. This is critical to comprehend as a saint, and that is what you are, Christian.

The Bible has two different contextual purposes for these words. One for *flesh* and the other for *the flesh*.

1. **Flesh.** Our body. Physical matter of skin, bone, muscle and more, which temporarily houses our spirits. Our original ancestors, Adam and Eve, produced all flesh from *their* flesh after God placed them here on Day 6 of Creation.

2. **The flesh.** The parasitic power of sin *through* our physical body, even our brain, which results in ungodly actions, attitudes, and thoughts. Sin, which is a noun in the original text–the Greek word, *hamartia*–it entered this physical realm when Adam and Eve chose to no longer believe God. *It* comes to life *through* us and must have physical members to use (hands, feet, mouth, brain). When it has the opportunity to manifest itself, and it does–even inwardly, in our thoughts–this is called the flesh. As Christians, our spirits have been taken out of the flesh and placed into the Spirit of Christ, but our mortal bodies are still susceptible to its influence (see Genesis 4:7, Romans 5:12, 7:21-23, 8:9, Ephesians 1:13).

Sin, hamartia, is not a verb. *Sinning* is the verb-tense of hamartia. Sin through our flesh is *the* flesh, but *our* flesh–our body–is not sinful. As a child of God, it can sin–our body–therefore expressing sin, but it *still* is not sinful. Remember, Paul told the Thessalonians that our spirit, soul, *and body* is blameless.

The power of sin is a parasite and needs a host. Our physical body is just that. Sin is *in* our body but not *part* of our body. Like a splinter, it's a foreign object. Even our brain can be influenced by the power of sin, causing sinful thoughts which are contrary to God. In turn, causing *you* to not walk according to your true holiness as a saint (see Galatians 5:17).

The flesh is not simply heavy drinking, fornicating, getting tattoos and cursing, as the legalists want to claim. There is good-looking *religious* flesh too. The Pharisees were the perfect example. The most well-behaved people on earth were chewed out by Jesus left and right because He knew their sinful thoughts. Those *thoughts* were the flesh (see Matthew 9:3,4, 12:24,25, Philippians 3:4-6, Galatians 3:3).

Once more for emphasis because this personally took me a while to grasp: the flesh is not *our* flesh. It's sin–hamartia–quickening through our body.

The flesh can even express itself in our brain as sin which can't be seen. But just because it can't be seen that doesn't mean it's not the flesh. Coveting, lust, fantasy, superiority, silent criticism, unforgiveness, same sex attraction, philanthropy done in pride, Law observance, and other *inward* flesh which is not expressed *outwardly* for others to be able to see and point out is *still* the flesh. For example, Paul struggled with jealousy, yet his contemporaries thought he was blameless. They could not *see* the flesh Paul was dealing with. I'll stay on track here, but the Law of Moses *excites* the flesh rather than douses it, and the Ten Commandments are *in* the Law. That should tell us something (see Romans 5:20, 6:14, 7:7,8, Philippians 3:6, 2 Corinthians 3:6-18, Deuteronomy 4:2, Galatians 3:12).

Paul goes to great lengths explaining the flesh in Romans 7 and 8, and in Galatians 5. Read all three chapters with the following information in mind: *the flesh is not you, Christian.* Not once was he referring to believers being "at battle" with our physical bodies. In fact, he said we are to care for our bodies, not fight them:

"After all, no one ever hated their own body, but they feed and care for their body, just as Christ does the church" (Ephesians 5:29)

To make matters worse–even more confusing–in the early 1980's a version of the Bible was released called the NIV which stands for *New International Version.* This is an amazingly clear, easy to read Bible, but it had a huge flaw in the text. In order to make it more readable the words *the flesh* were changed to *sinful nature.* Yet the flesh does not mean sinful or nature. It means *the flesh.*

This Bible became a bestseller but such was catastrophic for the Christian world in regard to understanding our identity. Why? Because we do not *have* a sinful nature! We have God's *own* nature! (See 2 Peter 1:4). We have flesh–our body–and then there's *the* flesh. They are not even *remotely* the same thing but people were reading them not only as *one* but also as our "natural sinful bend" as children of God! What a disaster! The flesh being changed to sinful nature–mind you, in the infallible Bible–caused many to believe *we* are naturally sinful! Wrong, *so* wrong!

For Christians, God has taken *out* our naturally sinful heart and replaced it with a good heart, a heart like His. We've been recreated in Christ as holy children of God with new hearts–new spirits. Holy children of God cannot have a sinful nature, that's impossible. We've been reborn *of* God, of His own supernatural loin! (See Ezekiel 36:26, 2 Corinthians 5:17, 1 John 3:1,9, Colossians 1:22, John 1:12, 3:6,7).

After much advice the publisher changed sinful nature back to the flesh, but the damage was done. Lots of unlearning must now take place because countless Christians think they have a "naturally sinful side"–when they don't–all because of this minor text change.

Can you see how we can't fall at the feet of a book and must allow the Spirit to be our true guide while *reading* the Bible? Plus, the Bible is only 1,600 years old, the Holy Spirit is eternal. He has no beginning or end. Further, how do you think mankind knew God before the world *had* a Bible? The same as today! By His very Spirit!

Don't get me wrong, before salvation, yes, we did have a sinful nature. But not after. Now we are partakers in the *divine* nature of God Almighty–not later, but right now. Peter explains:

"Through these he <u>has given us</u> his very great and precious promises, <u>so that through them you may participate in the divine nature</u>" (See 2 Peter 1:4)

The original Greek word for the flesh is *sarx*. Remember, the flesh–sarx–doesn't mean sinful nature, or sinful, or nature, or *physical* flesh. Sarx's definition in our language is *the flesh*–that's it. We simply do not have an English translation of sarx to unpack it perfectly. Therefore we must put our confidence in the Spirit within us to translate the flesh in unspoken ways as we read Scripture.

He does this for us all the time. That knowing? That's Him (see Hebrews 8:10,11, John 14:26).

On the other hand, Satan was ecstatic to see the flesh being changed to sinful nature because now there were millions of Christians walking around believing something was naturally sinful about themselves:

> "What better a reason to sin? After all, I have a sinful nature. One
> more won't hurt."

To top off this lie, Romans 7 gets used out of context, when Paul said, "I'm doing the very thing I don't want to do!" However–Paul was *not* describing his "sinful nature" as a Christian nor giving himself an excuse to sin. He was detailing how the power of sin (hamartia) came to life through his thoughts–birthing *the flesh*–as he "tried" to obey the Mosaic Law during his *past life* as a devout Pharisee. "Thou shalt not covet!" was causing the flesh *to* covet. Just start at the beginning of chapter 7 and read all the way through. He's explaining his past battle as a non-believer struggling to follow commandments which condemned him–but keep going–*then* you'll see his conclusion in Romans 8:

THERE IS NO CONDEMNATION FOR CHRISTIANS!

Why? Because we've died *to* the commandments in the Law *so that* we can live for Him! The Law hasn't died but we've died to it! As a result, Jesus has changed our nature! Our nature is good! We might not always *act* good, but when we *don't* act good, it's just that–an act. God has recreated us as holy people who sometimes sin but *we* are not sinful in any way. That is, in our identity. Our spiritual genetic makeup is just like Jesus Christ's (see 1 John 4:17).

God cannot live in sinful places, so He gave us a new sinless identity, so He could join our spirits forever. The first time this happened was in the upper room at Pentecost, recorded in the book of Acts. Before the apostles' literal possession of the Holy Spirit of Jesus, God had been *with* people and *on* people but not *in* people–inside their very body and spirit permanently. But because of the Cross, all of humanity now has the opportunity to become one with God in spirit and body by grace through faith! (See Acts 2:1-4, Romans 6:6-10, 2 Corinthians 5:21, Galatians 2:20, Colossians 3:3, 1 Corinthians 6:17,19, Ephesians 2:8,9).

This could not happen if we had a sinful nature. Like oil and water God and sin don't mix. So He *had* to make us brand new, not a better version of ourselves but a reborn version; a whole new creation who's completely spotless from the power of sin (see John 3:6,7, 1 Corinthians 6:11, 2 Corinthians 5:17, Colossians 2:9,10).

This is why the flesh is not part of a Christian. *Flesh* is–our body–but not *the* flesh. Unfortunately, due to this mistake by the publishers of the NIV, the word *flesh* has become a dirty word. Not just the flesh but *also* flesh. Commingling the two in Scripture became a normal thing, so now we must begin to separate them based on context. Only then will we be able to understand there's nothing wrong with our bodies.

One last example to prove that our bodies are good. In Philippians 3, Paul said he had no confidence in the flesh but he isn't referring to his physical body. He's talking about his legalistic lineage of living by the Law, also known as religious flesh. Obviously Paul had confidence in his body. His body took him many places to preach the gospel. Friend, do you see it? He puts no confidence in his old, sinful, self-righteous way of living, apart from Christ.

Even for myself, for so long I believed that *I* was at battle with my flesh. Because of poor teaching and my NIV Bible, I thought I had to fight my body each day. This was not right. Instead, my *mind* was being renewed each day *to* my holiness; a holiness which came as a result of my one-time faith in the Cross (see Hebrews 10:10,14, Romans 12:2, 2 Corinthians 3:18).

Truth be told, not only are we not at battle with our flesh, but even *the flesh* we're not supposed to fight. The Holy Spirit *in* us is at battle with the flesh but *we* are not. We are told to rest. At no point in Scripture are we instructed to fight the flesh–that's an unwinnable war. Hamartia is here to stay until God burns this place up. The Bible says the flesh and the Spirit are at battle with one another, not the flesh and us (see Revelation 21:4, 22:3, 2 Peter 3:10, Galatians 5:13-26).

We can give *in* to the flesh and walk *according* to the flesh, which are old ways of coping and contrary to our divine nature. And if we do, if we sow to the flesh, we will reap to the flesh. The flesh will be birthed in our life. Just the opposite, if we walk *out* our true nature, therefore sowing to the Spirit, we will reap everything the Spirit has planned for us! (See Galatians 5:22,23, 6:7,8).

So today, my friends, know this: In my NIV Bible I've put a straight line through all the passages which read *sinful nature* and wrote *the flesh* above it because this is the truth. Sarx means the flesh. It doesn't mean sinful and it doesn't mean nature. It also doesn't mean physical flesh or human body. It means the flesh. Even more, Christians don't have a sinful nature because we have God's nature. The flesh is not us! Our natural actions and attitudes will always result in the Spirit of Jesus Christ living through us!

A prayer for you: *Dad, thank you for showing me the difference in my body and the flesh. What an amazing relief. I know at any point I can walk according to the flesh, but that's just dumb because I'm faking who I am. I'm holy. I'm like just you. Teach me more, Father. Right now, I lift up all who are reading this, directly to you. For those who believe they have two natures or they are fighting their body, give them peace in their minds. Through your Holy Spirit, help them to understand the power of sin is the enemy and not their flesh. Show them who you've recreated them to be in Christ and empower them to walk it out. Let them know it's okay to be themselves if they've placed their faith in Jesus. Give them confidence. I ask these things in Christ's name. Amen.*

Day 22

A Letter to Myself on My Wedding Day

*"And walk in love, as Christ loved us and gave himself
up for us, a fragrant offering and sacrifice to God."*

Ephesians 5:2

Today is August 23, 2019, my 15-year wedding anniversary. Here's what I'd say to 23-year-old me on his wedding day.

Matt,

I'm so happy for you! You're making one of the best decisions of your life by marrying Jennifer! She is such a gift from God to you! If you think she's beautiful now, just wait. She will become even more gorgeous, not just on the outside, but within. You are so blessed!

I know you wanted to have a big lavish wedding. I know Jennifer didn't want to be pregnant on her wedding day. I know you wanted to give her the beautiful dress and have everyone there. But don't be hard on yourself. God knows you can't afford it right now and *He* is there. He sees you honoring her, and Him, by making this official. He's the only one who truly matters when it comes to bringing two people together as one. He's a master at this. Not just with marriages, but He does the same thing with us and Himself. This has already happened to you and you'll learn a lot more in your 30's about your oneness with God. In fact, you'll write books about it.

Matty, you're very wise for not going into debt to have an expensive wedding. What you're saving now will help you establish your business, which will provide for your family. I know you feel less-than, I know you think you've let Jennifer down, but you won't always be living in Phil's basement. In just about a year you'll have enough money to move out and start building a life for your family. No, it's not ideal, but be grateful for such a kind father-in-law. His help will allow you to you save up. It won't always be like this buddy.

The drive you have inside will cause you to do amazing things! It's God working *in* you, combined *with* you! Together, you'll achieve so much! You might not believe me because you're cutting coupons and counting change just to go to Long John Silvers, but Alarm Security will take off soon. All those things you're doing now will be worth it! Keep going! Those countless doors you knock on, all the late nights, the stress, discouragement, and tears? Keep, going. I already know you will.

Speaking of those tears, Jennifer will be your greatest comfort when they flow. She'll always be your number one supporter. God is giving her to you for a reason. She'll be what you need every single day, when you're weak and wore out, wanting to give up. She's so sweet, steady, smart, courteous, a wonderful mother, and her best gift is comforting *you*. You're a McMillen, so you know you need someone who's the exact opposite. That stunning woman in front of you is she. Be easy on her. Give her a break on the days you want her to be more like you. She's not like you, and you're not like her. You both fit together, perfectly.

She will ease your mind in so many ways, soothing you is her gift. She loves children, puppies, catalogs, non-sexual cuddles, and sunsets. She doesn't want you to waste your money on flowers, but you will anyway. She likes it when you just stand in the kitchen as she cooks. When she says, "Come here and look at this sunset," for the millionth time, do it with a smile and a warm hug. Did I say she likes sunsets?

She also likes clouds, a lot. Just look at the clouds and say, "Wow, babe, that's nice," okay? And mean it, because you love her.

Listen to her without saying anything. Be willing to be wrong. Be willing to be misunderstood. Kiss her softly every night before you go to sleep. Let her vent and don't correct her when she's venting. Serve her with all your heart. Forgive to the point of understanding Christ's forgiveness for you. Be kind, even in disagreements. No, especially in disagreements. Watch what you say and be meaningful when you say *important* things. I repeat, watch what you say. Take your time with Jennifer. She's never in a rush unless she's late. She will be late, a lot. Sit on the couch and don't be salty. If you're in the car waiting, don't honk the horn to make her go faster, it will backfire.

One of the main reasons why I believe God matched you up with Jennifer is to teach you more about who *you* are. You're a saint. I know, I know, that's weird, but it will make sense later on. That's New Covenant stuff.

Also, I don't want to go into the pain which will happen in the future, but during those seasons God will teach you that He is the true Comforter. You'll both lean into Him when you aren't leaning into each other. The enemy will attempt to rip your family apart, but God won't allow it.

HE WILL MAKE IT STRONGER THAN EVER.

During your dark times of trial, the Holy Spirit within–that Spirit you think keeps coming and going based on your religious performance (He never leaves, by the way)–He will teach you things I cannot express in typed words. You'll type a lot of words in the future. You'll have an actual social media ministry and reach millions of people each week. Social media? Oh yes. This platform will change how the world connects and communicates. I don't have time to explain it now, but God is currently using it to spread the gospel in ways unlike ever before.

I know you're 23 right now, but by the time you're 38, God will have taken you much deeper into the knowledge of His grace and the New Covenant. It's "called" the New Covenant, but it's very old and you're already enjoying it! You just don't realize it!

As you grow and mature, those around you will benefit greatly from a restful version of yourself, which is actually authentic. *Rest*, Matt. Please, take time to rest. Delegate responsibilities. You don't have to do it all yourself. Trust people. No, they won't do it like you, but it's worth the rest. For years, you will battle addictions because of your refusal to rest and let others take things off your plate. So please, make every *effort* to rest.

Your drive is a double-edged sword, causing you to become extremely successful in business and ministry, but also causing you to look to alcohol to shut off your brain. There will be many great years for your company, but many terrible years for your marriage. So *please* rest. As your attention is shifted toward the New Covenant, rest *will* happen. I can't explain much more to you now, but know that God will use all your heartache and poor choices for a good purpose.

Today marks a wonderful day for you! You put the cart before the horse by getting Jennifer pregnant, but that little baby inside her belly? Just wait! Her name will be Grace! All the best characteristics of you and Jennifer–plus a great personality–will come to life! She's so much fun and she's going to melt your heart!

Matt, if I could just get you to remember that most of the things you stress over will never happen, you'll sleep better. Please enjoy each day, breathe in the fresh air, and look to your beautiful bride's care-free attitude for inspiration. *Join* her care-free attitude more often. She'll tell you many times, "Everything's going to be okay," as she holds your face, and she's right.

You're going to make a lot of mistakes, so forgive yourself, a lot. If it's past 6pm don't have any serious conversations, go to sleep. Not at 6pm, but you know what I mean. A good night's sleep changes a lot in your mind.

Express your feelings, set healthy boundaries, and value yourself. Never insult yourself. Never think you have a good side and a bad side. You only have *one* side, a holy side—a holy heart—and your mind is being renewed to your holiness. Yeah, you're holy, and you can't change this. More New Covenant stuff, buddy.

Cherish the amazing gift God has given you, your wife. You're about to embark on a wonderful, crazy, heartbreaking, loving, fulfilling life. It's gonna be a good one, with this beautiful woman. I'll see you in 15 years.

A prayer for you: *Heavenly Father, thank you for Jennifer. After all these years together she still makes my heart jump when she walks into the room. Her sensitive and kind soul will forever amaze me. What a treasure she is. I look forward to another 50 years with her, and more, if you'll let me. Right now, I lift up all who are reading this, directly to you. For many of them what they've just read resonates. The same Spirit within Jennifer and me—your Spirit—lives in them too. So they can relate to our story. Continue to bless them in great ways! But then again, others might have gotten sad, as their marriage has failed. Dad, give them peace today in the assurance that their identity has never been in marriage, but in Christ. He can never be lost, and He will never leave us. Let them know you'll bring beauty from their pain, somehow, in this life or the next, and their tears won't be wasted. Continue to teach us how to walk in your love and express your glorious Spirit! We love you so much! Amen!*

Day 23

———— ⊶⊷⊶ ————

But What About… (Part 2)

*"For the Law was given through Moses; grace
and truth came through Jesus Christ."*

John 1:17

I don't usually ask this, but would you please glance back up and reread that opening verse?

Now, based on that passage, what if we had it all wrong? What if Jesus was *not* really full of grace and truth and the Law of Moses was still meant to guide our lives? What *if* the 613 commandments weren't just for the Jewish people but for the entire world today? Would things be different? Would these commandments keep humanity in check? Would peace on earth be a reality?

Paul, a former devout Mosaic commandment-keeper, he said the opposite; that these commandments would *increase* sin, not decrease it:

"For sin, seizing an opportunity <u>through the commandment</u>, deceived me, and through it killed me." (Romans 7:11)

By way *of* the commandment–one of the Ten Commandments, "Thou shalt not covet" (see Romans 7:8)–sin went to work in Paul's life; therefore killing him *spiritually*. This proves we cannot legislate grace and truth through the Ten Commandments *or* the other 603 in the same Law package. Why does this matter? Because Jesus *is* grace and truth and He is the only option on this side of the Cross.

As you can see in the opening verse of this devotional, John pit Moses' commandments against Jesus Himself–as opposites. Law versus a Person. Moses had 613 commandments and Jesus had two. Do a quick Google search of "What are the 613 commandments in the Law"–which Moses gave–and you'll have to get up and make a sandwich before you finish reading half of them. And if you want to *live* by them, first, you must be Jewish, second, you must do *all* of them. No picking and choosing what you like, or what you *think* you can do. Eat all 613 or eat none (see Galatians 3:10, James 2:10).

When Jesus came He gave us two new commandments, believe and love (see 1 John 3:23). Jesus' commandments are not *added* to Moses' commandments because the Law is unchangeable (Deuteronomy 4:2, Matthew 9:17, Hebrews 8:13). Also, Jesus' commandments are simple, they're not burdensome like Moses'. Believe and love are the *only* commandments of Christ.

If you love Him you will keep *His* commandments *not* the commandments of Moses. Even better, if you love Him, believe and love are a part of who you are. So there's no need to "try" to do either. Just be yourself each day because believe and love is Christ in you.

Unfortunately the grace-confused people have a goal to stress others out about doing *both* as much as you can, as *hard* as you can, until you prove you're on "their level" of faith. Overlook their mistakenness with gentleness and respect.

Jesus, on the other hand, wants you to simply *be* who He's already made you to be (Hebrews 4:11, 2 Corinthians 5:17). The truth is, after salvation Jesus *becomes* your faith, so there's no pressure on you whatsoever (see Hebrews 12:2). Don't worry, Christ in you isn't passive. Things will happen in your life but it won't be because you're trying to "increase" your faith. Only unbelievers have a need for such. You just need to be you (see 2 Peter 1:3, John 15:5). Grace and truth flow through you like a river, the Spirit of Jesus Christ.

This is part two of my *But What About* devotionals. As the Spirit renews our minds we naturally have questions.

"But what about this?"

"But what about that?"

By staying focused on Jesus—on grace and truth, not Law—Scripture becomes an effervescent fountain of confidence in which we can drink from. Here's five new questions:

1. **But what about when Paul said "I die daily"? (See 1 Corinthians 15:31).** The behavior-focused folks have taken this verse out of context for centuries in an attempt to cause a believer to *think* they have to kill themselves each day in an effort to not sin. Satan loves this because he knows it's impossible. We only die in spirit *once* from the moment of faith in Christ. Our minds are renewed daily, but we are not dying daily (see Romans 12:2, Philippians 1:6). Yes, Paul said, "I die daily," however, a more contextually authentic translation of the original text is "I face death every day." Why? Because Paul was explaining the *physical* dangers he faced while traveling to preach the gospel. He even said in the *following* verse he was attacked by wild dogs on the road to Ephesus. God is not wanting us to die daily! He's wanting us to renew our minds to who we really are—and live!

2. **But don't we need to die to self?** No. Those words are not in the Bible. The closest thing is "our old self died" or "our old self *was* crucified"—past tense—found in Romans 6. Christian, you don't need to *die*

to self. You already died when you believed Jesus forgave you. You've received a new self. You simply need to learn more about the fact that you *have* died, in spirit, you *have* received a new spirit, and Jesus' Spirit has *joined* your spirit never to leave again! You have a good self so *be* yourself! (See Romans 6:6-11, Galatians 2:20, 2 Corinthians 5:17, Colossians 1:22, 3:3, 1 Corinthians 6:17).

3. **Don't I need to ask for forgiveness each day?** If you're a Christian why would you ask for what you already have? God isn't handing out forgiveness at our beckon call because forgiveness requires a bloody death. Our Creator has never forgiven anyone based on asking, but *only* on blood and our one-time faith in it (see Hebrews 9:22, John 3:16). Why do you think the Cross was such a big deal? Friend, the words *ask for forgiveness* are not in the Bible. Think about it, some people don't have a tongue nor a voice box. They don't have the *ability* to ask. Will our loving Father not save them? Of course He will, if they believe (see John 1:12). God forgives us based on faith in Jesus' blood, not words. We *receive* forgiveness not by speaking but by *believing* Jesus has forgiven us (see Galatians 3:2). Yes, there's a verse in Romans which reads, "If we confess with our mouth and believe in our heart Jesus is Lord we will be saved" (see Romans 10:9); but Paul is writing to the *Roman* Christians. Those who had to constantly confess with their mouth that the *government* was lord. Further, you can see he mentions the heart. The heart is what justifies us with God, not our mouth. Another verse, 1 John 1:9, might also come to mind over this topic. John wrote, "If we confess our sins, He is faithful and just to forgive us our sins and to cleanse us from <u>all</u> unrighteousness." I've underlined *all* because all means all. This is a one-time deal. Secondly, John is writing to *unbelievers* in this verse. He's evangelizing in the opening of this letter. He's inviting people to join *us* in fellowship with

Jesus by *first* admitting they *need* forgiveness. If you'll start from the beginning of the chapter and read down for context, you'll see. In chapter two, he *then* begins to address the believers. Whoever placed this chapter break in John's letter picked a great spot to do so. God doesn't forgive us by babbling or begging but by faith in His Son's perfect blood (see Romans 5:1, 6:23, 1 John 1 [all of it], 2:1,2, Hebrews 1:3, 7:25, 10:10,14, Matthew 6:7, John 19:30).

4. **But won't we be judged according to our words?** Only if you don't believe in Jesus. It can't be both. If it were both–our words plus the Cross–how can we be sure we've said the right words and *not* said the wrong words throughout our lifetime? And what percentage is our words in reference to the blood of Jesus? This is a classic example of Covenant-mixing double-talk. A self-centered person will spout off the following passage in order to push people down, "But I tell you that everyone will have to give account on the day of judgment for every empty word they have spoken. For by your words you will be acquitted, and by your words you will be condemned" (Matthew 12:36,37). Jesus isn't talking to Christians in these two sentences but to some idiots who just compared Him to the devil. Start back up in verse 22 and work your way down. You'll see that these type of people *will* be judged according to their words. You, Christian, will be judged according to the Cross! Be confident because it was a huge success!

5. **But what about when James said teachers will be judged by God more severely? (See James 3:1).** This is true, they *will* be–*if* they are teaching the Law. That's the context of this passage in James. Keep in mind, James was an apostle to the Jews, not to us Gentiles (see James 1:1). So he's primarily chastising unbelief in Messiah to his own race. Yes, there would be many people who would read this letter and *hear* it read over time (Christians and non-Christians) but it was

originally directed toward the Hebrew people. This is why he opens up the letter with "to the twelve tribes." Who were the twelve tribes? Israel. The Jews. The people group who followed Moses out of slavery in Egypt, through the Red Sea floor. To create order, Israel was split up into twelve tribes. So what were the Jews teaching in which they *would* be judged more severely? The Law, *not* grace and truth. 613 *Thou Shalts* given by Moses at the base of Mount Sinai. What's the takeaway then? Well if we're not Christians and we're teaching Law we *will* be judged more harshly, both by God *and* by those who *live* by the Law (see James 2:10, Galatians 3:10,11). Christians aren't judged by what we teach, but by our identity. We are children of God and we live by grace. Sometimes we don't teach proper things and that's okay because we're all learning and growing in the knowledge of Jesus Christ. But we won't be judged for that. Why not? Because improper things to God are called sins, and Jesus has removed those from us (John 1:29, 1 John 3:5). Teach away, my friend, and don't be afraid. Grace and truth will prevail if you are one with the Son of God!

A prayer for you: *Heavenly Father, thank you for grace and truth. Thank you for Jesus. Thank you for sending Him here to remove all of my sin punishment for good! Please teach me even more about Him. Right now, I lift up all who are reading this, directly to you. So many of these dear readers have been taught a mixture of Law, grace, and truth. Please begin to help them sift through this terrible concoction. Teach them how to remove the stuff they shouldn't be thinking about, and strengthen the stuff they should be. Help them grow each day. Amen.*

Day 24

The Prosperity Gospel vs. The Social Gospel

"Praise be to the God and Father of our Lord Jesus Christ, who has blessed us in the heavenly realms with every spiritual blessing in Christ."

Ephesians 1:3

"God never promised we would be healthy, financially secure, vindicated, or happy. He promised to never leave us and His grace would be enough to get us through anything."

Recently I posted this on Facebook and Instagram, what I didn't expect was the response to be so colossal. Having a social media ministry, I post several times a day. But this meme went viral, going on to be shared thousands of times. Most were agreeing with the quote, however, a small percentage got very upset. I even had to block one person because they wouldn't stop attacking me. I gently responded a few times, but the idea that God never promised to grant all our wishes like a magic genie made them really mad.

This person attempted to use Scripture to back up God's desire to make everyone rich, instantly healed, and effervescent all day long. Each passage was pulled way out of context. This is the result of the prosperity gospel being preached. It's very enticing.

The blame doesn't lie solely on the prosperity gospel. There's an antithesis preached which is just as bad, the social gospel. I'll get to this in a moment. But first, the prosperity gospel tells us God will make every situation turn around for the better and if it doesn't it's *our* fault. We didn't have enough faith, tithing, obedience, church attendance, or pastoral respect. We weren't "on fire" enough. We didn't "fully sell out."

"If you want to break the curse then stop robbing God! Sow your seed! *Use* your faith!"

"Name it, claim it! It's yours!"

"There's your confirmation from God that it belongs to *you*!"

Although this give-to-get, butter-God-up snake oil is terrible, in my opinion the social gospel might be worse. At least the prosperity gospel is focused on having a positive mental attitude, albeit misaimed. If I was an unbeliever that rah-rah stuff in itself would be very appealing to me.

I want to be perfectly clear: Neither is the gospel.

The social gospel says you're not allowed to have anything nice, "We don't believe in that blab-it-to-grab-it garbage!" It says you can't be comfortable financially, or physically, or emotionally. Martyrism and woe-is-me floods the halls of their churches. There are no boundaries. People-pleasing, codependent behavior, and abuse is rampant. Your church can't be too big, all other churches are against you, and you need to give most of your possessions away if you want to look good. Covenant-mixing theology is foundational and unselfish behaviors will "prove" your holiness. Seminary degrees are more important than being led by the Holy Spirit and you will be attacked with cobra-like strikes if you express how you feel. Deacon boards determine your worth, not God. Pulpits are "protected" by an elite group who are confused about what the Cross has actually accomplished.

False humility is the flapping flag of the social gospel. "Look at how humble they are," others will say, as a person continually talks bad about themselves.

"What a godly man."

"What a *strong* Christian woman."

The Pharisees were masters at this. While constantly trying to appear humble in public, behind closed doors they enjoyed prosperity a whole lot more. Most of our prosperity teaching comes from pulling Old Testament Scripture out of context and slapping the American Dream on it. A person with excellent sales skills up on stage, good looking, gifted communicator, funny, able to pull our heart strings; they sell us a bill of goods and use Bible verses written to Jewish people under the Law to close the deal.

It makes for really good sermons, people clap and shout–people *feel* good–and when you feel good you'll give more money to the church. The formula is simple but the audience is clueless. Myself included for many years.

In context, Israel, the Jews, *they* were informed they'd be rich, healthy, and prosperous *if* they obeyed the Law of Moses (see Deuteronomy 30:9,10). This does not apply to Christians, nor Americans. Our country is not even 250 years old whereas these Scriptures are thousands of years old. We were never given the Law, so we can't copy-paste the words written to the Hebrew people and apply it to getting ourselves out of debt or "expanding" our territory (see Ephesians 2:12).

Yes, God will give us wisdom but not from the Law. We have *no* relationship with the Law. Our only access to anything having to do with our Creator is through the Spirit. It's fine to know the Law, but even gleaning from it is foolish and immature (see Romans 6:14, 7:4, Galatians 2:19, 3:1-3, 1 Corinthians 13:11, 2 Corinthians 3:7-17).

Truthfully, even for the Jews, this was an all-or-nothing deal. The Law, 613 commandments, had to be obeyed perfectly in order to be blessed by God.

They were doomed from the beginning and true Law prosperity would never be achieved. That goal–being prosperous–like today, was meant to get them to lean toward faith in God alone (see Deuteronomy 4:2, Galatians 2:16, 3:10).

This is exactly why Jesus said it would be easier for a camel to fit through the eye of a needle than for a rich man to make it to heaven (see Matthew 19:24). This has nothing to do with us having too much money, as the social gospel preachers will claim. Jesus said this to a devout Law-follower who had been taught all his life to do everything Moses commanded, and if he did, he'd be rich and righteous.

We're not righteous–and we don't enter God's Kingdom–because of the size of our net worth, or lack thereof. Jesus was just asked a Law-based question so He gave a Law-based answer.

"You gotta put God first and *truly* surrender!" is wrong and small thinking. We Christians haven't just put God first, we've become one spirit with Him. Further, there's no need to surrender to someone who's loving us (see 1 Corinthians 6:17, John 3:16).

The same applies to the passage in which Christ said, "What good would it be to gain the whole world, yet lose your soul?" (See Matthew 16:26). This was before the Cross, and the disciples, who were under the Law, they were being taught the true cost of placing their faith in Him. Too much financial success was not the frame of reference.

Mosaic Law prosperity falls flat when we look at how a person is rich after coming to faith in Christ:

"Praise be to the God and Father of our Lord Jesus Christ, who <u>has blessed us</u> in the heavenly realms with <u>every spiritual blessing</u> in Christ."
(Ephesians 1:3)

Spiritually. We are blessed *spiritually*. Paul, who had tasted both feast and famine, contentment in Christ *in* him was his strength (see Philippians

4:11-13,19). Christians are like Warren Buffett when it comes to being blessed in our spirits. Why? Because we house the Spirit of Jesus Christ, the Son of God! (See 1 Corinthians 6:19).

Anytime Jesus referred to abundance, or life, or having what we need, He was talking about Himself, His very Spirit. How much more wealthy can a person be than to have God Almighty inside of them?

If God fixed everything instantly, healed everyone at our asking, made us all financially filthy rich, and nothing bad ever happened, what would be the need for heaven? What would be the need for a new physical body? What would be the need for faith in Christ at all or any relationship with our Creator? We would need football stadiums for churches because everyone would be there for stuff. Not Jesus, but just *stuff*.

Can God heal people? Yes. Can He cause a person to become rich? Yes. Can He vindicate us in front of others? Absolutely. There are many stories in Scripture to back this up, but for Christians, these *things* are not the authentic focus of our faith. These *things* may or may not happen, so we don't worry about them. We pray, trust, and hope, but we *know* that we have *all* we need by way of God's grace, Christ's Spirit within.

We *have been* blessed with every spiritual blessing!

For many years I followed prosperity preachers, mainly because I just didn't know any better. Motivational speaking mixed in with Jesus? Count me in! This was how I thought because of my immaturity. Although I felt really good after a sermon–motivated to achieve my dreams and God backing me up–it was all vapors. There's no substance in prosperity preaching. Why not? Because the focus isn't on Jesus Christ. It's on *more*.

Jesus came to give us rest, but there's no true rest in prosperity preaching. Expansion is their obsession. We are taught to reach for the dangling carrot of "being as successful as the pastor," but we can't all be pastors so how is this possible? What if we just have a normal life?

If you don't like what they have to say, leave. You're a drop in the bucket. No, the pastor isn't going to return your email, he's too busy. But you can sign up for a hand-shaking event in three weeks. Their bodyguard will be there too, so you behave, of course.

Prosperity preaching is accessed through a revolving door of emotionalism. I'm all for emotions, but we have to mature into realizing emotions are not the foundation of our faith. Our foundation is in Jesus and we have Him in full as believers from the moment of salvation. There's no need to whine and beg God for what we already have, or *who* we already have. You can't get "more" of God, no matter how many songs you sing about it.

The Holy Spirit won't allow prosperity preaching to sit well with us for very long. For a time? Sure, but not permanently. We don't need to attack prosperity preachers or even be sarcastic about them. We need to treat them with love and respect. We need to express the truth, gently, not slander their names. They could very well be saved, just confused, as we all are at times. We must show them grace. We must understand that God can *use* error to save people and to get them to a better place in their lives.

Paul said the same:

> "Some indeed preach Christ from envy and rivalry, but others from good will. The latter do it out of love, knowing that I am put here for the defense of the gospel. The former proclaim Christ out of selfish ambition, not sincerely but thinking to afflict me in my imprisonment. What then? Only that in every way, whether in pretense or in truth, Christ is proclaimed, and in that I rejoice." (Philippians 1:15-18)

Paul didn't care if Jesus was being preached about by selfish and competitive people in a pretentious way, as long as Christ was proclaimed. Another Bible translation says, "as long as Christ is preached."

The paper-thin prosperity stuff never really got to the root of my issues. I needed to learn my identity and grow in Christ, not just attend an "amazing service" with lights and fog. Don't get me wrong, I liked the lights and fog, I enjoyed the creativity. It was first-class all the way and it helped me *feel* better. But I became addicted to "needing" church and wanting the autograph, notoriety, and approval of celebrity pastors. I was wrong. I was immature. I love them to this day, but it was time to move on.

When I was still stooped in the prosperity stuff, one thing I noticed was that the social gospel always attacked the prosperity gospel. These people *hated* all prosperity preachers. Yes, hated. Large churches were treated as if they were nasty nightclubs. If you were a "true" Christian you'd sit down, shut up, be stiff as a board, and God forbid you have a concert-style worship service.

They spout, "God is not here to entertain you!" and no, not necessarily. But He's also not here to make people fall asleep in the pews.

If you dressed nice, had a nice home, or if you had a nice car, you're just trying to look better than others. Therefore you *better* purchase the shanty house, dress like you just got off the Oregon Trail, and buy the brown beater. Pastor will call you out in his sermon if you refuse. And don't you *dare* try to have any type of ministry apart from the church's approval.

The social gospel is preached by pastors who simply don't understand the struggles of 99% of the population. They live in a religious bubble and can't relate at all to what we deal with; and if they do struggle, they lie about it, sweeping mishaps under the rug which would actually make them relatable. They always use themselves as their best example of holiness, not Jesus. Bomb-shelters which protect their patrons from the world is more of what their church is about. We disgust them even though their own families mess up and we all know about it.

You'll get kicked out for even *asking* certain things, "How dare you question Pastor!"

They don't really want to deal with you unless you're "acting" like a Christian. They'll stroll by you in Walmart, look you in the face, say nothing, and keep walking. They believe passive-aggressiveness or the silent treatment should straighten you out.

They just want to have *church* and they want *you* to be sure you commit every waking moment to *their* church, *then* they'll be friendly with you. You're a backslider and you've lost your salvation and/or fellowship if you don't do what they say. *They* come from holiness and their family has *always* been doing stuff for God. Catch up, if you'd like to try.

Jesus? Oh yeah, Jesus. They'll bring Him up occasionally, but just like *only* "dreaming big" is the center of the prosperity message, church, church, church, church, churrrrrrrrrrrch is their main focus. Don't pick on the church, don't stop coming to church, or Jesus will getcha.

Both, the prosperity and social gospels are wrong. *Neither* are the gospel. The gospel is the gospel of grace. That's what Paul called it in Acts 20:24. The gospel is not about how much worldly success you can achieve, nor is it about the exact opposite. It's about God's grace. Paul wasn't hung up on how much money he could earn, but at the same time, he wasn't focused on being a patsy. God's grace was always his calling card:

> *"But by <u>the grace of God</u> I am what I am, and <u>his grace</u> to me was not without effect. No, I worked harder than all of them—yet not I, but <u>the grace of God that was with me</u>." (1 Corinthians 15:10)*

> *But he said to me, "<u>My grace is sufficient for you</u>, for my power is made perfect in weakness." Therefore I will boast all the more gladly about my weaknesses, so that Christ's power may rest on me.*
> *(2 Corinthians 12:9)*

"For it is <u>by grace</u> you have been saved, through faith–and this is not from yourselves, it is the gift of God–not by works, so that no one can boast."
(Ephesians 2:8,9)

"It is good for our hearts to be strengthened <u>by grace</u>"
(See Hebrews 13:9)

It's not official that Paul wrote Hebrews, the last passage from above, but even in that book which was written to the legalistic Jews, grace was the focus (see Hebrews 10:29). Jesus Christ *is* grace. We can replace the word Jesus with grace, and grace with Jesus, all throughout the Bible and the same context would be the result!

So today, my friends, know this: The gospel is the gospel of Jesus Christ. There are many Christians all throughout the world who live in poverty, they're sick, shunned socially, and ostracized from their families. They're not happy. They have joy, but not happiness. These people have prayed countless times and begged God for change, yet their situation remains. It's not their fault. It's not because of sin or lack of faith. It's not because they didn't tithe on their birthday money. In some countries, many Christians don't even know how old they are or the day of their birth. The *fault* is the fact that we live in a fallen world, we have flawed DNA, and unregenerate people along with the enemy's army runs rampant. This is not our permanent home. Rich, poor, or in-between, healthy as an ox or on our deathbed, well-fed or hungry, we have all we'll ever need in Jesus. His grace is enough.

A prayer for you: *Heavenly Father, thank you so much for teaching me about the value of your grace. This truth has set me free in my mind in so many ways. Your amazing grace is the world's answer for every problem. Right now, I lift up all who are reading this, directly to you. So many of them are confused because of certain styles of teaching. Thankfully, your Spirit is the ultimate Teacher and you'll guide them into all truth, gently, and with grace. We thank you for your Spirit of counsel. In Jesus' name, amen.*

Day 25

The Truth About Holy Communion

"Do this in remembrance of me." ~*Jesus*

See Luke 22:19

E motional music is playing softly, the lights are dimmed and Pastor speaks, "If you have sin in your life let this cup pass from you and do not partake in the bread. If you are a child, and know not what salvation is, do not partake in this holy communion. But, if you find yourself worthy of no judgment, please, join us in consuming the body and blood of Jesus Christ our Lord."

Communion. Oh my goodness how it's been slaughtered by today's church. What was meant to be a celebration and reminder of Jesus bringing in the New Covenant, has been massacred. By who? By those who find *themselves* worthy–by their own standards. To them, unless you've performed properly and repented well enough, you can't take communion. Some are even claiming we're ingesting Jesus' *literal* blood and body into ours. I'm not joking.

Even more diabolical, some groups claim if communion is consumed a person will receive physical healing. And I gotta say, yes, sometimes miracles happen after communion is taken, but Christ is not involved. These are miracles from the devil to make us think communion caused the miracle. Jesus mentioned the same type of miracles in Matthew 7:21-23 to the unbelievers who were focused on their works. God does not perform miracles because we eat and drink, but because He loves us, and because He wants those who witness the miracles to believe in Jesus (see John 3:16, 10:38, 14:11).

I try to keep an even keel and be sensitive about the subjects I write about, but it's sickening when I think about what's happened to communion. The twisting of 1 Corinthians 11, the contorting of Luke 22, Matthew 26, and Mark 14–it's all wrong.

Like water baptism–an event which achieves nothing but reminds us of something wonderful–drinking grape juice and eating a piece of a saltine cracker has shipwrecked the faith of many. Some denominations use wafers, some dip the bread *in* the juice, some stand in line and some pass trays. But these can all be turned into demonic details when the *reason* is wrong.

"God! I'm so sorry! I *know* I'm not on the level I should be so I won't eat or drink!"

I've been there. Tears and snot coming from my face as my head hung low. Heavy remorse for the entire church to see. Communion reminded me of *my* sin–and as a believer, this was never its intent. For those who actually claimed to have no sin in their lives, it was always a great day. They got to shine bright in front of us terrible Christians. Communion made everyone aware of *their* "spotless" lives. No awareness of Jesus, not His body, not His blood–but them.

Communion was specifically reserved for those who didn't need Jesus.

Now that I understand communion has always been meant to be done in remembrance of Him–not my sin or ability to not sin–I fear for their salvation. Are these people *not* saved because of this immature behavior and thinking? I doubt it. Just like me, I have wrong thoughts and choices too, and I'm still saved. If they've ever believed Jesus has forgiven them, they're secure, just confused due to their church's tradition.

At the Last Supper, Jesus said to do this in remembrance of *Him*, not in remembrance of ourselves (see Luke 22:19). This is enough for me to buck tradition and stand up to those who push a quasi, sin-focused communionism on me and others—respectfully of course. As my friend Andrew Farley says, "We must be anchored, not angered."

Let's take a step back and establish why there even *is* a Lord's Supper, what many call holy communion. The Jews used the blood of animals to *remind* them of their sins once a year at the Day of Atonement (see Hebrews 10:1-4). Each time they broke *one* of 613 commandments given by God through Moses, they *remembered* how poorly *they* performed as they handed off the animal to the Levitical priest. At the temple, that priest would take the sacrifice behind the curtain, kill it on the altar, and present the blood to God for that individual's transgressions of the Law (see Hebrews 9:7).

That animal *cost* the Jewish person money and time—and REMEMBERING OF THEIR SINS—as they made this trip once a year.

This was *their* sacrifice given *to* God for their sins. This didn't make them holy, but forgiven. Only God was holy up until Pentecost. Now believers are holy too, just like God, because of the *bloody* death and resurrection of perfect Jesus (see Hebrews 6:19,20, 7:25, 10:10,14,20,21, 2 Corinthians 5:21).

The blood of animals was the only way a Jewish person could receive forgiveness (see Hebrews 9:22). Not confessing to a priest, not repenting of sins, not saying sorry, not by forgiving others, but blood offered up, annually. This is why the Sermon on the Mount upset so many Law-following legalists. Jesus upped the ante against their self-made perfection. Further, blood did not take away sins, but atoned for, or *covered* sins, until they walked down the stairs from the temple and broke another Mosaic command. Immediately their sin tally began to add up, then they'd have to make *another* trip, year after year after year (see Hebrews 10:1-4).

> Side note: These sins were left unpunished until Christ came because all sins require a death by the person committing them–every sin, from gossip to murder. They were forgiven by the animal blood but not *paid for* by death. It was only by the individual's faith were they justified with God. This should answer the questions of, "How were non-Jews saved before the Cross, and even the Jews before Jesus?" Jesus' blood payment–His death–goes forward and backwards because He isn't bound by our notion of time (see Romans 1:29-31, 3:25, 4:3, 6:23, Galatians 2:16, 3:11, James 2:23, Hebrews 11:13, 2 Peter 3:8, John 8:58, Revelation 13:8).

The Jews knew that only animal blood given annually could forgive them with God, yet Christ the Messiah came along and eliminated this! He made it to where they didn't have to make this annual trek any longer! His blood wouldn't *cover* sins, as the animals' did, but banish them *once* and for all time by *one* sacrifice–Himself! The blood of the Son of God would replace the blood of animals forever! (See Hebrews 10:5-14).

The Last Supper signifies this event.

These Jews sitting around Jesus knew how important this final meal was but only *after* Jesus came back to life! As they passed around the bread and wine, they had no clue this would be a celebration, a remembrance! They were still in the dark because Christ had not yet offered Himself up!

But they would, oh…they would. I could just see their faces when the epiphany hit them long after the Last Supper. Remembering Him, as they ate and drank together, understanding the effect which would happen for all who would ever believe:

COMPLETE FORGIVENESS FOREVER, BY GRACE, THROUGH FAITH.

NO MORE BLOOD SACRIFICES.

ACCESS TO THE NEW COVENANT.

The question I had for so long was, "How can a person be completely forgiven forever if they still sin?"

The answer changed my view of people, myself, and life, and it came from the truth of the New Covenant:

> *Only blood forgives and Jesus will never offer up His blood again. He finished the world's sin problem once and for all time and now it's our job to believe in His achievement, once.*

For the Jews, animal blood reminded them of their sins. For us Christians, Jesus' blood reminds us of our righteousness. This is the true meaning of communion. Communion is meant to bring us to remembrance of our complete forgiveness, the New Covenant (see Luke 22:19,20).

So where have we fallen off course? As with most instances the blame lies on poor interpretation of Scripture and, "How my parents did it." Tradition. Tradition does not equal truth, it simply means it's old. Islam is old too, and it's a cancerous, demonic plague, sweeping our planet founded by a murderous pedophile who saw demons and therefore created a cult. I'm not saying all Muslims are bad people, of course not. And we should love and respect them. There are countless, caring individuals who are confused because of their traditions, Christians included. What I *am* saying is this particular *religion* is from hell—as is all religions not based on Christ. When you get to the deepest roots of Islam it's easy to see Satan is the author. Research it back to the beginning for proof. Research *all* religions back to their beginning for proof of fallibility. Only the God of the Bible has no beginning.

In 1 Corinthians 11:17-34, what many churches are using as instruction to take communion, we should *not* be doing so. Why? Because such is not the context. Paul is correcting the church, not giving doctrine. The Corinthians, who were prone to gluttony and debauchery, their immature behavior had spilled over into the partaking of the Lord's Supper. Paul called it "an unworthy manner" (see 1 Corinthians 11:27).

How was it unworthy? Was it because they had sin in their lives? No. If that were the case they'd never have the Supper–no Christian ever would. It was two primary reasons:

1. They were eating all the bread and drinking all the wine while not waiting for others to get there. This caused many to become sick and drunk. Some even died due to their alcoholism and overeating.
2. They were judging *each other* harshly and creating factions because of this poor behavior.

Back then, communion wasn't like it is today. It was a full meal. While we get a thimble of juice and corner of a cracker, for some, this was the best meal they'd get all week. They looked forward to it, even depending on it, but rude people were showing up early and binging while not waiting on others. This is why Paul said, "If you're that hungry eat at home so you don't get judged by others for eating all the food" (see 1 Corinthians 11:34).

In the middle of this rebuke, Paul reminds them of the whole reason they *have* communion:

The Lord Jesus, on the night he was betrayed, took bread, and when he

had given thanks, he broke it and said, "This is my body, which is for you;
do this in remembrance of me." In the same way, after supper he took the
cup, saying, "This cup is the new covenant in my blood; do this, whenever
you drink it, in remembrance of me." (See 1 Corinthians 11:23-25)

In remembrance of me, in remembrance of me. Do you see it, friend?

Paul, a formerly devout Jew, he understood how God forgives. He knew
that what goes *into* a person's body has nothing to do with God's judgment.
The judgment he was talking about in this section of Scripture was the church
judging *each other* for abusing the Lord's Supper.

"You jerk! You didn't leave me anything to eat or drink!"

In fact, Paul educated the church in Colossae on this very thing:

"Therefore do not let anyone judge you by what you eat or drink, or with
regard to a religious festival, a New Moon celebration or a Sabbath day."
(Colossians 2:16)

When we rightly divide the Word, he's clearly *not* saying God will judge
us harshly if we partake in the Lord's Supper because of sin. We all sin as
Christians, a lot, and the blood of Jesus has already taken those sins away (see
John 1:29, 1 John 3:5).

So eat. Drink. Remember the New Covenant, like Jesus said.

If I could shout this from the rooftops I would:

1 CORINTHIANS 11:17-34 IS ABOUT MANNERS!

"Have some scruples, would you? Stop with the gluttony and eat at home.
Stop passing out during communion because you drank all the wine and your
stomachs hurt. Stop judging each other and love as Christ has loved you.

Come together, remember Jesus, and celebrate in a worthy manner. Have some order."

Now *this* was Paul's emphasis.

There's also a *single* passage in the previous chapter, 1 Corinthians 10, which states:

> *"You cannot drink the cup of the Lord and the cup of demons; you cannot partake of the table of the Lord and the table of demons."*
> *(1 Corinthians 10:21).*

Many legalists will use this as a weapon against their congregations' mishaps. But in context, Paul is advising the church to not participate in offerings which are made to demons. Read from verse 14 down and you'll see this has nothing to do with our sins, as Christians, nor the Lord's Supper.

So today, my friends, know this: Communion isn't about remembering our sins, it's about remembering Christ's sacrifice *for* our sins. It's a celebration! Communion is meant to remind us of our righteousness and the New Covenant! Partake! Enjoy! Remember what Jesus has done *for* you and *to* you *through* His body and blood!

A prayer for you: *Dad, thank you for teaching me the truth about communion. By understanding how powerful Jesus' blood is, and how He finished my sin issue on the Cross, I'm free to remember this at any time—even in church. Right now, I lift up all who are reading this, directly to you. So many of these dear people have felt the pressure of communion guilt on Sundays. Ease their minds in knowing that communion is all*

about remembering Jesus, not their sins. Give them a clear conscience and refocus their thoughts. Children and unbelievers should be able to join us in communion too, as this celebration might cause them to believe. Teach us more about your grace, about Jesus, about ourselves, and the freedom we have. In His name, amen.

Day 26

Is the King James Bible the Best Version?

"In the beginning was the Word, and the
Word was with God, and the Word was God.
He was with God in the beginning."

John 1:1,2

Another person has died and stands before Jesus Christ.
"Oh it's so good to be here!" they yell and run toward Him.

"Stop." The Son of God puts out His hand, not letting them get any closer.

"Wait. Why?"

"I never knew you." Christ replies.

Confused, they begin pleading their case.

"But I had a seminary degree...I was the pastor of a church...Jesus, I fought for you! I was committed to you! I had more works than anyone I knew! I helped people achieve their dreams by what I taught! I even spoke in tongues!"

"I'm sorry. I never knew you. Yes, you told people you knew me as you talked *about* me, but we never had a personal relationship. You never believed me. You only believed in what you did *for* me."

"No! Please! I followed you better than anyone! I baptized hundreds! I repented every single time I sinned! I confessed *all* my sins *all* the time! I even visited the Holy Land! Jesus, I *never* missed a chance to let people know about how hot and torturous hell is! I preached repentance *and* faith—together! I pointed out all the idols in everyone's life and set a wonderful example of conservatism! I *showed* my entire congregation how to live! I even put those nasty sinners in their place as I preached from the one true word of God, King James only!"

"I'm so sorry. I never knew you, and you never knew me. Goodbye."

On average, two people die each second. Around 50 people will stand in front of Christ before you finish reading this paragraph. For those who have believed in Him for forgiveness they will get to enter into eternity with Him. For those who haven't, they will not. What's really sad is a lot of devout church-going folks will be turned away. They placed all their eggs into their own basket and not in Jesus Christ's.

"I" is their reasoning for being allowed into heaven rather than "He." That won't work for God.

Perhaps the most tragic are those who have placed their faith in a book called the Bible in lieu of Christ Himself. I don't want to be misunderstood. The Bible is an extremely valuable piece of literature, but even *that* statement upsets those who praise biblical sacred writings above Jesus. By their own stubbornness, they simply cannot fathom God being bigger than words on a page. Or, that God is *older* than words on a page.

"We gotta have God's word!" they'll shout. "And it has to be the King James! Who could possibly know Him if we don't study the most *authentic* holy word?!"

These individuals believe *without* being able to read the KJV in black and white, and red in some versions, the world couldn't possibly understand who our Creator is. When someone asks them about Jesus they talk about their Bible and *not* Jesus. That, or they talk about a pastor who preaches from the King James Bible but fail to mention a word about *who* saved them.

"You don't know what you're talking about! I would reach out to wise counsel if I were you! You'd do well to find a pastor who knows the King James and he will steer you right! Be careful!"

These people won't be saved if they never believed Jesus. I'm not grouping them all together and saying they're *not* saved, but many have believed a book *instead* of Jesus. There's a huge difference.

Muslims worship their religious book on the same level as their god. They literally see the Quran as we see Christ. You could be killed for destroying it when Islam is walked out in its purest form based on the words *in* the Quran. The word Islam means *submission*. It does not mean peace. For Christians, this cultish behavior of book worshiping is no more prevalent with any version of the Bible than with the King James translation. I've never seen anything like it with any other version.

Here are some common phrases I've had spout at me over the years:

"1611 or you ain't going to heaven!"

"I'm a *true* Bible believing Christian! King James only!"

"You need to be quoting from the King James or else you're sending people to hell! False prophet!"

"Blood will be on *your* hands for changing the word of God! That's exactly what you're doing when you don't quote from the King James!"

"Don't add to God's word or take away from it! You've been warned!"

"Well my Bible says *this* because it's the King James Version so it's right!"

"Nope! False teacher! You gotta have the *Authorized* King James!"

"You're only a Christian *if* you've believed in the KJV!"

King Jamesism infects many people. Why is this? The Bible wasn't even compiled into an actual book until 400 years after Christ, and King James' translation wasn't complete until 1,200 years after that. So how are we going to place all our faith into an English king who lived 1,600 years after Jesus, 3,000 miles away from the area Jesus lived, in text written in Early Modern English, yet, the original biblical manuscripts were written in Hebrew, Aramaic, and then Greek?

Do you see it?

Further, rumor has it King James wasn't a Christian but had the Bible translated so he could become famous. It's also scuttlebutt that he struggled with homosexuality. Not that this sinful tendency would mean he wasn't a Christian, but just to give some background on him to those who fall at the feet of King James Only.

So if not King James, which version of the Bible is the most accurate? Which one is 100% perfect? The answer is simple: *Only the original manuscripts from the hands of the authors, not any single Bible.*

The printing press wasn't invented until the 1400's. Before this, woodblock printing was used, and from the time of Jesus–and earlier–people known as *scribes* would make copies of literature by hand. Scribes made transcripts of the original biblical manuscripts. Then another scribe after that scribe. Then another scribe after him. Then another. Handwritten copies of copies, of copies, of copies. This was the only way to mass-produce Scripture.

As the decades and centuries went on, sometimes scribes would make mistakes in their transcripts. Not that the first manuscript was wrong, but them *copying* it was, and then the next scribe making a copy of the *mistake* was. Like the telephone game–only with written words–the older the transcripts of the pages of the Bible, the more accurate.

These are called *earlier transcripts.*

Since 1611, when King James had the Bible translated into English, earlier transcripts of Scripture have been found, therefore replacing subsequent text.

This is why King James' Bible is not the Holy Grail of Literature. It's good, but not perfect. It has flaws in the translated text just like every Bible does.

This truth should cause the body of Christ to stop with the faction of King James Only. We must repent of making a law out of translations and allow the Spirit to teach us from within.

Some people become furious in church, or walk out, all because the words on the pastor's screen don't match their King James perfectly. Others want a word-by-word translation but a "word level" from Greek to English will read in a chopped up manner. Certain Greek words cannot be expressed in English.

For example, Eskimos have about 50 different words for snow. We have *one* word. For the Bible, there are Greek words in which we English speakers have the same unpacking issue. Now apply this to translating Scripture in *any* language, let alone English, with approximately 800,000 words. Scholars have done their best but it's impossible to have scalpel precision. This is why we can't get mad when people read from different English translations. We all need to chill.

What's more is, if you translate Greek into a *phrase* level, rather than a word level, it's even more difficult because we don't have an English equivalent for certain Greek phrases.

For the scribes–the ones down the line making copies of the Bible–first, they were *not* writing in English. Second, they sometimes made mistakes. They were human just like you and me. However, that doesn't mean the Spirit who inspired the *first* writings made mistakes. That same Spirit–God's Spirit–guides each Bible reader today! The Holy Spirit is older than any written word! He is eternal!

Through *His* guidance many who read the Bible will believe Him, yet others will refuse. For them, no matter how much they read or memorize they'll never be born again by their own choosing. They don't think they need to be forgiven and their works are saving them. They sure can quote Scripture verbatim, especially from the King James, but Jesus does not know them.

Juxtapose, countless Christians will never read a single word in the Bible yet they'll be welcomed into heaven with open arms. They trusted Jesus to forgive them of their sins, once, and they knew their greatest works were like filthy rags in comparison to Christ's.

Disturbingly, some *inaccurate* text translations have had catastrophic consequences. In one version of the Bible the words *the flesh* were changed to *sinful nature.* Yet in the original manuscripts the words *the flesh* didn't mean sinful and didn't mean nature. It also didn't mean our physical flesh. It means *the flesh.* That's it.

These two words together is like an indescribable English word for a version of *snow* for Eskimos. Our language can't express it with pinpoint accuracy. It doesn't exist in our native tongue. Therefore, we need to just let it be and allow the Holy Spirit to extract the context in unspoken ways.

But in an effort to do what only the Spirit could, we translated the flesh into something it's not. We changed it, trying to make it more understandable, yet it did not work! Instead, this caused a multitude of Christians to believe a lie about themselves! That we have two natures and we're at battle with our body! No way! Oh how the devil loved this! Friend, the flesh is *not* us!

The publishers have since changed sinful nature back to the flesh after much advice. But as you can see, this minor English tweak–IN THE INFALLIBLE BIBLE–caused a myriad of God's reborn children to think they have a sinful nature and that their physical bodies are sinful too. Wrong.

Poor interpretation of a foreign language is to blame. Only *unbelievers* have a sinful nature, not us. We have God's nature (see 2 Peter 1:4). Our bodies aren't sinful either but beautiful and amazing instruments. They are tools which can be used in any way, righteously or sinfully, by what we decide on a moment by moment basis. But our flesh isn't sinful. Our flesh is holy, blameless, and God's idea. *The* flesh isn't, but *our* flesh is (see Genesis 1:27, 1 Thessalonians 5:23).

For years, what I didn't understand was that God's Spirit doesn't speak to me in King James English. There's an entire world out there and the majority of humanity does not use *thee, thou, shalt, cometh, speaketh, brethren,* so on and so forth. I mean no disrespect if you prefer to talk or read in this manner, but God's Holy Spirit speaks to each *human's* spirit in a language they can understand.

Do you think we'll all be speaking King James English in heaven? I don't think we will, so we must stop pounding this version into the heads of so many with militant force.

Those who struggle with legalism have been taught the KJV or the New KJV is the only Bible we should read, which is incorrect. If we think about the King James Only mantra even deeper, what did Christians do before it was available—or unbelievers for that matter? If we digress even *further* what did the early church do for the first 400 years without a canonized Bible at all? They were lucky to have one transcript of one letter, and 70% were illiterate.

This proves a relationship with God has always been about the Spirit, not anything physical. Is this making sense? If legalistic demons pester a person over "the power of *the word*" then it's probably got their mind spinning. But the truth will set you free!

The truth is the Word always *has* been and always *will* be! The Word is a person not a book! The Word is Jesus! Jesus is everything God wanted to say to us from the beginning of time! The Bible simply records those words and events! Just look at this!

> *"In the beginning was the Word, and the Word was with God, and the Word was God. He was with God in the beginning." (John 1:1,2)*

The beginning is Creation! Genesis chapter one! This was the start of anything physically existing! John is about to say the Word became flesh! JESUS! JESUS IS THE WORD IN HUMAN FORM, NOT A BOOK!

Mike Kapler, a friend of mine and author of *Clash Of The Covenants*, he recently posted on Facebook the same point:

The Word did not become pages published in a book, the Word has always been in existence and He became flesh. Grace and truth is realized through Him, not our theology nor our opinions about the pages. You can be filled with a plethora of Bible knowledge and cite verses out of context to infinity and beyond without ever discovering the eternal Source of Life. Scripture doesn't give life, it merely points us to the One who does.

The Source of Life whom Mike mentioned informed the unbelieving Jews of this same thing only *they* were hung up on some Scriptures of the Old Testament. Rather than admit their oracles all pointed to Jesus, they hated Him and His exegesis. Christ rebuked them for their hard hearts:

"You search the Scriptures because you think that <u>in them</u> you have eternal life; and it is they that bear witness about me, yet you refuse to come to me that you may have life." (John 5:39,40)

Today there are hundreds of versions of the Bible, yet there's no life in any Bible. The Bible has been translated into more than 2,000 languages, yet there's no life in any specific language. Life is in faith in Christ alone, by grace. Life is in realizing our need for His forgiveness, one time.

How can we know which version of the Bible to use? If every version has translation flaws, which one is the most accurate? Friend, it's the one you'll read. Don't worry, the true Word, the Spirit of Jesus Christ, He will always guide your heart *as* you read. The stuff that doesn't sit right with you He'll make clear, eventually. If you still don't understand certain passages on this side of heaven, in the twinkling of an eye, when you meet Him face to face you'll grasp it.

Every book in the Bible was inspired by His Spirit as it was written by each human author. God used 40 different people over the course of 1,500 years—all with different styles, temperaments, and personalities. Their written words will help you know more about the character of God and *your* character too, saint. The reality is, if you've believed in Jesus, you already know Him in full in your heart. The Bible simply backs up your supernatural knowledge in words you can read.

In every version there's a consistency. Each translation points to Christ from beginning to end. The Old Testament reveals Creation, the Fall, and our need for a Savior. It records God's broken relationship with Israel. It encapsulates the shadows of Jesus and what only His blood could permanently do. The New Testament reveals the Messiah Himself! It lays out the New Covenant! It teaches us that God is now available to live inside of all who will believe in His Son! Ultimately, it uncovers what will happen when time ends as we know it! We win! We get to live on forever with God in a place that cannot be described in *any* language!

So today, my friends, know this: The most *authentic* version of the Word is Christ in you! He's our true teacher! Trust Him to guide you with His Spirit! Read the book to enforce what you're learning! It's a marvelous resource! It will help you mature in great ways! But always remember that Jesus is the reason the Bible exists. Put your confidence in Him, not simply words on a page, because *He* loves you, those pages do not.

A prayer for you: *Heavenly Father, thank you for your written words. We're so blessed to have the Bible. It's amazing to me how I get to live in this era of technology. I can search words in the Bible at ease and find passages in a snap. But I'm even more thankful for Jesus. He is the real Word. It is His Spirit who guides me as I read. Thank you so much for letting Him live in me. Right now, I lift up all who are reading this, directly to you. Dad, like me, I know a lot of them are having a hard time separating your Spirit from the Bible, but we must begin there. Teach them through your grace that if they never read another sentence from the Bible you love them just the same. You're never disappointed in them, and you live in them—that is, for all who have believed Jesus. And for those who have shunned the Bible because they're afraid of it, or because legalism was shoved down their throat, ease their minds today. You love them deeper than my words can describe, yet your Bible does a masterful job at explaining this. Teach them how to read the Bible in context and with confidence, through your Spirit within. In Jesus' name I pray, amen.*

Day 27

Can Christians Get Divorced?

"Marriage should be honored by all"

See Hebrews 13:4

Does this situation justify a divorce?

"Mom, last night, Dad came into my room and touched me there again. He said he wouldn't do that anymore. Why won't he stop? It hurts. Please do something."

This isn't the first time he's molested his daughter, and this isn't the first time she's come to her mom for help. Yet he continues to sexually abuse her because he knows his wife will never divorce him–because she's not allowed. "The Bible says you can't! It's not adultery!"

He's not a believer but he's memorized Scripture and understands there's no passage on "divorce for molestation." So he rapes his own child repeatedly with no plans to quit all because his spouse's religion won't enforce any healthy boundaries.

Another situation: "I don't know what to do, Grandma. He hit me again. I guess I should've watched what I said and not made him so mad. I'll just keep quiet the next time he's drinking and stay out of his way. I have to submit, that's what the Bible says. So I'll keep serving him. I need to be obedient to God's Word."

The physical abuse and alcoholism has been going on since their second year of marriage. Five years into her vows, she never knew her husband would treat her so badly and use the Bible to back himself up. "Sit down, shut up, and submit! Woman!"

No signs of heavy drinking or abuse happened when they dated, he was very loving. But now, cursing loudly, calling her disgusting names and slamming doors–all in front of the kids–she feels trapped. Each time she considers leaving, her devout church-going grandmother gives the same advice, "You'll never enter into the kingdom of God as an adulterer. That's exactly what you'll be if you divorce him. He's the head of your household so do what he says. It's better you suffer now than to go to hell later. Carry your cross and deal with it."

Another situation: "Pastor, this is the sixth time she's cheated on me. All of her affairs started on social media with so-called friends. I found the messages on Facebook, I saw the Snapchats on her phone while she slept in the middle of the night, I even pulled our phone records. The texts and phone calls to these men were numerous–pages worth. But when I confronted her she became enraged and told me to not be so jealous. She said these are her *friends* and I have no right to control her. Now it's happening again. This is how her cheating always starts out, on her phone. The men flirt and she eats it up. The pain I feel is so deep! I *hurt* knowing she's slept around with no remorse! She's had an excuse each time! She's never even said sorry and I keep forgiving her! It feels as if I have something sitting on my chest! She's had sex with people in our own home and I keep doing what the Bible says–FORGIVING! I don't want to feel this way anymore! She refuses to be faithful to me!"

A committed husband sits in the office of his pastor, sobbing in his own hands. His wife has no respect for boundaries whatsoever, nor does she take her vows as of any importance. She plays the victim on social media while constantly looking for attention. Damaging her husband's reputation quite often, their family is in shambles. She lives with no filter and acts as if she's never heard the word honor before. Picking and choosing what she likes from the Bible to suit her needs, this woman's emotional cheating has led to physical cheating multiple times. But she doesn't care. Her girlfriends and relatives never give any godly advice but encourages her to "be happy" and "Don't worry about what your husband needs."

"God hates divorce," the pastor says. "But, biblically, you *are* allowed to divorce her because of her adultery. I wouldn't take the chance though. There's no guarantee you'll stay saved yourself. After the divorce you might fall out of God's will for your *own* life and be in danger of the fires of hell. Hang in there, lest you fall too."

Another: "Dad, she won't stop spending all we have. The bounced check fees alone are killing me. Our credit cards are maxed, she refuses to work, and I can't seem to catch up. Her shopping, trips, eating out, and giving our money to her family whenever they ask for it is ruining us. She won't even *attempt* to keep our home clean, it's a pigpen. I'd gladly clean it but I don't have time because I'm working so much. She stays up late *every* night watching trash on TV and Netflix–and she's severely addicted to her phone. She won't contribute to our family in any way. She's crushing us Dad, and I'm miserable. I don't know what else to do. I've begged her to go to counseling and I *want* to talk and work things out, but she gives me the silent treatment for months and won't communicate. We haven't even had sex since last year."

Reaching out for wise counsel from his father–who's a deacon at his church so he's supposed to know more–his dad replies, "Son, I'd say you need to get a divorce but I'd hate to see you not make it to heaven. No matter what, the Bible says you can't divorce her unless she commits adultery. The misery you're in is not worse than the misery you'll feel while burning in hell. You don't want to lose your salvation over losing a marriage, do you? Count it all joy and keep storing up your treasures for your next life. You'll get a bigger mansion, too, when you die, for your sacrifice."

... All of these people giving marriage advice are wrong. They might mean well, but they're incorrect, biblically.

There are countless circumstances of marital strife and tragic situations where a spouse just doesn't care anymore. But the threat of becoming a sec-ond-class Christian or banished from heaven completely because of a divorce is a lie from hell. Such is only "true" when we read the Bible from a discom-bobulated perspective. God does not judge us based on our marital status but on our supernatural identity.

However, when Scripture is twisted out of context, there are only two rea-sons to "justify" a divorce: adultery or death.

Let's go over both based on the truth of the New Covenant to prove these are fallacies. The truth always sets us free and error always binds us–in our minds.

Satan has ruined many lives by making people *think* divorce is unpardon-able without adultery or death, but there's no New Covenant law against di-vorce. This is completely absent from all New Testament text when the text is read in the proper context. If this weren't the case then the New Covenant would be more stringent than the Old Covenant. Why? Because even in the Old, divorce was legal *without* adultery or death (see Deuteronomy 24:1-5).

So where are we getting this theology? That divorce is an unforgivable sin without someone cheating or dying? Several places in the New Testament *but only* when Scripture is taken out of context. Satan loves out-of-context biblical explanation. He even tried to pull this card on Christ Himself (see Matthew 4:1-11). But each time he contorted Scripture, Jesus straightened it out contextually. We should do the same.

In Matthew, Mark, Luke, and John, Jesus is asked about divorce and He taught on it too. Each time He was *asked* it was by a legalist who wanted to find an excuse to rid themselves of their wife *or* to trap Jesus in His own words. Each time He *taught* about divorce it was to enforce the impossibly of living according to the Law so the hearer would turn from the Law and repent toward faith in Him alone. Over a dozen times divorce is referenced in these four letters and not once was He teaching a *believer* how to be married or stay married (see chapters: Matthew 5, 19, Mark 10, Luke 16, John 8). New Covenant instruction for Christian marriages can be found in Ephesians 5:21-33 but not before the Cross. The context is completely different.

Therefore, using Jesus' teachings as grounds to stay married if adultery or death has not occurred is wrong. Remember, anytime Jesus was asked a Law-based question He gave a Law-based answer. And when He wanted to bury a legalistic crowd in their own hypocrisy He would teach the true standards of the Law, the very Law they failed at following *perfectly* which is required if a person wants to follow it (see Matthew 5:48, Deuteronomy 4:2). We Christians are not under the Law but under grace (see Romans 6:14, 10:4). So none of these marriage passages in the four gospels are for us. Sting as it might, because of what our relatives and church leaders believe, this is the truth.

Adultery was always the justification behind a Law-lover's excuse to kick their significant other to the curb. This is *so* prevalent in these four books, Covenant-mixing theology is taught in our churches today, ad nauseam. As a result of such terrible teaching, some Christians *want* their spouse to cheat *so that* they can "biblically rationalize" a divorce.

I even watched a Dateline–or 48 Hours episode, not sure which one–where a lady tried to have her husband killed because he *wouldn't* have an affair. She needed a reason to get rid of him so death was the only other option. This woman couldn't bear what a divorce would do to her reputation at church. Her husband's death seemed like a much better alternative. After all, she'd get sympathy rather than rejection.

"I wish you *would* cheat so I could call up my lawyer! Go ahead! You are free to sleep around!" This statement isn't out of the ordinary for some. So, to answer the title of this devotional: Can Christians get divorced? Yes.

"Matt, you're a liar! You're just telling people they can get a divorce whenever they feel like it! How dare you! You're telling people to run away from their problems and never commit! You don't respect marriage!"

Friend, no. That's not my opinion at all. Here's my own personal advice about marriage:

Do everything possible to save it. Do whatever the crisis demands. Feel the pain, and forgive. Feel the pain, and forgive. Feel the pain, and forgive. Never stop doing this. Set boundaries and enforce them with love and respect. Sacrifice your time, sleep, energy, reputation and finances to save your marriage. FIGHT HARD FOR YOUR MARRIAGE! FIGHT! Do everything possible ON YOUR PART to save it. Say sorry when you want to give excuses–THEN DO IT AGAIN, AND AGAIN, AND AGAIN! See their side, their point of view, and their needs as extremely important. Serve them with all your heart. Get counseling. Get more counseling. Get MORE counseling–but make sure it's Christian counseling. Reach out to advocates. Ask for advice. Look for those who have successful marriages and ask them to pray for both you and your spouse. PRAY HARD. THEN, WHEN YOU'RE FINISHED, PRAY HARDER. SCREAM AND CRY AT THE FOOT OF YOUR BED AND BEG GOD FOR HELP.

Fight. FIGHT! Fight FOR your marriage as if your life depends on it! Get counseling for yourself too, without your spouse, repeatedly. Go without sex. Go without respect. Go without validation. Deal with the debilitating loneliness and lean into the comfort of Christ. CRY. Feel your pain. Don't turn to addictions or lovers or porn. Don't post about it, tweet about it, DM or IG. Don't put it on your Story. Just cry. Be sad. It's okay to be sad. Never numb your sadness or pain—feel it, and ask God for solace. Tell your spouse how much you love them and how you want to save your marriage. Tell them how important they are to you. Educate them, kindly, on the healthy changes which must be made, but that you're still there for them and you care. If you lose your cool forgive yourself and start over the next day. Keep your kids out of this completely. Do NOT talk to your kids about your marriage problems, ever, on any level. Honor your spouse whenever you mention them in front of your kids. Don't let your kids talk bad about your spouse. Don't act passive-aggressive toward your spouse in front of your kids. DON'T BE SARCASTIC ABOUT YOUR SPOUSE TO YOUR KIDS. Watch your body language and keep them secure. Don't believe the names your spouse calls you. Don't scramble trying to defend yourself to the people they lie to about you. Overcome evil with good and hateful remarks with love. Don't get even. Don't think God is getting even FOR you. He loves them too. Their attitude toward you doesn't mean they are no longer saved. Tell them you don't want a divorce, repeatedly. Repeatedly. Repeatedly. Repeatedly. Say I love you. Get a legal separation if you have to, but don't file just yet. Give it time. BE KIND. HOLD YOUR TONGUE. BE PATIENT. When you're tired, don't talk or text about anything serious, go to bed. Be cordial to those who are trying to rip your marriage apart. Tell your spouse a divorce is NOT what you want, but healthy changes must be made. Don't tell them what to do, tell them what YOUR boundaries are. Boundaries are not ultimatums. They are see-through fences, not walls.

They have gates which are meant to let people in, and out, and also for taking out our own trash. Tell your spouse how much you love them every day, even if they go months without saying it back. DON'T get a divorce if you can help it. As far as it depends on YOU fight tooth and nail for your marriage and trust God with your actions and attitudes.

But sometimes, even after your best efforts, it just doesn't work out. Sometimes, even after you've done everything you possibly *could* do, they still leave, or they still refused to make the healthy changes your family needed... so you had no other choice.

Friend, life doesn't end in those ashes. Lamenting won't last forever and Jesus Christ is *still* there, with you. He feels your pain on a deeper level than even you do—He knows. He *knows* (see John 11:33-35). He was there the entire time and He held you every moment. He saw your effort. He saw the changes *you* made to save your marriage. He saw you stand up to unacceptable behavior properly, with gentleness and respect. He saw you mature. He saw you grow. His arms were wrapped around you every lonely night. You were never really alone... ever.

Just give it time. Just give it truth. Life will go on and happiness will happen again. God will use this pain for a greater good, somehow, someway. Using pain for purpose is His specialty. Just look at the Cross. The darkest day in history turned out to be the brightest.

He didn't cause this pain, but He'll use it.

Your heartache and tears will not be wasted.

Sadly, in Romans 7, some grace-confused Christians see verses 1-3 as a law in which we are bound to our spouse until they die. According to their incorrect interpretation, if divorce happens and our ex-spouse is still alive, we're adulterers until they croak. Let's clear this up to ease your mind. Here's the Scripture:

"Do you not know, brothers and sisters—for I am speaking to those who know the Law—that the Law has authority over someone only as long as that person lives? For example, by law a married woman is bound to her husband as long as he is alive, but if her husband dies, she is released from the law that binds her to him. So then, if she has sexual relations with another man while her husband is still alive, she is called an adulteress. But if her husband dies, she is released from that law and is not an adulteress if she marries another man." (Romans 7:1-3)

THIS HAS NOTHING TO DO WITH MARRIAGE ADVICE. If I could type that sentence in a larger font I would. The two words I've underlined—*For example*—gives the context. If an example is being used we must look to what the topic is and not solely the example. What's the topic? Paul is explaining to the Jews their *relationship* with the Mosaic Law. This is obviously not written to Christians because we've never had a relationship with the Law but only with Christ.

Let's highlight the parts of Romans 7:1-3 to prove this:

1. **"for I am speaking to those who know the Law"** – who knew the Law? Only the Jews, not us Gentiles.
2. **"the Law has authority over someone only as long as they live"** – so the Law is the context, not marriage.
3. **"a married woman is bound to her husband as long as he is alive, but if her husband dies, she is released from the law that binds her to him"** – He's explaining a Jewish person's link to the Law. They must die *to* the Law so they can be joined *to* Christ. This is backed up in verse four, which I'll get to shortly, but look at it this way: I can't marry someone else, legally, if I'm still married to my spouse. If they die, or I die, the union is no more. The Jews had to consider themselves dead to the Law so they could join themselves to the Spirit of Jesus.

Sexual relations is mentioned as an example of "intimacy with the Law," juxtapose, "intimacy with Christ." Not literal sex but oneness and being legally bound to. Paul is saying, "Pick one. Be joined to the Law or joined to Jesus. You must divorce the Law if you want to be married to Christ."

Just look at the following passage for context. You'll see this has no instruction for marriage, but instead, it's about a Hebrew person's relationship with the 613 commandments given by Moses, the Law:

> "Therefore, my brethren (anytime Paul says brethren he's referring to his Jewish race), you also were made <u>to die to the Law through the body of Christ, so that you might be joined to another,</u> to Him who was raised from the dead, in order that we might bear fruit for God... But now <u>we have been released from the Law</u> (just like a woman is released from her husband if he dies) having <u>died to that</u> by which we <u>were bound,</u> so that we serve in newness of the Spirit and <u>not</u> in oldness of the letter (the letter is the Law)." (Romans 7:4,6, my notes added)

This section of Scripture should never be used in the context of marital counsel but for teaching people they have no relationship with the Law. They've died to it in order to be *able* to join Christ's Spirit by faith. We are released from the Law *so that* we can be bound to Jesus. Truth be told, unless we're Jewish we were never given the Law to begin with. *But* we can still use it to point out the dirt on an unbeliever's supernatural face if that person thinks they are actually following the Law (see Ephesians 2:12, Matthew 15:24, John 5:39,40, 1 Timothy 1:6-11, Galatians 3:1,2,12).

Jesus won't share you with Moses so you must cut that relationship off. When we "try" to follow any of Moses' commands–ten of which are the Ten Commandments–we are committing adultery, spiritually.

I don't want to be misunderstood. The Law has not died but we've died *to* the Law. It has no authority over us *because* of our faith which joined us to Jesus. I want to stay on track here, but briefly, this is what I mean:

> If you're on trial for a crime but you die during that trial you've died to the law which has the ability to convict you. Therefore that law now has no authority *to* convict you. You're dead. The trial is over. Based on that law you can no longer be found guilty because you've died to its jurisdiction to condemn you for your crime. Now, think about this, when *you* died did the law die? No. It's still there, ready to convict the next person who breaks it who is *under* it. Same with us and the Law of Moses. Our spirits have died to the Law from the moment of our salvation. We were crucified, buried, and rose again, forever connected to Jesus' Spirit (see Romans 6:6-11, Galatians 2:20, 2 Corinthians 5:17-21, Colossians 3:3, 1 Corinthians 6:17).

In Romans 7, that's Paul's point, not scaring divorced people and definitely not creating codependent husbands and wives.

The Bible also says no adulterer will enter the kingdom of heaven in 1 Corinthians 6:9-10, and in Galatians 5:19-21. Many will compound these passages with Romans 7:1-3 by saying, "If your ex-spouse is still alive and you've been remarried, you're an adulterer and so is your new spouse!"

So tell me, if this were the truth, what *should* they do? Should they divorce their new spouse and go back to the previous one? That would mean they'd be divorced *again*. Would this cancel out their second divorce if they go back to their first marriage? And what if the previous spouse doesn't want anything to do with them because they've moved on?

Do you see the stupidity in such a creed?

The truth is, in both 1 Corinthians 6 and Galatians 5–the "not inheriting the kingdom" verses–Paul is referring to the identity of non-believers, not Christians. He's speaking about contrasts of *nature*–not actions and attitudes in order to *identify* someone. Again, context is key and behavior-focused teaching is to blame.

At the end of Galatians 5 he said "against such things there is no law" after comparing a Christian's nature to those who are not of the Spirit. This proves we are not described in the bad-natured list above this verse because we are not under the Law. And if we read the following passage in 1 Corinthians 6, right after Paul's sin-filled laundry list, he's clearly describing their past, not who they now *are*:

> "And that is what some of you <u>were</u>. But you <u>were</u> washed, you <u>were</u> sanctified, you <u>were</u> justified in the name of the Lord Jesus Christ and by the Spirit of our God." (1 Corinthians 6:11)

Past tense. Were, were, were, and were.

"Yeah right, Matt! If they didn't repent of their sins they are still in them!"

No, that's wrong. If this were the case we'd all still be in our sins because we all have sins we've not repented of perfectly. If we say this isn't true, we're lying, therefore we've not repented of lying and no unrepentant sin can enter heaven–according to this falsity. We are saved by repentance of unbelief in Jesus as our Savior. This happens once. We are *not* saved by continual repentance of sinful actions and attitudes. Again, why not? Because we will all go to our grave with unrepentant sinful actions and attitudes. If you say you *don't* have unrepentant sin, I would doubt my salvation if I were you. It sounds as if you've never fully trusted Christ.

The demonic mantra of "You're only forgiven if you repent!" makes no sense at all. It spits on the Cross and says, "Jesus only forgives you of your sins when you stop sinning." Satan *loves* this because it takes our focus off Christ's finished work and puts the emphasis on what *we* stop or start. He'll even make you think it's too *late* to repent of certain sins. The legalists call these sins, *sins of omission*.

"That ship has sailed! It's all your fault! You had your chance! You're doomed! You might as well ignore God because He hates you and is disappointed in everything you do!"

Don't believe these lies.

Changing our immature actions and attitudes is healthy but cannot forgive us anymore than we already are. This would negate the Cross if it weren't true. Repent, yes, every single time you sin, but not to *be* forgiven. Instead, to *be* yourself.

In 1 Corinthians 6 and Galatians 5, Paul is speaking about their spirits—not actions, not attitudes—but who they *were* and what *has* happened. Christians have been taken *out* of sin and placed *into* the Spirit of Jesus Christ (see Romans 6:3-14, 8:9). No Christian is *in* sin because we are *in* Christ. We might be sinning but we aren't *in* sin. Understanding this supernatural epiphany causes us to *act* sinful a whole lot less because we know it's an act.

We are holy. We are blameless. We are righteous. We are children of God (see Colossians 1:22, 2 Corinthians 5:21, John 1:12,13, 1 John 3:1). Sinning will never make sense to us permanently. Just try it out and you'll see. A bottle-rocket of thrills might happen, but after, we realize that short-lived sin-spurt was dumb and unsatisfying.

Let's go over one last passage about divorce.

In 1 Corinthians 7, Paul seems to go back and forth on his view of marriage. In essence, saying, "If you're married, don't seek to get a divorce. If you're unmarried don't seek to get married—but then again, if you can't control your sexual urges, go ahead and get married."

Out of context, this chapter can seem strange, but Paul pens something which is key and explains his wishy-washy writing:

"Nevertheless, each person should live as a believer <u>in whatever situation</u>
the Lord has assigned to them, just as God has called them."
(See 1 Corinthians 7:17)

In whatever situation. Paul is giving advice for living a peaceful life in whatever situation a person is currently in. This is not doctrine for marriage but a kind mentor admonishing the Corinthian church. "Don't seek greener pastures. Be content with your present circumstances. Whatever happens, happens, but be satisfied with where God has placed you."

Paul was always preaching to himself as well. As he traveled relentlessly to teach the gospel, he knew such a dangerous lifestyle would be hard on a wife, so he stayed single. But he knew he was free to marry if he wanted to (see 1 Corinthians 9:5-10). 1 Corinthians 7 is not Paul being nutty about marriage and divorce. His heart is saying, "Think about how your decisions will impact those whom you love, and yourself, based on your surroundings. Then move forward with caution. You are free. Make good choices."

So today, my friends, know this: Approximately 50% of non-Christian marriages end in divorce. Approximately 40% of Christian marriages end in divorce. Does this mean 40% of those who claim to be Christians won't enter heaven? Does this mean they are perpetual adulterers? And if we're free does this mean we should throw up our hands at the drop of a hat and look for a new spouse? No, no, and no. It means *don't find your identity in your marriage but in Christ.* If we're looking to our marriage for identity, when it's threatened or not what we want it to be, we'll fall apart. Our identity is in Christ and nothing else! We are secure! Let your marriage–or your singleness–reflect your security and live in love!

A prayer for you: *Heavenly Father, thank you for giving me your Spirit through Christ. You've completed me. I've learned so much from you and marriage has been a great lesson you've taught. Thank you for MY marriage, and for being with Jennifer and me these past 15 years. Keep guiding us and teaching us more about you, and about ourselves. I'm so grateful for the wife you've given me. Right now, I lift up all who are reading this, directly to you. So many of these dear readers have been divorced and feel like you don't love them anymore. Ease their minds today in knowing you don't love them because of their marriage, or lack-thereof, but because they're your child. What kind of a parent would give up on their children because a marriage didn't work out? Only a bad parent–and YOU are a good, good Father. You never give up on us, no matter what happens in our lives.*

And Dad, for those who are on the brink of a divorce, help them. Maybe they've filed the papers. Maybe they've believed the lies of their ungodly divorced friends or loved ones who hate their spouse–those who never respected their marriage–I'M ASKING FOR A SUPERNATURAL INTERVENTION, RIGHT NOW! Don't let them give up! Because of Christ, they're infused with the strength they need to fight! By your grace, their marriage can be saved! By your grace, new boundaries can be set and wholeness can come! CHANGE CAN HAPPEN! They can leave a legacy for their children and break the cycle of divorce by saying, "I didn't give up. I stuck it out and God came through for us." Teach them more about how to enforce healthy changes! Teach them more about who YOU are! Send new people into their lives–advocates who care for both them and their spouse! REMOVE THE PEOPLE WHO ARE DESTROYING

THEIR FAMILY! Open up the eyes of the spouse who has hardened their soul and won't talk! Save their marriage, God, please. I rebuke Satan from their home and thought life–right now! In the name of JESUS, help them! Keep them together! Teach them both how to love one another and how to forgive just as you've done for them in Christ! In His name I pray–please, USE this difficult time for a greater good. We trust you. We love you. Amen.

Day 28

What's Wrong with Today's Church?

*"And He has qualified us as ministers of a new
covenant, not of the letter but of the Spirit; for
the letter kills, but the Spirit gives life."*

2 Corinthians 3:6

I want to be clear from the get-go: the church is the body of Christ, not a building. After all, Jesus destroyed the need for a building to have access to God. He also replaced the requirement of a human middleman to receive forgiveness, with Himself.

Yes, it's still a healthy thing to gather with other Christians, to love and encourage one another. But the church is you and me, believer. Not once was a church *building* referred to in the New Testament but only *groups* of Christians. However, for this devotional I'll be using the word *church* in the context of our building gatherings. I'd like to point out some unhealthy characteristics of today's churches so we can repent and grow into the full measure of the knowledge of Jesus Christ.

People are leaving churches in droves. According to a recent survey, more than two million have left their church, every year, for the past seven years. 62% of churches either have no growth or their congregations are declining.

What's strange is, on Christmas and Easter our churches are packed. So why not during the rest of the year? The answer is simple: *the message.* The message isn't the gospel. The gospel is good news, not bad news, and it's hard to find good news being preached to us non-Creasters.

Christmas and Easter sermons are normally about the birth and resurrection of Jesus, which is good news. But why can't we hear good news sermons all year long? Because the message is changed the other 50 weeks. We've believed the lie of the enemy, that good news might lead to bad behavior. The reality is, bad behavior is already happening plenty with not-such-good-news preaching.

It's as if many churches think God is naive, or that He baits and switches us, before and after salvation. For them, once you're saved, the good news turns into really bad news. As a result, we get behavior improvement sermons, sin management sermons, "Just be like me, I'm your best example of holiness" sermons, and of course, "Try harder, do better, surrender more!" sermons. None of which is good news.

Churches aren't normally filled to capacity 50 Sundays of the year because many of them turn back into a country club for members only. Volunteer requirements, tithing to be blessed, and pastoral worship replace the simplicity of the gospel. Sometimes you won't hear the name of Jesus an entire teaching, but the pastor will repeatedly talk about how influential they are, or how we need to rebuke the devour by giving until it hurts.

To add insult to injury, many churches want to "keep things balanced" by placing *us* into the Old Covenant while ignoring the New Covenant completely–as if it never happened. This is subtle, but deadly. If microscopic pieces of glass are placed in our food, even though we can't taste the glass because it's so small, ingesting it will eventually harm us in great ways. When the Covenants are mixed the Old Covenant becomes those shards. Most don't realize *what* they're being fed, they think because it's coming from a person on stage it has to be the truth. Unfortunately, Covenant-mixing theology is destroying many lives.

Here are a couple examples of what I mean:

1. **The praise and worship team begs God to "Fill this place with His Spirit."** This is completely Old Covenant. God is not filling any geographical place with His Spirit because *we* are now the place. According to the Old Covenant, God filled the temple with His presence. The Jews called this temple His *house* (see Psalm 27:4). We are now the temples. We are now the house of God, not any building. Both our spirit and our physical body is His abode (see 1 Corinthians 6:17,19). The Holy Spirit *in* us goes into the church building *with* us. We aren't going there to find Him. He's not bound by two-by-fours, bricks, or man-made walls (see Acts 17:24). He's everywhere at all times, and for believers, inside us. There's no need to "call God down into this place" because He's already *in* each believer evenly. The first time this happened was at Pentecost, recorded in Acts 2. This is extremely important because when we *think* we have to keep begging God to fill up the church with His presence we neglect the truth. He always dwells in our presence. Even deeper, in our very being (see Acts 2:4,17, John 12:32, 14:23).

2. **Old Covenant patriarchs and prophets are used as our best examples of righteous behavior.** This can be very confusing because most of them followed the Law of Moses. They *delighted* in the Law, *meditated* on it day and night, and were instructed they'd be healthy and wealthy by doing so (see Psalm 1:1-3, Romans 7:22). What's odd is, although obsessed with the Law, much of the writings in the Old Testament

expressed their infatuation *and* frustration with the commandments *in* the Law. This is not how the New Covenant works. In fact, Jesus put the hypocritical Jewish health-wealth preachers to shame. He said, "What good would it be to gain the whole world yet forfeit your soul?" to those who had grown up being taught the Law's principles (see Matthew 16:26). He said, "It would be more difficult for a camel to fit through the eye of a needle, than for a person who's gotten rich from following the Law to enter heaven" (see Mark 10:25). He also said, "Healthy people don't need a doctor" to the Pharisees, basically calling them sick (see Matthew 9:9-12). On this side of the Cross, Jesus' *Spirit* is our example of holiness and righteous behavior, not Law-followers nor anyone from the Old Testament. It's good to respect and glean from *parts* of their lives, but they longed for what we now have! God's presence in us, guiding us, and keeping us secure forever! We are spiritually rich and healthy! (See Romans 6:14, 10:14, Galatians 3:24,25, 2 Corinthians 3:7-17, Hebrews 11:39,40, Ephesians 1:3).

Easter and Christmas are the open houses to attract new members but if the New Covenant isn't being preached all year long the sermons are of no deep value. The Bible says we are *only* qualified to preach the New Covenant, and nothing else. The New Covenant is complete reconciliation with God through faith in Jesus Christ (see 2 Corinthians 3:6, Ephesians 2:8,9, Romans 5:1). Therefore, if we aren't teaching people about the peace they *have* with God, right now–or *can* have instantly–there's no competency to our message (see 2 Corinthians 3:5). Our churches have got to start preaching the good news *every* time because it's the goodness of God which leads people to change their actions and attitudes (see Romans 2:4).

"Matt, you just want pastors to tickle ears!" one might say. "Our planet is in terrible shape because of ear-tickling sermons!"

Friend, I'm not saying tickle ears, I'm saying preach the good news. There's a huge difference. This planet isn't in bad shape because of the good news being preached but the opposite. In fact, Paul told pastor Titus it's the good news–the grace of God–which will teach people how to live authentically as saints:

> For <u>the grace of God</u> has appeared that offers salvation to all people. <u>It teaches us</u> to say "No" to ungodliness and worldly passions, and to live self-controlled, upright and godly lives in this present age (Titus 2:11,12)

Paul never said, "That's too much grace! Balance it with Law!" No, he said *it*–grace–is what teaches us *how* to live godly, self-controlled, upright lives. Pastors don't need to talk out of both sides of their mouths, confusing their flock. They need to preach grace. I've never seen anyone who has finally understood the grace of God shout, "I've got a license to sin! Sweet!" It just doesn't happen.

God knows this and that's why He wants us to *think* we're holy so we'll *live* holy:

> "As a man thinks in his heart, so is he." (See Proverbs 23:7)

You *will* act like who you think you are. If you think grace empowers you to live in a godly manner, guess what will happen when you embrace grace as the air you breathe? A life of godly choices and thoughts inspired by His Spirit within.

What's more is, grace is not cheap, as the self-centered person will yell. They *think* it's cheap–as did the Jews who refused to believe Jesus was Messiah (see Hebrews 10:29)–but God's grace is the most expensive thing ever and Christ paid for it in full at the Cross. Grace only becomes cheap when we try to water it down by adding to it through our own efforts or feeble attempts at Mosaic Law observance (see Romans 11:6, Galatians 3:2,3, 5:4).

Titus 2 is overwhelmingly powerful Scripture in regard to God's mighty grace and what it does for His children on a moment by moment basis. If our churches wouldn't dabble in grace, but instead, dumped it on the crowds in buckets, sinful lifestyles wouldn't stand a chance. If you don't understand this fact reread Titus 2:11 and 12 daily until you do.

GRACE. EMPOWERS. US. TO. LIVE. PROPERLY.

I don't know how much simpler God could have made it.

Yet still, most churches won't teach this. Rather than water their parched people with grace, they heap flies into sticky ointment. Fear-mongering, guilt trips, and scorekeeping of sins-to-good-deeds are their hallmarks. Scattering both the lost and saved alike, they'll say, "Oh yeah, we teach grace, but Pastor does it with righteous anger."

What? Are you kidding me?

Grace insults the most sanctimonious folk because it's completely unfair. "These newcomers need to repent and be like us! We ain't going crazy on grace!"

We *should* be going crazy on grace.

Paul calls the gospel, the gospel *of* grace, in Acts 20:24; and if we look into Scripture, the only time ear-tickling is mentioned is in 2 Timothy 4. And guess who were the targets? Non-believers, not Christians, "Those who turn away from the truth." Who is the truth? Jesus (see John 14:6). It's impossible for a Christian to turn away from Jesus because God has hidden us inside of Himself *with* Jesus. Nobody can snatch us out of His hand and we can't jump out either. He's combined our spirit with His Spirit forever. The only way this could possibly be undone is if Christ dies again. That will not happen (see John 10:28, 14:19, 2 Timothy 2:13, Colossians 3:3,4, 1 Corinthians 6:17, Hebrews 7:25).

So who really wants their ears tickled? The people who spit on the Cross. Those who want teachers to give them more spiritual disciplines and stuff to improve their completeness *with* God. Those who want to *prove* to God how holy they are by what they start and stop—and through "gifts." Those who are bored with Jesus and want more sermons of Jesus-plus-this and Jesus-plus-that.

It's impossible for a *Christian* to have itching ears because we have the same ears as God because we've been reborn *of* God (see John 1:12,13, 1 John 3:1). But most churches won't teach this. They teach us we're at battle with God, even as His own children. This is wrong. This is not the gospel.

The gospel is Jesus. The gospel is grace. The gospel is good.

So today, my friends, know this: If today's churches would preach the message of the undiluted gospel they'd be overflowing all year long! What Jesus has done *for* us so He can do *to* us so He can do *through* us—this is good news! 52 messages a year *should* be good news!

A prayer for you: *Father, today I pray that our churches will begin to embrace the simplicity of your grace through faith in Jesus, as well as our new righteous identity. I pray that the message changes into what you want it to be. I pray for a new revelation to sweep the minds of behavior-centered church-goers, those who belittle your grace and the work of Jesus. Right now, I lift up all who are reading this, directly to you. So many of these dear readers have experienced harsh, double-talk teachings. The craziness of Covenant-mixing has harmed their thought life tremendously. I ask for you to begin revealing just how much Jesus has accomplished on their behalf, according to the New Covenant. As they grow in this grace, teach them how to be their true selves day by day, moment by moment. In Jesus' name, amen.*

Day 29

What Does Sanctification Really Mean?

"By this will we have been sanctified through the offering of the body of Jesus Christ once for all."

Hebrews 10:10

" Yeah, you're saved by grace but you still have to sanctify yourself! You *will* keep changing through sanctification!"

At first glance this statement would seem to be fine, minus the exclamation points. The problem is, Christians do not change. We've *been* changed—past tense—and *we* are only sanctified *once*.

Most of us simply don't realize there are two types of sanctification. Separating the two brings us peace of mind because we won't confuse our *who* with our *do*:

1. Sanctification of identity (happens once)
2. Sanctification of actions and attitudes (happens until we die)

Number two cannot happen until number one is complete. Number one is complete at the moment of salvation. Number two cannot change, alter, improve, nor sustain number one.

When we don't understand their separateness, we will praise people whom we *think* are more sanctified than us, and look down on those who "aren't." Eventually we'll get frustrated as we try to become "more" sanctified through what we do and don't do. Then, because we're placing our identity in actions and attitudes, our identity will be threatened when we fail.

We *will* fail, all the time, because we're human. This is why Christ had to die.

Failure in our quest to be more sanctified will digress into anger, lies, hiding, hypocrisy–or we'll give up altogether as the devil dangles the carrot of sanctification far out of reach.

Friend, it doesn't have to be this way.

First, let's define sanctification, or sanctify. It simply means *to set apart*. This is also another word for holy. The word saint is the noun version of sanctify. Saint means *holy person*. THAT IS WHAT WE ARE, AS CHRISTIANS. This cannot be achieved nor given from human votes. We are all holy people *in* our identity, *in* full, evenly, as children of God.

Nobody has individual higher status or less status. Such would nullify the Cross. This should give you a good grasp on the demonic doctrine of some denominations. I'm not saying entire *groups* of people aren't saved, I'm saying there's a turd in the punchbowl and the enemy is the culprit. His goal is to remove rest and freedom and he's doing a fine job through religion.

Hierarchies are not from God. Order is, leadership is, but not "levels" of holiness. Even the disciples argued over individual greatness in Luke 9, and Jesus corrected them. He pointed to the example of a child. Children aren't worried about such things.

Each and every believer is a saint, proportionately. This is why I call people saints in my books and social media posts. This is also why Paul addressed his letters, "To the saints in _____," to some seriously misbehaving, immature people. Whether they were struggling with licentiousness or legalism he knew their identity: *holy people* (see 1 Corinthians 1:2, 2 Corinthians 1:1, Romans 1:7, Ephesians 1:1, Philippians 1:1, Colossians 1:2, 1 Thessalonians 3:13, 2 Thessalonians 1:10).

Saints are sanctified spirits inside physical human bodies. Christian, that is what we are, right now. What has God done *with* us, as holy people? He has set us apart from the world, sin, and death by placing us inside of Himself. He has sanctified us. We've been taken *out* of Adam and placed *in* to Christ (see Colossians 3:3, 1 Corinthians 6:17, Galatians 2:20, Romans 5, 6, and 8).

Like Noah and his family in the Ark were saved *from* the world, by being placed in it, this is how we are saved from the world too, by being placed in the Spirit of Jesus (see 1 Peter 3:20-22). We couldn't be placed in Him without first being remade as holy. So, we were crucified with Him, buried, and raised as a holy, new creation. Then we were inserted inside Him. Another word for this is baptize, which, supernaturally, has nothing to do with water but our spirit. Paul goes into great detail about baptism in Romans 6 and not once does he mention any liquid. He's talking about Jesus! (See Romans 6:3-11, John 14:20, Galatians 2:20, 2 Corinthians 5:17,21).

Therefore, we've *been made* holy. Our spirit—which is our identity—*has been* sanctified!

1. Sanctified = you
2. Ongoing sanctification = your actions and attitudes but *not* you.

Just look:

"And that is what some of you <u>were</u>. But you <u>were</u> washed, you <u>were</u> <u>sanctified</u>, you <u>were</u> justified in the name of the Lord Jesus Christ and <u>by</u> <u>the Spirit of our God</u>." (1 Corinthians 6:11)

"By this will we <u>have been sanctified</u> through the offering of the body of Jesus Christ <u>once for all</u>." (Hebrews 10:10)

Do you see what made us sanctified? What made us holy? The body of Jesus. ONE SACRIFICE. Christ's bloody death. What *we* do—or refuse to do—can never cause us to *be* sanctified nor maintain sanctification as holy people. If this isn't true then Christ died for nothing and the Cross is weak. He would need our help. Yet He does not. By grace through faith is our only lifeline to Him.

Now that our identity is new—sanctified—our mind is being renewed by the Spirit of Christ (see Romans 12:2, John 14:26, Romans 8:9). Our mind leads our actions and attitudes. Consequently, yes, our actions and attitudes *are* being sanctified—we are maturing, not changing—but such cannot make us more sanctified than *who* we already are. Why not? Because Jesus will never sacrifice Himself again and that's the only way to become sanctified in your spirit, again. It's finished. You are complete!

So today, my friends, know this: Christian, you are completely sanctified. Now learn more about who you are and grow, gracefully.

A prayer for you: *Good morning, Father. It's beautiful here as the sun is just now peeking out. What a wonderful way to wake up. Thank you for*

another day alive on your planet. I'm grateful to be here. Right now, I lift up all who are reading this, directly you. I ask that you begin to open up the minds of these dear readers to the context of your Word. As they read the Bible, make it clear to them who is being addressed—believer or unbeliever. Take them deeper into the knowledge of your grace, confidently, knowing that if they are Christians they've been sanctified and are faultless. Enforce the truth in their thoughts. They lack nothing and are being empowered by your Spirit to grow each day—not change, but grow. Teach them more, Father, about who you are and who they are. In Jesus' name I pray, amen.

Day 30

⌒⦚⦚⦚⌒

God's Dream for You

"I want you to know all about Christ's love,
although it is too wonderful to be measured. Then
your lives will be filled with all that God is."

Ephesians 3:19

"Come here you little biscuit. You're so stinkin' cute. Did you know Daddy loves you?"

When Grace was younger I spoke to her this way. Now that she's almost 15, I still treat her the same, only she prefers to not be talked to like an 8-year-old. She wants to be regarded "as mature, because she is." Her words.

Jennifer isn't fully on board with treating Grace like a grown up, nor am I, to be honest. But I can hide this a lot better than my wife. She's still in mourning for not having a toddler in the house. Withholding overbearing cuddles, baby-talk, and constant doting, it's not been easy for either of us as we see this beautiful young lady in place of our baby. We both know Grace won't be living in our home forever and we're preparing our minds for the day she leaves. I'll be sad but glad, honored to raise this spectacular person.

I've enjoyed every stage of her life so much. From the moment I met her as the nurse laid her under the lamp, holding her tiny feet in my hands; to the days of teaching her how to walk and say, "Dada!"; to swimming with her in our pool as she held onto my neck and I ran in circles. It's been *such* a delight raising Grace.

Going to her dance recitals, watching her play the sax, shooting hoops in the backyard and running full court at the Civic Center. There are so many fond memories of this child. She's funny, smart, gets nearly perfect grades, and now she's a freshman in high school who's about to start driving. I'm ready for that too. I'm ready for the next stage of her life as she grows. I'll enjoy it. I'll enjoy *her*.

My dream for Grace is for *me* to be able to enjoy *her*. I want to be a part of every phase of her life. As her dad, my dream is also for *her* to enjoy others, herself, and her own life too.

God's dream for us is the same. Him enjoying us and us enjoying Him, people, and ourselves. This is all accessed through the love of Jesus Christ by grace through faith. Even for unbelievers this is His desire. God longs for them to believe in Jesus too, so they can become His child. He wants none to suffer (see Ephesians 2:8,9, 3:19, 2 Peter 3:9, 1 John 4:19, Romans 8:17, John 3:7,16).

Grace has her own dreams too, and I know that. Her dreams are my dreams because I love her. We, as God's children, have *our* own dreams too. These aspirations don't nix God's dreams for us but *His* dreams empower and center our own. They go hand in hand.

The prosperity gospel has given dreams a bad rap when there's nothing wrong with dreaming. The "Sow your seed to get your need!" preachers have made dreaming big the center of our faith, rather than Christ. They've made

Jesus a footnote to our goals and see God as a karma dealer. Now *this* is wrong. But not dreaming in itself.

God wants us to dream, He just doesn't want us to shipwreck our faith over ambitions by taking the focus off Christ. To be clear, shipwreck doesn't mean we are lost. It means we have broken *thinking* and our thoughts have placed us on an island in our minds. Legalism does the same. A dab of Law here, a sprinkle of Judaism there. The storm blows in and twists the bow, smashing our faith into the rocks. Thankfully, even when we do shipwreck our belief system, Jesus is on that island with us. He never leaves, ever. No matter what error we are struggling with.

As for dreaming, where do you think we got this from? Our Father dreams! He dreamt up this universe, dinosaurs, the animal kingdom, sea life, plant life, and humanity! He dreamt up gravity! He dreamt up seasons! He dreamt up *you*! He dreamt up the intricacies of the human body and how it would interact with the oxygen, food and water, on this planet—among a bazillion other things! Dreaming is normal, healthy, and wonderful! We're being like God when we visualize where we want to be, the health we want to be in, and the relationships we want to have! When we establish new objectives and are creative we're expressing our Creator! Why do you think He's called the Creator? You are creative too!

Having a vision, both short term and long, is inspiration from God. This isn't selfish, it is good. Dream, friend. Dream big, dream medium, dream small. To your loving Heavenly Father it's *all* good when you dream. He's extremely proud of you no matter what the world might say or how others measure your dreams.

Never believe the lie that God doesn't place certain longings and goals in you, because He does. False humility is the cancer of dreams. You don't need the approval of others. Plan it. Do it. Take steps and move forward, continually shaking off the discouragement through the strength of Christ within. His grace is always enough. It's everything you need and you have all of it. You lack *nothing*.

God works in us and through us, toward our ambitions. But in my opinion, more than anything, He wants us to know who we are. There's nothing *I* want more, for Grace, than for her to understand who *she* is. If Grace can comprehend her identity as a righteous saint–which she is because she's accepted Christ–she'll enjoy the abundant life He's already given her. Identity solves so many of our problems because it gives us a base to always stand on.

Identity determines value. God's dream for you is to understand His appraisal of you. Believer or not, your worth is *so* great to Him He gave you Jesus. For the unbeliever, the offer is on the table, stretched out, sitting in front of them. When we *receive* Jesus, we receive God's love. We don't earn this, maintain this, nor do we help Him give this. We are not to reach out and *take it* as some denominations teach. We open up our hands, receive, and say, "Thank you."

From then on out our identity is not the same as it once was. We learn, mature, and grow. We don't *change* but develop. Our changing only happened once, from the moment we believed and received (see 2 Corinthians 5:17,20,21, Galatians 2:20).

God's Spirit, who is now in us, is constantly renewing our minds to the truth of who we've become. From the millisecond of faith in Christ's ability to forgive us, we were born again in our spirit and now we blossom over the course of our lifetime. When a flower blossoms it's not changing, it's flourishing. Same with you.

The enemy knows our identity just as much as God does. For this reason he likes to make Christians think certain passages in the Bible are directed at us. Context-twisting is his specialty, applying Scripture pointed at unbelievers, to us. He wants to remove the firm foundation of our identity from our minds.

The good news is God's Spirit teaches us the truth! Any passage which creates shame, fear, guilt, or condemnation is not for us. We should know it, but also know who *we* are. The Counselor makes this perfectly clear in our hearts (see John 14:26, 1 John 4:18, Romans 8:1).

All of our shame, fear, guilt, and condemnation was placed on Jesus, on the Cross. He looked down the timeline of our lives, yanked it all up, and allowed the Pharisees and Roman government to nail them onto Himself (see John 1:29, 19:30, Romans 8:1-4, 1 John 2:12, Revelation 13:8).

As for *your* children, if you have any, would you ever use the threat of disowning them to motivate them? As if they'd no longer be your son or daughter if they didn't perform in certain ways? Absolutely not. You'd be respectful and set healthy boundaries out of love, but you know nothing can "change them" from being your child. Birth is final despite how they act. They've been born *of* you. Same with us and God. He warns us about dangers, but nothing can separate us from His love or spiritual DNA. Whereas our kids were born with our physical DNA, we are reborn with God's spiritual DNA. Both births are unchangeable and why Jesus told Nicodemus, "You must be born again" (see John 3:3, 1 John 4:10, 5:4).

Let's talk about feelings. Feelings do not determine identity. Would you ever instruct your children to *feel* different? No. You would listen to them and address their feelings in a wholesome way. Further, no matter *what* they feel, they'll always be your child. The same goes for us and our Heavenly Dad. The Bible never tells us to feel certain ways. Juxtapose, it constantly refers to the renewing our mind, fixing our thoughts, and *thinking* differently (see Romans 12:2, Philippians 4:8, Colossians 3:2, 2 Corinthians 4:18, 10:5, Hebrews 3:1).

God knows our feelings will follow our thoughts, so He wants us to center our thoughts on Jesus and our true identity. Feelings prove nothing except for how we feel. Although very important, feelings are not barometers of truth nor discernment. Sometimes we can even feel off because of something we ate yesterday or a movie we watched.

What about telling your child they have a reprobate mind? I know you nor I would ever do such a thing, and God wouldn't either. Only unbelievers have reprobate minds, not us. We, in fact, have the mind of Christ because we are one with Him (see 1 Corinthians 2:16, 6:17). Some grace-confused folks will use Romans 1:28 to make a saint think our mindsets prove salvation. No way. Again, this verse isn't directed at us. The first five chapters of Romans is about all of *humanity's* problem apart from Christ. Paul explains the dilemma of both the legalistic Jews *and* us Gentiles. The faithless Hebrew people were condemned by not obeying all of the Law perfectly. We Gentiles were condemned by our consciences, not by the Law.

Chapter six then gives the solution! Die in spirit, get buried in spirit, and resurrected in spirit–all three with Christ!

Lastly, would you ever tell your child they have a wicked, sinful heart, but they better live holy? In essence, "You're a wicked person but you better not act like it! Fake your good behavior until the day you die!" No you would not. You're better than that. The reality is, Christians have a new heart, a good heart, and we should live *from* the heart.

Covenant-mixing theologians are to blame. There's not a single New Testament passage which accuses Christians of having a wicked or deceitful heart. However, according to the Old Covenant, the prophet Ezekiel foretold what would happen *after* Messiah came. We would get new hearts! (See Ezekiel 36:26). God isn't giving us new hearts and then taking them away, nor is He giving us half-good hearts.

By grace through faith God takes *out* our old sinful heart–our spirit–and gives us a new, tender heart; an actual holy spirit of our own combined with His Holy Spirit! (See John 14:20, 15:5, Colossians 1:22, 1 Corinthians 6:17, Romans 6:6-11).

God *had* to do this–remove and replace our heart–because He can't live in wicked, sinful places. Jesus said a house divided will fall, so God tore down the house and built a new one on top of the solid foundation of Christ (see Mark 2:25, Matthew 7:24-27). He then moved in permanently and now He's cleaning up our mess *with* us. Not *us* but our mess, our old habits, coping mechanisms, and attitudes. We have a good heart, an obedient heart, a loving heart just like God's (see Romans 6:17, Ephesians 6:24, Galatians 5:22).

So today, my friends, know this: Ultimately God's dream for us is Jesus. Receiving Him, knowing Him, and growing in His love. His aspiration for us is to express Christ by expressing ourselves. His Son is a gift to us, but we must accept Him freely. Many will miss out on Jesus because they don't know how to accept a free gift. They want to pay for it somehow or at least leave the tip. They feel obligated to hand over their own gift before accepting God's gift. They want a spectacular exchange and He won't have it. If that's you, friend, keep your payment. Let our Heavenly Father bless you with Jesus. This is His dream for you.

A prayer for you: *Dad, you're a much better father than I am because sometimes I put pressure on Grace. I want her to succeed, I want her to learn a strong work ethic, and I want her to be prepared for a harsh world. In this devotional I've used our father and daughter relationship and compared it to your Father and child relationship with us. But I understand our human relationships can't always be correlated to yours. You are God, not just Father. You never treat us wrong nor pressure us as we sometimes do our children. Even though we make mistakes, you never do. You're such a good parent. Your pressure is perfection, and that*

perfection was placed on Jesus. He succeeded for us and now you simply call us to rest. Thank you for Him! Right now, I lift up all who are reading this, directly to you. Let them know from the state of resting in Christ they can achieve their dreams. They can enjoy you, others, themselves, and their lives. Take them deeper into the knowledge of your dream for them, their new identity. Amen.

Dear friend,

Thank you so much for spending time with me through this book. I hope I was able to bring you a sense of peace and confidence in knowing more about what Christ has truly done. My prayer is for you to grow into even deeper revelations of your identity as a believer. Lastly, it would mean the world to me if you'd leave a kind review on Amazon.com, Goodreads.com, Barnes & Noble's website, or wherever you've purchased this book. Your opinion is very important and encouraging to me. I always look forward to reading reviews.

May God continue to bless you greatly, with even more knowledge of His love for you through Jesus!

In Christ,
Matt

The Christian Identity, Volume 1: *Discovering What Jesus Has Truly Done to Us*

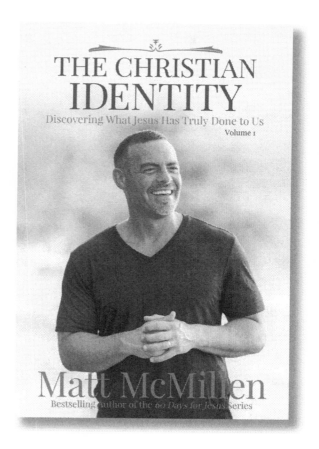

"Matt brilliantly explains the supernatural transformation that happens when we become believers in the finished work of the cross. His writing style makes this easy to understand as he answers some of the toughest questions that are on so many Christians' minds today." *-Amazon Customer*

60 Days for Jesus, Volume 1: *Understanding Christ Better, Two Months at a Time*

"I really like Matt's writing style. He makes understanding the gospel simple and real. I have found his daily devotions to be very helpful in guiding my walk with Christ. I highly recommend his book." -*Amazon Customer*

60 Days for Jesus, Volume 2: *Understanding Christ Better, Two Months at a Time*

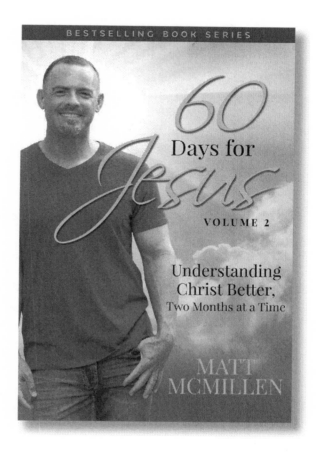

"This book is exactly what I needed to understand more about Jesus. I couldn't put it down. Thank you, Matt McMillen, for sharing your story to help strengthen others!" -*Amazon Customer*

60 Days for Jesus, Volume 3: *Understanding Christ Better, Two Months at a Time*

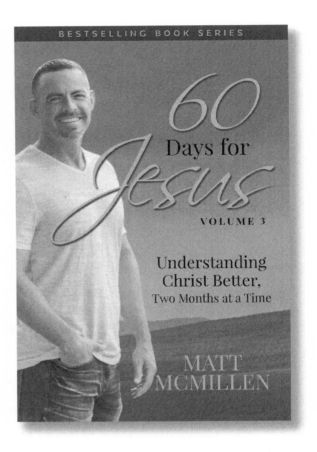

"Matt does an excellent job of providing clarity on many difficult issues every believer walks through on a daily basis. He does this by clearly articulating the scriptures to reveal the truth that really does set us free. This Volume, like the ones before, is an excellent devotional book to help any believer with their walk with God. Every page of this book is filled with the good news of God's unconditional love and grace. If you read one book this year, make it this one!" *-Amazon Customer*

True Purpose in Jesus Christ: *Finding the Relationship for Which You Were Made*

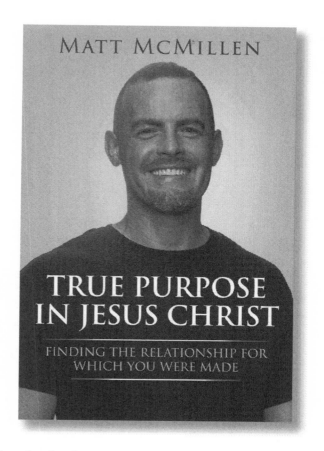

"One of the best books I've ever read! Matt's honesty about his life and what Jesus did to redeem him is amazing! He uses Scripture throughout his book to back up everything he talks about. I bought 20 books so I could share with the lost. Absolutely life changing! Thank you, Matt, for writing this book!"
-Amazon Customer

Made in the USA
Coppell, TX
03 December 2019

12293966R00169